VERSIONS OF BAROQUE

Versions of Baroque

EUROPEAN LITERATURE IN THE

SEVENTEENTH CENTURY

by Frank J. Warnke

New Haven & London
Yale University Press, 1972

In Memoriam
Lillian C. Warnke
1891–1964

Contents

Preface

Any writer on Baroque literature is bound to be indebted to a
large number of other scholars in that complex and controverted field. Most of my debts will be apparent in my text and
its notes, but I should like to mention some works that either
escaped my attention until this book was completed or appeared
too late to enable me to benefit from them. Among the former
are Werner P. Friederich's "Late Renaissance, Baroque or
Counter-Reformation?" *JEGP* 46 (1947): 132–43, reprinted
in his *The Challenge of Comparative Literature and Other Addresses* (Chapel Hill, 1970), pp. 78–95, and Tudor Vianu's
"Din istoria unei teme poetice: lumea că teatru," in his *Studi
de literatură universală şi comparată* (Bucharest, 1963). I am
grateful to Dan Grigorescu of the University of Bucharest for
drawing my attention to the latter scholar's essay on the theatre-
topos, and also for supplying me with a translation from the
Rumanian. Among the works that appeared after the comple-
tion of my book, I think especially of Rosalie Colie's *My Ecchoing Song* (Princeton, 1970), one of the most learned studies of
Marvell's poetry; Robert J. Nelson's *Immanence and Transcendence: The Theater of Jean Rotrou* (Columbus, Ohio, 1969);
M. J. Hanak's "The Emergence of Baroque Mentality and Its
Cultural Impact on Western Europe after 1550," *JAAC* 28, no.
3 (Spring 1970): 315–26, an essay which, despite differing em-

phases, employs an approach in several ways like mine; and Helmut Hatzfeld's "Literary Mannerism and Baroque in Spain and France," *Comp. Lit. Stud.* 7, no. 4 (December 1970): 419–36, in which that master of Baroque studies continues to elaborate and refine insights derived from many years of research and thought.

Some scholars whose work has been of general illumination to me are cited in my apparatus, but without reference to certain specific works. I should like to mention them: Carlo Calcaterra, "Il problema del Barocco," in *Problemi ed orientamenti critici di lingua e di letteratura italiana,* ed. A. Momigliano, vol. 3 (Milan, 1949), pp. 405–501; J. M. Cohen, *The Baroque Lyric* (London, 1963); Rocco Montano, "Metaphysical and Verbal Arguzia and the Essence of the Baroque," *Colloquia Germanica* 1 (1967): 49–65; and Franco Simone, "I contributi europei all'identificazione del barocco francese," *Comp. Lit.* 6, no. 1 (Winter 1954): 1–25.

Many friends and colleagues have helped me through conversation or through the recommendation of pertinent works: Jules Brody, Joachim Dyck, Claudio Guillén, Frank Kearful, Monika Köhler, Eric La Guardia, Wolfgang Leiner, James Siemon, Arnold Stein. I received most special help from Louis L. Martz, who, as often before, having read my work gave me the benefit of his learning, taste, and critical insight; from Janice Davis Warnke, my wife, who read the text with her customary alertness for any sloppiness of thought, feeling, or expression; from Elizabeth Dipple, who gave the final manuscript a critical reading and also "the lowliest duties on herself did lay," giving it an initial proofreading as well.

It's an academic convention to attribute one's virtues *(wenn schon!)* to one's friends and to arrogate one's vices to one's self. I really mean it. Several of the mentioned friends think that one, or two, or many of my contentions are faulty, or just plain crazy. The craziness I acknowledge mine.

I've been fortunate in the technical help I've received: from D. Twyla Warren, who initially typed my manuscript; from Marie Farr, who typed the final draft and also cast a trained editorial eye on it; from Monica Hill, secretary of Comparative Literature at the University of Washington, my co-worker and friend, who handled all sorts of details during my several absences in Europe.

Some of my research expenses were defrayed by a grant from the University of Washington Graduate School Research Fund in the summer of 1968. I want to thank my university for that help.

Chapter 3 of the book appeared, in rather different form, in *Colloquia Germanica* 1 (1967): 38–48. Most of chapter 4 appears in my "The World as Theatre: Baroque Variations on a Traditional Topos," in *Festschrift für Edgar Mertner,* ed. Bernhard Fabian and Ulrich Suerbaum (Munich: Wilhelm Fink Verlag, 1968). A portion of chapter 5 was published in *Arcadia* 4, no. 3 (1969): 225–37, under the title "Das Spielelement in der Liebeslyrik des Barock." I'm grateful to the editors of *Colloquia Germanica,* to the editors of *Arcadia,* and to the Fink Verlag for permission to reprint.

F. J. W.

Seattle, Washington
August 1971

Terms and Concepts

A desirable preliminary to a study of the literature of the Baroque age is that the writer indicate what he means by the chameleonlike adjective he has adopted. What I mean by it can be said quite simply: the style dominant in European literature from the last decades of the sixteenth century to the last decades of the seventeenth—the style that appears tentatively in Tasso and Montaigne, reaches its fulfillment in Donne, Crashaw, Marvell, Browne, Milton, Corneille, Pascal, Vondel, Gryphius, Marino, and Góngora, and occurs vestigially in Dryden and Racine. As I shall use the word *Baroque*, it parallels the customary use of such period terms as *Renaissance, Neoclassicism,* and *Romanticism;* that is to say, it designates what René Wellek calls "not an ideal type or an abstract pattern or a series of class concepts, but a time section, dominated by a whole system of norms, which no work of art will ever realize in its entirety."[1] In other words, I shall use *Baroque* to denote not a precisely definable style but a period complex made up of a whole cluster of more or less related styles—a complex which, in its earlier phases (approximately 1580–1610), contains significant survivals of the preceding complex, or period style (i.e. the Renaissance), and,

1. R. Wellek and A. Warren, *Theory of Literature* (New York, 1949), p. 278.

I

in its later phases (approximately 1650–90), anticipations of the subsequent complex (i.e. Neoclassicism).

Among the hypotheses which the study will attempt to sustain is the argument that, despite the rich variety of its literary products, the age in question has a clear identity when set against the periods preceding and following it. I also maintain that, although the term *Mannerism,* used as a literary concept by a number of recent scholars, has some utility as the designation of a kind of stylistic option found recurrently during the Baroque, it does not designate a clearly discernible literary period intervening between Renaissance and Baroque (as is perhaps suggested by the conspicuous lack of agreement, among those using the term historically, as to just what authors are embraced by the Mannerist period; see below, pp. 5–11). One of my tasks in this opening chapter will thus be to indicate how my usage compares to that of other writers on the Baroque and Mannerism and to attempt to justify that usage.

Several writers on the Baroque use the term as the designation not of an entire literary period but of a single, strictly definable style. Few of these authorities, however, agree on the definition of that style or on the writers who should be classified as its exponents. *Baroque,* as a term in literary history, has occasioned an extraordinary and at times an amusing amount of controversy. Emerging first in the eighteenth century as a scornful epithet for the extravagant architectural and plastic creations of earlier eras,[2] it was stripped of its pejorative

2. R. Wellek, in *Concepts of Criticism* (New Haven, 1963), pp. 69–127, gives the best account of the history of the term and concept. See also L. Nelson, *Baroque Lyric Poetry* (New Haven, 1961), pp. 3–17; L. Nelson, "Baroque," in *Encyclopedia of Poetry and Poetics,* ed. A. Preminger, F. J. Warnke, and O. B. Hardison (Princeton, 1965), pp. 66–68; O. de Mourgues, *Metaphysical, Baroque and Précieux Poetry* (Oxford, 1953), pp. 67–75; A. Coutinho, *Aspectos da literatura barroca* (Rio de Janeiro, 1950). The derivation of the word *Baroque* has long been controverted: Wellek (pp. 115–16) asserts that there occurred a con-

connotations near the end of the nineteenth century by the
art historian Heinrich Wölfflin, who established it as a neutral
descriptive term for the style which, in art history, intervenes
between Renaissance and Neoclassicism. The same historian
went on to suggest, as early as 1888, that the term might usefully be employed in literary history.[3] In the second and third
decades of the twentieth century a number of literary scholars
in Germany and Italy followed this lead; by 1940 scholars in
other parts of Europe and the Americas were speaking of
Baroque literature; and in the last twenty-five years the term
has gained currency until it seems now, despite the recent com-
petition of the term *Mannerism,* firmly established as the
definitive designation of a specific concept in literary history.[4]

But, as I have remarked, the precise definition of that concept is far from clear. Even if we leave aside those conservative
authorities who have still not resigned themselves to the kid-
napping of the term from art history, even if we discount
those who would use the term for a recurrent constant in literary sensibility, not confined to any one historical period, we
find a wide divergence in the definitions of Baroque literature
which have been proposed. These definitions may be divided
into two categories: those which conceive of the Baroque as a

---

fluence of two different words—an Italian noun derived from *baroco,* a
particularly sophisticated type of syllogism, and a French adjective derived from the Portuguese *barroco,* an irregularly shaped pearl.

3. H. Wölfflin, *Renaissance und Barock* (Munich, 1888), pp. 83–85.
See Wellek, *Concepts,* pp. 71–73.

4. French literary scholars have been the most reluctant to adopt the
term, probably because of the prestige of French Neoclassicism (cf. H.
Peyre, *Le Classicisme français* [New York, 1942]), but during the last
two decades a spate of titles indicates an ultimate acceptance (cf. de
Mourgues, *Metaphysical;* J. Rousset, *La Littérature de l'âge baroque en
France* [Paris, 1954]; M. Raymond, *Baroque et Renaissance poétique*
[Paris, 1955]; *Revue des Sciences Humaines* 55–56 [1949]: special issue
devoted to the Baroque).

single style, distinguished by the consistent occurrence of specific devices, emphases, and ideas (sometimes interpreted as implying a definite cultural or religious orientation),[5] and those which conceive of the Baroque as a complex of related styles constituting a distinct period in European literary history.[6] My commitment to the latter usage is already clear: if *Baroque* designates the style of an entire period, it is parallel in its level of designation to such terms as *Renaissance, Neoclassicism*, and *Romanticism;* none of these refers to a single, unified, and simply definable style, and yet their utility as conceptual tools is virtually beyond question. The literature of the seventeenth century has sufficient internal consistency to make a comparable period term desirable, and *Baroque* has already established itself as such a term (and the study of seventeenth-century literature has supplied us with a wealth of limited terms which, taken together, make up the Baroque: e.g. *Metaphysical style, préciosité, marinismo, conceptismo, culteranismo*). In the case of the Baroque it is perhaps especially unrealistic to attempt to arrive at a stylistic definition which is at once precise and historically inclusive, for the Baroque era, like the Romantic, was notable for the variety and individuality of the literary phenomena which it embraced.

The very richness of the age in question has something to do with the terminological squabbles which surround its study.

5. H. Hatzfeld, "Die französische Klassik in neuer Sicht. Klassik als Barock," *Tijdschrift voor Taal en Letteren* 23 (1935): 213–81; Hatzfeld, "A Clarification of the Baroque Problem in the Romance Literatures," *Comparative Literature* 1 (1949): 113–39; B. Croce, *Storia dell' età barocca in Italia* (Bari, 1929); M. Praz, *Secentismo e marinismo in Inghilterra* (Florence, 1925); W. Sypher, *Four Stages of Renaissance Style* (Garden City, N.Y., 1955); Rousset, *Littérature de l'âge baroque;* de Mourgues, *Metaphysical.* The list could be made much longer.
6. Wellek, *Concepts;* Nelson, *Baroque Lyric Poetry;* F. J. Warnke, *European Metaphysical Poetry* (New Haven, 1961); R. A. Sayce, "The Use of the Term Baroque in French Literary History," *Comp. Lit.* 10 (1958): 246–253.

Confronted by such diversity, the historian (haunted as he habitually is by Bacon's Idols) feels compelled to reduce it to some kind of orderly system, positing a sequence of shorter periods within the time span 1580–1680 in order to explain its baffling profusion. But the fragmentation of the concept of the Baroque as a period is attended by perils. To posit a Mannerist *period* in literature is, in a sense, to undo the valuable work of a great many writers on the Baroque during the earlier part of this century and to leave us, finally, in a position rather similar to the one we were in before they performed their labors—a position in which the earlier episodes of the Baroque are assimilated to the Renaissance and the later episodes to Neoclassicism. Viewing European literary history as a whole, we can, I believe, see that the works of Donne, Milton, Corneille, Gryphius, Vondel, Marino, Góngora, and Calderón, radically different as they are from one another, differ far more significantly from the works of Ariosto, Ronsard, and Spenser in the age preceding and from the works of Dryden, Pope, Voltaire, and Lessing in the age following. To destroy the unity of the concept of Baroque is to blur our perception of this central fact and thus to render more difficult the already formidable task of literary periodization. A brief review of some of the literature on the concept of Mannerism will perhaps clarify my argument.

Wylie Sypher, working from analogies with the visual arts and limiting himself to English and French literature, conceives of a Mannerist period intervening between Renaissance and Baroque and embracing such authors as Donne, Montaigne, Webster, Marvell, the Shakespeare of *Hamlet* and *Measure for Measure,* and the Milton of "Lycidas." The title of Sypher's work—*Four Stages of Renaissance Style*—is in itself significant, implying as it does that Mannerism and Baroque (as well as "Late Baroque") are to be conceived of as episodes in the larger unity of the Renaissance. The process of what might be called expansion-through-fragmentation is typical of the proponents of Mannerism as a historical concept. Helmut Hatzfeld, using the Romance literatures as a point of departure, argues powerfully for a complex stylistic sequence of Renaissance-Mannerism-Baroque-"Barroquismo," and maintains, further, that the sequence occurs at different times in different national cultures.[7] Thus, for Hatzfeld, the sequence is epitomized as follows: in Italy, Ariosto (fl. 1520), Michelangelo (fl. 1550), Tasso (fl. 1580), Marino (fl. 1620); in Spain, Luis de León (fl. 1580), Góngora (fl. 1600), Cervantes (fl. 1600), Calderón (fl. 1650); in France, Ronsard (fl. 1550), Malherbe (fl. 1620), Racine (fl. 1670), Fénelon (fl. 1700). He sees Mannerism as a transitional stylistic phase intervening between the two great, fully developed styles of Renaissance and Baroque, and he identifies it with features of artificiality, distortion, and exaggeration contrasting with the organic unity and the moralism which he finds typical of the Baroque.

Hatzfeld's system, though far superior to Sypher's in inclusiveness, perception, and logical rigor, nevertheless presents a number of problems. The virtual contemporaneousness of Cervantes and Góngora, for example, does little to help his contention that Mannerism and Baroque, in any given national culture, are clearly separable historical epochs. Even more troublesome are some of the collocations with which we are presented. Ariosto, Luis de León, and Ronsard are all demonstrably practitioners of Renaissance poetic style, but

7. H. Hatzfeld, *Estudios sobre el barroco* (Madrid, 1964). This study in Spanish synthesizes and summarizes the views toward which Hatzfeld has been working for four decades and which he has adumbrated in numerous earlier articles. A related though less schematic view is expressed by E. B. O. Borgerhoff in "'Mannerism' and 'Baroque': A Simple Plea," *Comp. Lit.* 5, no. 4 (Fall 1953): 323–31.

can we do much with the assertion of a stylistic identity between Michelangelo and Góngora? In Hatzfeld's scheme, Michelangelo, Góngora, and Malherbe are Mannerists; Tasso, Cervantes, and Racine are the greatest of Baroque writers; and Marino, Calderón, and Fénelon are all *barroquistas*, practitioners of a Late Baroque style. It is possible to make stylistic distinctions with such precision that Marino and Góngora are seen as exponents of different styles, but in that case it is difficult to maintain that Tasso, Cervantes, and Racine are exponents of the *same* style, or that Marino and Calderón belong together stylistically.

If one conceives of a literary period in Wellek's terms, as "a time section, dominated by a whole series of norms," it is reasonable to group together as belonging to the same period all the writers classified by Hatzfeld as Mannerist, Baroque, and *barroquista*. If, on the other hand, one requires that a style be defined more rigidly, one is obliged, it seems to me, to justify more plausibly than does Hatzfeld the groupings for which he argues.

Like Sypher, Hatzfeld ends by proliferating stylistic distinctions until he blurs the central and important distinctions— between Renaissance and Baroque and between Baroque and Neoclassicism. Another eminent champion of the term and concept *Mannerism*, Arnold Hauser, simply expands the range of reference of that term until it includes virtually all authors traditionally classified as Baroque, together with a good number of late Renaissance figures. For Hauser the Baroque has shrunk to a brief episode involving Milton, Racine, and a few others. His weird grab-bag of Mannerist authors includes Tasso, Marino, Cervantes, Góngora, Calderón, Scève, d'Aubigné, Marlowe, Shakespeare, Donne, Herbert, Crashaw, Marvell, Michelangelo, Montaigne, Malherbe, Gryphius, and Hofmannswaldau. It is difficult to see that this use of the term *Mannerism* does us much good: Hauser seems to use it, as Hatzfeld does *Baroque,* as a kind of honorific designation for the works he admires most. Hauser inquires, with some acerbity, how it is possible to label his "Mannerist" authors Baroque, since the latter term designates the style of Milton, Dryden, Racine, Bossuet, Chiabrera, and Guarini.[8] The question is puzzling. If one can, without hesitation, see Tasso, Calderón, Shakespeare, and Crashaw as practitioners of the same style, it ought to be easy enough to add Milton and Racine and throw in Snow White and the Seven Dwarfs.

The point is, of course, that Hauser, like Hatzfeld, is caught between two opposed conceptions of the nature of a literary period. On the one hand, he sees it as a time section marked by the coincidence of a certain large variety of technical devices and thematic concerns. On the other hand, he sees it as a specific, precisely definable style. At one and the same time he denies the concept of a large and broadly inclusive Baroque period, on the grounds that the figures claimed for that period do not practice the same specific style, and argues for the concept of an even more broadly inclusive Mannerist period, on the grounds of general spiritual kinship. Significantly, he identifies Mannerism as intellectual, Baroque as emotional.[9] But are these terms in any sense justifiable as elements in the concept of a literary *period?* Every age displays some writers who are predominantly intellectual, others who are predominantly emotional. To attempt to define a period in terms of its emotionality

---

8. A. Hauser, *Mannerism: The Crisis of the Renaissance and the Origin of Modern Art,* 2 vols. (London, 1965), 1:275. The authors who make up Hauser's truncated Baroque seem a strangely assorted group. Even if one is willing to be persuaded that Milton, Racine, and Dryden share the same style, it is frightfully confusing to find the early Baroque Guarini (fl. 1590) placed in their company. Guarini, one might note in passing, is seen as definitively "mannerist" by John Shearman, *Mannerism* (Baltimore: Penguin, 1967), pp. 91–86.

9. Hauser, *Mannerism,* 1:274–75.

or intellectuality is to end by destroying altogether the concept of period. (One might note, in passing, that Hauser's formulation involves certain inconvenient implications: his Mannerist Tasso, for example, is presumably intellectual, and his Baroque Milton, presumably emotional.)

A literary period cannot be conceived of as a time span populated by authors expressing themselves in virtually identical styles, style itself being too individual a phenomenon to allow for such a conception. A literary period is, rather, a time span in which underlying shared spiritual preoccupations find expression in a variety of stylistic and thematic emphases. It will be the task of this study to attempt to trace the emphases and locate the preoccupations of the Baroque age, an epoch extending from Montaigne to Milton and clearly distinguishable from both Renaissance and Neoclassicism.

My choice of the term *Baroque* in preference to the term *Mannerism* can, I believe, be justified on two bases. An enormous body of twentieth-century scholarship, in all the Western languages, has employed the term and concept *Baroque* and, despite numerous individual differences of emphasis, with sufficient agreement to have created a useful and coherent historical concept.[10] Furthermore, the chaotic divergence in the applications of the term *Mannerism* by its various champions makes the "querelle du manièrisme" far outstrip the "querelle du baroque" in the proliferation of mutually exclusive individual formulations. The various classifications applied to a sampling of sixteenth- and seventeenth-century writers will demonstrate what I mean: Donne is Mannerist

10. Among the many scholars of the period to whom I am variously indebted, I might cite particularly Morris Croll, Fritz Strich, Karl Viëtor, Richard Alewyn, Raymond Lebègue, Jean Rousset, Odette de Mourgues, Rocco Montano, Dámaso Alonso, R. A. Sayce, Blake Spahr, René Wellek, J. M. Cohen, Imbrie Buffum, Lowry Nelson, Jr., Franco Simone, Carlo Calcaterra, and Afrânio Coutinho.

(Sypher, Hauser) and Late Renaissance (L. L. Martz); Crashaw
is Baroque (Sypher, Martz) and Mannerist (Hauser); Shakespeare is Renaissance (the traditional view), Mannerist (Hauser), Baroque (Oscar Walzel), and, at various stages, Renaissance, Mannerist, *and* Baroque (Sypher); Tasso is Mannerist
(Hauser) and Baroque (Sypher, Hatzfeld); Marino is Mannerist (Hauser), Baroque (the traditional view), and Late
Baroque (Hatzfeld); Cervantes is Renaissance (the traditional
view), Mannerist (Hauser), and Baroque (Hatzfeld); Góngora
is Baroque (the traditional view) and Mannerist (Sypher,
Hauser, Hatzfeld); Calderón is Baroque (the traditional view),
Mannerist (Hauser), and Late Baroque (Hatzfeld); Milton is
Baroque (Hauser) and, at various stages, Renaissance, Man-
nerist, Baroque, *and* Late Baroque (Sypher). Milton's "Lycidas,"
to choose a single text, is Mannerist (Sypher) and Baroque
(Martz).

It seems to me that a gratifying degree of historical clarity
and accuracy is achieved if, in considering the writers listed
above, one recognizes that Tasso and Shakespeare are figures
in whom Renaissance survivals and Baroque features coexist
and that the others are all classifiable as Baroque, the rich
variety of their individual styles cloaking but not masking
profound similarities of both attitude and technique. One is
thus spared the chronological embarrassments that plague
Hatzfeld's historical argument and vitiate Hauser's.

Nevertheless, the concept of a Mannerist style is perhaps
convenient as the designation of one tendency found recurrently throughout the Baroque. Louis Martz employs it sen-
sitively in a recent book to denote the style that allies Thomas
Carew and Andrew Marvell. It is only when Martz goes on to
posit a Mannerist *period* that his argument crumbles in the
manner of Hauser's: the Mannerist Carew follows the "Late
Renaissance" Donne but is followed in turn not only by the

Baroque Crashaw but also by the Mannerist Marvell—whose style, most readers agree, strongly resembles Donne's. Aware of the problem, Martz points out that "all the great currents of revival that had grown up gradually on the Continent over a period of more than two hundred years suddenly flowered in England [during the earlier seventeenth century]. . . . As a result, all the styles and stages of the European Renaissance were compressed and recapitulated in England during this brief time. Even more than on the Continent, the phases of style that we call Renaissance, Mannerist, or Baroque all flow together and in England become inseparably intermingled and simultaneous."[11] But the simultaneity of which he speaks was fully as marked on the Continent as in England, if we consider the phenomena variously called Baroque and Mannerist. In England as on the Continent, the Renaissance was clearly over by the time the Baroque (and/or Mannerism) came to their full flourishing. The imaginative world of Spenser and the sonneteers belonged unequivocally to the past during the age of Carew, Crashaw, Marvell, and Milton, just as the world of Ariosto and Ronsard belonged to a past recognizable as such during the age of Marino, Góngora, Calderón, Malherbe, and Corneille.

Like Sypher, Martz blurs the distinction between the Renaissance and the period—whatever we choose to call it—that follows it. Like Hauser, he attempts to discern two separable stylistic periods during a single time-span dominated by varied, "inseparably intermingled," and ultimately related stylistic currents. The fragmentation of the concept of the Baroque period leads again to the breakdown of the identity of that concept and threatens the historical picture cumulatively achieved by a large number of scholars of the period.

The variety of literary phenomena during the Baroque age

11. L. L. Martz, *The Wit of Love* (Notre Dame, 1969), pp. 113–14.

is, I have proposed, the source of the arguments over terminology that so often obscure its study. At least two trends, or, as
I have called them, options, are recurrently perceptible amid
this variety—the spare, witty, intellectual, paradoxical trend
typified by Donne, Herbert, Marvell, Sponde, Quevedo, Huygens, and Fleming; and the ornate, exclamatory, emotional,
and extravagant trend typified by Crashaw, Gryphius, Marino,
d'Aubigné, Góngora, and Vondel. The latter option—for
many authorities the quintessential Baroque—might for con-
venience's sake be designated as "High Baroque." The former
option—the style of "Metaphysical" poetry—might be designated as "Mannerist."[12] The latter term would, so used, have
the advantage of including not only the Metaphysical poets
but also such figures as Webster, Gracián, Sir Thomas Browne,
Pascal, and the early Corneille. The question of the interrelatedness of the two stylistic options will concern us later
(see below, pp. 54–64).

The Baroque age simply will not lend itself to any simple
schematization as far as its style, or styles, are concerned. But
the example of Romanticism is again illuminating: the varied
and contradictory phenomena of that period do not invalidate
the concept of Romanticism, for there is, beneath the exuberant disparity of nineteenth-century styles and attitudes, a
unity of style and attitude, although one which cannot be
expressed in a simple formulation.[13] A comparable unity lies
beneath the seeming chaos of seventeenth-century styles and
attitudes, and it will be the task of the following chapters to
attempt, without undue simplification, to identify that unity—
one which is finally spiritual rather than technical.

Before undertaking that task, however, one further usage

12. For a more detailed discussion of "High Baroque," see my *European
Metaphysical Poetry.*
13. Cf Wellek, *Concepts,* pp. 128–98.

of the terms *Baroque* and *Mannerism* requires notice. Ernst Robert Curtius, rejecting altogether the notion of a Baroque period, contends that the literary phenomena of the age in question constitute simply one more resurgence of a Mannerist tradition perceptible recurrently throughout European literary history from antiquity on.[14] Curtius argues persuasively and with a formidable degree of erudition. His formulation is particularly tempting in view of what seems to be a fairly regular alternation, in Western literary history, between ages dominated by such criteria as imitation, realism, objectivity, and rationality ("classicist" ages) and ages dominated by such criteria as personal expression, fantasy, subjectivity, and a sense of aspiration which projects itself sometimes as paradox and sometimes as irrationality ("mannerist" ages). Nevertheless, the literary phenomena of the later sixteenth century and the seventeenth cannot really be viewed as a simple replay of Hellenistic or Medieval "mannerism" (any more than the phenomena of the eighteenth century can be seen as identical with those of Augustan Rome): as Hauser justly observes, any literary period is essentially unique.[15]

Some aspects of my usage, then, will be as follows: *Baroque* for the period in question, *High Baroque* and *Mannerist* for two of the major interrelated tendencies manifesting themselves during the period. The sweeping division of all writers, viewed ahistorically, into camps of "classicist" and "non-

14. E. R. Curtius, *Europäische Literatur und Lateinisches Mittelalter* (Bern, 1948). See also the work of Curtius's disciple G. Hocke: *Die Welt als Labyrinth* (Hamburg, 1957) and *Manierismus in der Literatur* (Hamburg, 1959). E. d'Ors, in *Du Baroque* (Paris, 1935), shows a similar distaste for the whole concept of period, but he uses *Baroque* rather than *Mannerism* to designate the recurrent constant. B. L. Spahr, in "Baroque and Mannerism: Epoch and Style," *Colloquia Germanica* 1 (1967): 78–100, makes the interesting recommendation that Baroque be used as the name of the literary period and Mannerism be used as the name of the style characteristic of the period.

15. Hauser, *Mannerism*, 1:38–40.

classicist" has, as Wellek remarks,[16] little utility, and it will
play effectively no role in this study of a historical style. One
might suggest, in passing, the term *mannerist* (lowercase) as a
workable designation for the nonclassicist tradition, to the
limited extent that the concept is useful.

Baroque literature includes the highly colored, ornate poetry
of which Crashaw is the chief English representative and of
which Marino, Gryphius, and Vondel are among the Continental practitioners; the ingenious, intellectual, witty poetry
which flourished in England with Donne, Herbert, and the
other Metaphysical poets, paralleled in France, Spain, Germany, and Holland in the work of Sponde, Quevedo, Fleming, and Huygens; the magniloquent prose of Sir Thomas
Browne and the familiar prose of Montaigne and Bacon; the
varied dramatic works of Webster and Middleton, Corneille
and Rotrou, Lope de Vega and Calderón; the monumental
creations of Milton and Góngora; and, at least to an extent,
the incomparable achievement of Shakespeare.

Baroque tendencies did not begin to appear at the same
time in the various European countries, nor did the Baroque
manners manifest themselves simultaneously in all forms of
literature. The earliest monuments of Baroque style are found
in Italy and France: Tasso's *Gerusalemme liberata* (1576),
Du Bartas's *La Sepmaine* (1578), and the first book of Montaigne's *Essais* (1580).[17] The first manifestations of the new

16. Wellek, *Concepts*, p. 97.
17. In his initial suggestion that *Baroque* might be used as a literary
historical term, Wölfflin, in *Renaissance und Barock*, proposed a contrast
between Ariosto as a Renaissance poet and Tasso as a Baroque poet.
T. Spoerri, *Renaissance und Barock bei Ariost und Tasso* (Bern, 1922),
investigated Wölfflin's insight in detail. Despite this study, and despite
the arguments of Hatzfeld, in *Estudios,* it seems to many readers that
Tasso's epic is mixed in style, displaying anticipations of the full Baroque
manner but also numerous vestiges of Renaissance style. See below, pp.
166–68.

age are thus in epic poetry and in prose. The Baroque lyric did
not emerge fully until the 1590s in England, France, Italy,
and Spain, and still later in Germany, Holland, and the Scan-
dinavian and Slavic countries. It was not until the 1600s that a
drama which might accurately be described as Baroque appeared. To some extent the closing years of the sixteenth century constitute a period of overlap between the emergent
Baroque style and the moribund Renaissance style: Spenser's
Faerie Queene (1589, 1596) is a monument of the earlier
manner, and the poems of Michael Drayton, many of them
written after the seventeenth century was well underway, remain unequivocally Elizabethan (i.e. Renaissance) in tone,
form, and technique. Elements of both period styles may be
perceived in Shakespeare, as a comparison of *A Midsummer
Night's Dream* with *Measure For Measure* or of *Romeo and
Juliet* with *Hamlet* suggests.[18] What is certain is that by the
1610s a period style, significantly different from that of the
Renaissance, had announced itself in European literature.

The idea that European literature of the seventeenth century constitutes a period—one as clearly defined as the Renaissance or the age of Neoclassicism, and unequivocally distinguished from both—has been slow in establishing itself. There

18. Shakespeare was claimed as a Baroque artist as early as 1916, in
O. Walzel's "Shakespeares dramatische Baukunst," *Jahrbuch der Shakes-
pearegesellschaft* 52, and several other German scholars have adopted this
position. In America, Sypher, in *Four Stages,* characterizes Shakespeare's
work as being variously Renaissance (e.g. *Romeo and Juliet*), Mannerist
(e.g. *Hamlet*), and Baroque (e.g. *Othello*). Sypher perhaps attaches his
labels too confidently and categorically; a period term is more usefully
employed as convenient shorthand to designate the dominant tendencies
of an age than as a pigeonhole in which to file specific works. The danger
of pigeonholing is particularly marked with a superlative artist like
Shakespeare or Milton, as Sypher himself (p. 18) partially realizes. One
might note, however, an increasing tendency among comparatists to regard Shakespeare as belonging to the Baroque age (e.g. L. Forster, *The
Icy Fire* [Cambridge, 1969]).

are good historical reasons for this slowness. The seventeenth century was conspicuously an age of controversy, warfare, and disorder; it was, above all, an age in which a new scientific and rationalistic world-view progressively ousted the old religious and symbolic world view which had conditioned European thought and art since the Middle Ages. Intellectual innovation is one of the major causes of the Baroque shift in sensibility, but the religious and political disturbances of the time explain more cogently why seventeenth-century men were generally unaware that such a shift was taking place: those disturbances had the effect of pushing the nations of Europe into a relative mutual isolation which contrasts with the vital cultural internationalism of the High Renaissance, with the result that literary men of the various national cultures could not perceive that their creations were part of a strikingly new international trend. Theorists of the age were, in general, unaware of the novelty of contemporaneous developments, and the attachment to a static and antiquarian ideal of Classicism inherited from the Renaissance made such awareness effectively impossible. Until recent decades a similar cultural nationalism —perhaps an intensified one—has prevented literary historians from formulating a conception of the literary Baroque as an international phenomenon.

In England certain local considerations, both during the seventeenth century and since, have further militated against thinking of that century as a distinct literary period. The relative indifference toward theory displayed by English men of letters of that period combined with the general antiquarianism and nationalism noted above to blur the recognition of significant stylistic innovation, and the late occurrence of the English Renaissance has since blinded many literary historians to the autonomy of the English Baroque: they have assimilated the earlier stages of that age to the Renaissance and the later stages to the Neoclassical period, acknowledging the facts of development and change only through the application of extra-artistic labels derived from the reigning monarchs (i.e. the various episodes of the English Baroque have been tradition-ally identified as "Jacobean," "Caroline," and "Common-wealth").

Historians of the Continental literatures have been guilty of similar blurrings. The eminence and prestige of French Neoclassical literature of the later seventeenth century has led many French scholars to ignore the existence of the Baroque, assimilating such pre-Classical figures as Corneille to the ideal Classicism of the age of Racine, Molière, and La Fontaine, and slighting, until recent decades, such unequivo-cally Baroque figures as Sponde, St.-Amant, and Théophile de Viau.[19] In Spain and Holland the Baroque era coincided with the greatest epochs of national culture, with the result that honorific terms have predominated in their designations for the seventeenth century in literature: the *siglo de oro* and the *gouden eeuw* have plated the Spanish and Dutch Baroque with a self-congratulatory gold which until recently has rendered difficult the recognition of links with general Euro-pean culture. Ironically, the term *Baroque* and the concept of that age as stylistically distinct established themselves first in the practice of German and Italian scholars, representatives of national cultures for which seventeenth-century literature is of relatively less importance: the German seventeenth cen-tury has the rawness of something not yet achieved; the Italian has the overripeness of something achieved distinctly earlier.

Thus, in an age in which intellectual innovation, political disorder, and religious controversy had combined to encourage

19. Among manifestations of the revision of the traditional French view may be cited the works listed in n. 4, above. See also *Le Préclassi-cisme français,* ed. J. Tortel (Paris, 1952).

a new international literary style, national isolation, cultural pride, and critical traditionalism conspired, both in the seventeenth century and later, to obscure the true dimensions of that new style. The question of critical traditionalism in the Baroque age itself will require some consideration.

The writers of the Baroque period give occasional indications of an awareness that something new is happening in the literature of their time. Thomas Carew praises Donne for his originality, for his "line / Of masculine expression,"[20] and other Englishmen refer, admiringly or slightingly, to the "strong lines" which have become fashionable by 1620. Théophile de Viau announces that it is necessary to write "à la moderne," and Marino and his followers exhibit an analogous emphasis on novelty.[21] The critics and literary theorists of the age are, on the whole, content to echo the assertions of the Renaissance Aristotelians; most Baroque writings on poetry concern themselves with such familiar subjects as fable and genre, and theoretical observations lay stress on the doctrine of imitation, the criteria of probability and decorum, and the obligation of literature to be *utile* as well as *dulce*. Baroque poetics, in short, remains classical in orientation, and its chief authorities remain Aristotle and Horace.[22]

The work of a few Italian and Spanish theorists, however, indicates an at least partial recognition that a new conception of literature was embodied in the work of the artists who were their contemporaries. Chief among these theorists is the Spaniard Baltasar Gracián, whose treatise *Agudeza y arte de ingenio* (1642) at times approaches being a manifesto of a

20. In his "Elegy upon the Death of Dr. Donne," in Carew, *Poems*, ed. R. Dunlap (Oxford, 1949), p. 72.
21. Théophile's phrase is quoted in Tortel, *Le Préclassicisme*, p. 264. For the modernism of Théophile, Marino, and others, see Rousset, *Littérature de l'âge baroque*, p. 77.
22. See Nelson, "Baroque," in *Encyclopedia*, p. 68.

new, anticlassical poetics. Similar emphases are found in the writings of the Italians Tesauro, Sforza-Pallavicino, and Pellegrini. At the heart of their writings is a radical emphasis on metaphor, more particularly the ingenious metaphor, or conceit (*agudeza, acutezza*), which establishes a relationship of similarity between seemingly disparate phenomena.[23] The chief poetic faculty, then, is what seventeenth-century English called "wit" (Spanish *ingenio,* Italian *ingegno),* the capacity for perceiving likeness beneath seeming unlikeness, and the essence of poetry becomes not so much the imitation of the phenomenal world as the imaginative modification of it.

Nominal classicists all, the theorists of *ingenio* felt obliged to cite ancient authorities for their contentions. Aristotle remained the chief authority, but significantly, the Aristotle of the *Rhetoric* rather than, as for the Renaissance, the Aristotle of of the *Poetics.*[24] Plato, too, could be cited to advantage, particularly the *Ion,* that dialogue in which Plato detailed his views on the *furor poeticus,* or divine madness, which is the soul of poetic invention. The concept of poetic fury, like that of taste, or *gusto,* is a necessary part of the foundation of a theory of poetry which stresses in a novel way the individual ingenuity of the poetic creator.

If *ingenio* theory emphasizes poetic individuality (and, at least implicitly, modernity), it emphasizes also the form of the work of art rather than its narrative content or moral sig-

---

23. For Gracián, see Curtius, *Europäische Literatur* (trans. W. R. Trask, *European Literature and the Latin Middle Ages* [New York, 1953], pp. 293–301). J. A. Mazzeo, *Renaissance and Seventeenth-Century Studies* (New York, 1964), pp. 25–59, explores most fully the theoretical implications in the writings of both Gracián and the Italians. Nelson, "Baroque," *Encyclopedia,* pp. 68–71, discusses the *ingenio* theorists but does not ascribe as much importance to their views as does Mazzeo.

24. In this paragraph, as in the preceding, I am particularly indebted to Mazzeo's work.

nificance.[25] One implication of this emphasis is that Baroque
poetry, in both its Mannerist and its High Baroque versions, is
more specifically form-conscious than is Renaissance poetry.
How this formalism relates to individualism is a question
which these theorists scarcely raise, but it is of interest to the
modern student of the age. It leads, for example, to a number
of larger questions: How is it that writers of the period, often
vociferously committed to a conception of art as either personal projection or utilitarian instrument (e.g. Donne, Bacon,
Browne, Montaigne), owe their immortality to the mannered
elaborateness or eccentricity of their styles? How is it that
Baroque style may be associated, and justly, with such seemingly opposed tendencies as formalism and colloquialism?
How is it, finally, that Baroque literature, unparalleled in its
cultivated sophistication, strikes us sometimes as almost primitive in its astonishing vigor?

The literary theorists of the Baroque age can give us no
help with such questions (not even Gracián, for example,
could wholly rid himself of the classical concept of metaphor
as decoration, despite the implications of his whole theory of
wit). For tentative answers we must turn to the works of art
themselves.

25. Both Sforza-Pallavicino and Pierfrancesco Minozzi specifically exalt
form over matter (Mazzeo, p. 31).

Appearance and Reality

T he literature of the Renaissance is committed to the
reality of the phenomenal world. This is not to say that
anything like a naïve naturalism prevails during the
period, for the great writers of the fifteenth century in Italy
and the sixteenth century throughout Europe are profoundly
aware of the claims of the spirit; it is rather to note that
Renaissance literature ascribes a firm validity to the experiences of the senses, which are both felt to be intrinsically
worthy of artistic celebration and believed to be true sources
of genuine knowledge. Hence the range and the gusto of so
much sixteenth-century literature—one thinks of Rabelais, of
Ariosto, of Marlowe. Hence too the fact that even works
which, like Spenser's *Faerie Queene,* are fervently dedicated to
the expression of abstract truths of religion or morality find
their natural terms for such expression in the vivid representation of the perceptible and palpable world of sense experience.
The most exalted and serious poems of the age seem to see
experience on two levels, the finally real level of the spirit and
the provisionally real level of the flesh.[1] The deeply rooted
symbolic habit of mind which the Renaissance had inherited
from earlier ages enabled its poets to speak of the ultimately

1. A fuller discussion of this point occurs in my *European Metaphysical Poetry* (New Haven, 1961), pp. 22–24.

real in terms of the phenomenally immediate, and one result was a poetic style which relies strongly on simile and its extension, allegory. Such a style, reconciling the seen world with the unseen, is free to develop a texture which is lovingly sensuous and representational. Appearance, in short, is an accurate, if approximate, mirror of an ineffable reality.

For the artists of the Baroque period this relationship between appearance and reality has broken down. The old symbolic cast of mind, with its assumption of an ordered and hierarchical cosmos, remains operative until well into the second half of the seventeenth century,[2] but an irritable doubt as to the precise relationship between seen and unseen worlds informs the Baroque, in both its typical works and its masterpieces. A thirst for the single reality behind the disparate appearances of experience is characteristic; no longer content with a double vision of reality, the Baroque poets and prose writers seek not to reconcile the two worlds but to reduce them to one. "The world that I regard is my self," wrote Sir Thomas Browne; "it is the Microcosm of my own frame that I cast mine eye on; for the other, I use it but like my Globe, and turn it round sometimes for my recreation."[3] The passage, with its turning away from the world of appearances to seek for truth within the inner life, might serve as a motto for many Baroque artists.

Not surprisingly, Baroque literature displays an obsessive concern with the contradictory nature of experience. In poetry, for example, simile largely gives way to metaphor and allegory to symbolic narrative, and the texture of that poetry, purged of the representational sensuousness of the Renaissance, is per-

2. For an exposition of the orthodox world-view of the Renaissance, see E. M. W. Tillyard, *The Elizabethan World Picture* (New York, 1943).

3. Sir Thomas Browne, "Religio Medici," in *Religio Medici and Other Writings,* ed. F. L. Huntley (New York, 1951), p. 85.

meated with the figures of contradiction—conceit, paradox, antithesis, and oxymoron. The compulsive search for the One enmeshes the poet in the complexities and contradictions of the Many.

The contradictory vision and the attempt to capture absolute reality constitute the unifying elements of Baroque poetry, but the poets of the age display these elements in widely varying ways. There are perhaps two general groups, however, into which these poets may be divided: the first is typified by John Donne with his cerebral and paradoxical art; the second is typified by Richard Crashaw in England and by numerous poets on the Continent, authors of a poetry which is highly sensuous in its imagery but phantasmagoric rather than representational in the effects created by that imagery. It might be useful to examine three fairly extended poetic passages, from Spenser, Donne, and Crashaw, in the hope that they will suggest something about the differences between Baroque and Renaissance style and between the two major subdivisions of Baroque style. The passages have similar subject matter—a vision of a soul's progress from earth to Heaven—and the expressed attitudes toward that subject matter may illuminate the shift from Renaissance to Baroque. The first passage is from Spenser's "Hymne of Heavenly Beautie" (1596):

> Beginning then below, with th'easie vew
> Of this base world, subject to fleshly eye,
> From thence to mount aloft by order dew
> To contemplation of th'immortal sky,
> Of the soare faulcon so I learne to fly,
> That flags awhile her fluttering wings beneath,
> Till she her selfe for stronger flight can breath.
>
> Then looke, who list thy gazefull eyes to feed
> With sight of that is faire, looke on the frame

Of this wyde universe, and therein reed
The endlesse kinds of creatures, which by name
Thou canst not count, much lesse their natures aime:
All which are made with wondrous wise respect,
And all with admirable beauties deckt.

First th'earth, on adamantine pillars founded,
Amid the sea, engirt with brazen bands;
Then th'aire, still flitting, but yet firmely bounded
On everie side with pyles of flaming brands,
Never consum'd, nor quencht with mortall hands;
And last, that mightie shining christall wall,
Wherewith he hath encompassed this All.

By view whereof it plainly may appeare,
That still as everything doth upward tend,
And further is from earth, so still more cleare
And faire it growes, till to his perfect end
Of purest Beautie it at last ascend:
Ayre more then water, fire much more then ayre,
And heaven then fire appeares more pure and fayre.

Looke thou no further, but affixe thine eye
On that bright shynie round still moving masse,
The house of blessed gods, which men call skye,
All sowd with glistring stars more thicke then grasse,
Whereof each other doth in brightnesse passe:
But those two most, which, ruling night and day,
As king and queene, the heavens empire sway.

And tell me then, what hast thou ever seene
That to their beautie may compared bee?
Or can the sight that is most sharpe and keene
Endure their captains flaming head to see?
How much lesse those, much higher in degree,
And so much fairer, and much more then these,
As these are fairer then the land and seas?

> For farre above these heavens which here we see,
> Be others farre exceeding these in light,
> Not bounded, not corrupt, as these same bee,
> But infinite in largenesse and in hight,
> Unmoving, uncorrupt, and spotlesse bright,
> That need no sunne t'illuminate their spheres,
> But their owne native light farre passing theirs.[4]

Spenser's "Hymne" is a philosophical poem, and the ideas on which it is based are clearly those of most common currency during the Renaissance: the conventional Platonism elucidated in the fourth of the quoted stanzas and a cosmology centered on the principles of order and hierarchy. The principle of order involves also the doctrine of universal correspondences, which enables the poet to speak of the unimaginable in terms of the phenomenal. Or, as Spenser's heir Milton was later to phrase it,

> ... what if Earth
> Be but the shaddow of Heav'n, and things therein
> Each to other like, more then on Earth is thought?[5]

Simile, then—that figure of comparison in which the entities compared exist in a relationship of mere similarity, each preserving its discrete and unmodified existence—is the mode of Spenser's imagination. Specific similes, appropriately enough, permeate the texture of his verse: the poet learns *of* the faulcon how to fly *like* the faulcon; the sky is sowed with stars "more thicke then grasse," and that sky in turn is somehow *like* the unimaginable heaven above it.

There is a curiously public quality to the passage. The voice is that of Edmund Spenser in his capacity as seer-poet, *vates*, and it addresses us in our capacity as a poetry-reading audience

4. Edmund Spenser, *Complete Poetical Works*, ed. R. E. Neil Dodge (Cambridge, Mass., 1908), pp. 754–55.
5. John Milton, *Poetical Works*, ed. H. Darbishire (London, 1958), p. 114.

(the relationship is essentially the same in Spenser's narrative and lyric poetry as well). The vision is experienced not by a dramatized character but by the imaginative and rational potential common to the human race (even if it takes a Spenser to express the vision).

The passage exemplifies other standard Renaissance features —the use of images with a built-in conventional value (e.g. light, flame, crystal), mythological reference (e.g. the sky as the abode of plural "gods"—angels, in Christian humanist terms), and metrical composition through regular stanzaic pattern (in this poem, rhyme royal). But before examining these features more closely it would be wise to look at some Baroque treatments of similar material.

Donne's two "Anniversaries" (1612) are his longest and most ambitious poems. Later we shall examine some of the complexities of these works in which the death of a fifteen-year-old girl becomes the occasion for a profound meditation on death, the decay of the world, and the immortality of the soul (see below, pp. 121, 126), but for the present a single passage from "The Second Anniversarie" claims our attention. In this passage Donne imaginatively presents the progress of the soul, liberated by death, to its reward in Heaven:

> But thinke that Death hath now enfranchis'd thee,
> Thou hast thy'expansion now, and libertie;
> Thinke that a rustie Peece, discharg'd, is flowne
> In peeces and the bullet is his owne,
> And freely flies: This is to thy Soule allow,
> Thinke thy shell broke, thinke thy Soule hatch'd but now.
> And thinke this slow-pac'd soule, which late did cleave
> To'a body, and went but by the bodies leave,
> Twenty, perchance, or thirty mile a day,
> Dispatches in a minute all the way

Twixt heaven, and earth; she stayes not in the ayre,
To looke what Meteors there themselves prepare;
She carries no desire to know, nor sense,
Whether th'ayres middle region be intense;
For th'Element of fire, she doth not know,
Whether she past by such a place or no;
She baits not at the Moone, nor cares to trie
Whether in that new world, men live, and die.
Venus retards her not, to'enquire, how shee
Can, (being one starre) *Hesper,* and *Vesper* bee;
Hee that charm'd *Argus* eyes, sweet *Mercury,*
Workes not on her, who now is growne all eye;
Who, if she meet the body of the Sunne,
Goes through, not staying till his course be runne;
Who findes in *Mars* his Campe no corps of Guard;
Nor is by *Iove,* nor by his father barr'd;
But ere she can consider how she went,
At once is at, and through the Firmament.
And as these starres were but so many beads
Strung on one string, speed undistinguish'd leads
Her through those Spheares, as through the beads, a string,
Whose quick succession makes it still one thing:
As doth the pith, which, lest our bodies slacke,
Strings fast the little bones of necke, and backe;
So by the Soule doth death string Heaven and Earth;
For when our Soule enjoys this her third birth,
(Creation gave her one, a second, grace,)
Heaven is as neare, and present to her face,
As colours are, and objects, in a roome
Where darknesse was before, when Tapers come.[6]

6. John Donne, *Poetical Works,* ed. H. J. C. Grierson, 2 vols. (Oxford, 1912), 1:256–57.

Most immediately striking, in contrast to the Spenser passage, is the quality of Donne's imagery. Whereas the Renaissance poet uses images conventionally associated with value or desirability, images derived, as it were, from a common storehouse of specifically poetic language, Donne utilizes a whole range of images with few or no particularly poetic associations—a rusty musket, a string of beads, the human spinal column, a room suddenly illuminated by candles. Some of these images—beads, candles—have vestigial associations of conventional value, but the poet studiously plays down such associations: our attention is directed not to the appearance or costliness of the beads or to the brightness of the candles but rather to the analyzable facts that the beads are strung on a string and that objects spring at once into visibility when light is brought into a room. Similarity, for Donne, is not a sensually perceptible resemblance of appearance but an intellectually perceptible resemblance of function. Spiritual experience—whether, as in the passage quoted, the vision of eternity, or, as in Donne's lyrics, love profane or sacred—is conceived of not in analogues of appearance but in analogues of intellectual comprehension. Hence, for Donne and the other Metaphysical poets, the characteristic instrument is the conceit, which implies that all sensuous appearance is illusion and that transcendent experience can be evoked only in intellectual terms.

Other deviations from Renaissance idiom might be noted in the Donne passage—the fact, for example, that Venus, Mars, and the rest have become mere planets, with, at most, a facetious identity as figures of myth. Of greater importance is the dramatic immediacy which informs the Donne passage. Spenser focuses on the content of the soul's vision; the soul which has the experience remains generalized, almost anonymous, and the manner of the passage is, appropriately enough, discursive and expository. Donne focuses on the fact that a particular soul is having the experience—the soul of the individual reader, who is, as it were, conjured into participating in the vision. The imperative constructions which open the passage prepare us for the sequence of brilliant figures which evoke no strongly visualizable content but rather a kinesthetic sensation of ineffably rapid movement. In the context of the "Anniversaries" the "she" who is the protagonist of the passage is further characterized, for the incantatory repetition of that pronoun earlier in the poems has already led us to associate it automatically with Elizabeth Drury, the nominal subject of the work.[7] The "she" who is transported in an instant from earth to heaven is, then, at once Elizabeth Drury and the soul of the reader. Individual inner experience is paradoxically identified with the experience of a protagonist who has already been equated with universal creativity and virtue.

Viewed negatively, the passage exemplifies the Baroque breakdown in unquestioning faith in universal correspondences. Much has been written about the "Anniversaries" as documentation of the impact of the new science on sensitive intellectuals of the early seventeenth century,[8] and, although it is surely inaccurate to see the new science as the true subject of the poem, these famous lines from "The First Anniversary" do help us to understand how, for Donne, the utterance of transcendent truth could no longer depend on the data of the earthly senses:

> And new Philosophy calls all in doubt,
> The Element of fire is quite put out;
> The Sun is lost, and th'earth, and no mans wit
> Can well direct him where to looke for it.

7. Divergent views of the true subject of the poems are given in M. H. Nicolson, *The Breaking of the Circle* (Evanston, Ill., 1950), pp. 65–104, and L. L. Martz, *The Poetry of Meditation*, rev. ed. (New Haven, 1962), pp. 228–48, 354–56.

8. For example, Nicolson, *Breaking of the Circle*, and C. M. Coffin, *John Donne and the New Philosophy* (New York, 1937).

And freely men confesse that this world's spent,
When in the Planets, and the Firmament
They seeke so many new; they see that this
Is crumbled out againe to his Atomies.
'Tis all in peeces, all cohaerence gone;
All just supply, and all Relation.[9]

The isolation of the individual sensibility is the point of departure for the Baroque imagination.

The third passage, from Crashaw's hymn "In the Glorious Assumption of Our Blessed Lady," combines the sensuousness of the Renaissance and the intellectual extravagance of the Baroque in a fusion which typifies one whole international tendency in seventeenth-century poetry:

Hark! she is call'd, the parting houre is come.
Take thy Farewell, poor world! heavn must goe home.
A peice of heav'nly earth; Purer and brighter
Then the chast starres, whose choise lamps come to light her
While through the chrystall orbes, clearer then they
She climbes; and makes a farre more milkey way.
She's calld. Hark, how the dear immortal dove
Sighes to his sylver mate rise up, my love!
Rise up, my fair, my spottlesse one!
The winter's past, the rain is gone.
   The spring is come, the flowrs appear
No sweets, but thou, are wanting here.
               Come away, my love!
               Come away, my dove! cast off delay,
               The court of heav'n is come
               To wait upon thee home; Come, come away!
               The flowrs appear.

9. Donne, 1:237.

Or quickly would, wert thou once here.
The spring is come, or if it stay,
'Tis to keep time with thy delay.
The rain is gone, except so much as we
Detain in needfull teares to weep the want of thee.
                    The winter's past.
                    or if he make lesse hast,
His answer is, why she does so.
If sommer come not, how can winter goe.
                    Come away, come away.
The shrill winds chide, the waters weep thy stay;
The fountains murmur; and each loftyest tree
Bowes low'st his heavy top, to look for thee.[10]

Crashaw's style here seems to resemble Spenser's both in its
vivid sensuousness and in its reliance on generally accepted images of value, but the cumulative effect of the passage is very
different. Spenser explicitly recognizes the incommunicability,
indeed the unimaginability, of the transcendent, but utilizes
the Platonic ladder of contemplation and the inherited doctrine of correspondences to frame a kind of imaginative para-
digm of it; Donne, obsessed with the absoluteness of his subject,
turns from the senses to the purified inner experience of the
aspiring soul. Crashaw constructs his transcendent world of the
materials of earthly experience—presented not as faint Platonic
shadowings of the transcendent but as its very substance. One
might be tempted to say, then, that Baroque art of the sort
typified by Crashaw asserts, to a greater degree than Renaissance
art, the reality of the phenomenal world, but reflection will suggest that Crashaw is here using imagery of the senses not in a
manner that significantly imitates or represents the world of ordinary experience but in a manner that constructs a phantasma-

10. Richard Crashaw, *Poetical Works,* ed. L. C. Martin (Oxford, 1927),
pp. 304–05.

goric heaven out of chunks of sensuous experience regarded simply as raw material for an artifact. In effect, he rejects the reality
of the phenomenal world as firmly as does Donne. It is worth
noting, for example, that the ascendant Virgin is *brighter* than
the stars and makes "a farre more milkey way," as it is worth
noting that the fanciful weather of heaven is a mere by-product
of her presence. For all its surface vividness, Crashaw's poetic
world is, like Donne's, almost completely internalized.

Perhaps as an aspect of this internalization, Crashaw's
celestial voyager, like Donne's, is specifically identified: not any
or every soul capable of imaginative speculation, but the specific
soul of Mary. In his dramatic concentration on an individual
protagonist, as in his rejection of the phenomenal, Crashaw is a
Baroque poet of the truest sort.

Nevertheless, any sequential reading of the quoted passages
from Donne and Crashaw makes it clear that two very different
poetic manners are involved, and one suspects that the differences are due to more than the individual idioms of the two
poets. Essentially they are due to the poets' respective adherences
to two different manners within the Baroque: Donne's, to the
spare, witty, conceptual Metaphysical style, of which he is,
though not the founder, the greatest practitioner;[11] and Crashaw's, to the expansive, hyperbolic, sensuous style, more common on the Continent than in England. Within the Baroque,
Donne adopts the Mannerist option, Crashaw the High
Baroque.[12]

11. For discussions of "metaphysical poetry" before Donne, see de
Mourgues, *Metaphysical,* pp. 12–25; Martz, *Meditation,* pp. xvii–xxv and
passim; my *European Metaphysical Poetry,* pp. 18–19. See also the intro-
ductions to two important recent anthologies: *The Metaphysical Poets,*
ed. Helen Gardner (Oxford, 1957), and *The Anchor Anthology of
Seventeenth-Century Verse,* vol. 1, ed. L. L. Martz, 2 vols. (Garden City,
N.Y., 1969).

12. A term for which I argue in my *European Metaphysical Poetry,*
p. 3.

The three passages I have chosen for analysis show the poets dealing with similar materials in very different ways. The general material itself—the actual or imagined ascent of a soul to the transcendent realm of absolute reality—elicits from the poets the expression of attitudes which help to locate them in different eras and different stylistic traditions. But one seldom finds Donne or Crashaw dealing with material similar to Spenser's, or in forms similar to his, and this fact in itself gives us something of the measure of the shift from the Renaissance to the Baroque period. Spenser's masterpiece is an epic: allegorical in mode, romance-derived in material, didactic in avowed purpose. It is difficult to imagine Donne, Crashaw, or almost any representative Baroque poet undertaking such a task. Spenser, to be sure, wrote distinguished lyrics as well, but there is an enormous gulf between the sonnets which make up his *Amoretti*—conventionally Petrarchan in stance, addressed, more often than not, to an audience whom he tells *about* his amorous sufferings or the beauty of his beloved—and the lyrics, profane or sacred, of Donne, Herbert, or Crashaw—dramatic and colloquial in accent, and almost invariably addressed directly to the beloved, to God, or to some specifically evoked individual figure.

A divergence between Renaissance and Baroque concepts of metrical form also makes itself strongly felt. For Spenser, as for Sidney, Daniel, or almost any of the Elizabethans, the fixed form of the sonnet, and the fixed stanzaic patterns of rhyme royal and ottava rima (and, of course, the flexible and versatile stanza which Spenser invented for his *Faerie Queene*), operate as preexistent containers into which the poetic material may be poured. For most typical Baroque poets, on the other hand, material makes form, and the individual poetic utterance, particularly in the lyric, assumes a unique prosodic form, suitable for it and for it only. Donne's *Songs and Sonets* are remarkable for the variety of stanzaic forms they employ (many of them once only),

and Donne is excelled as a prosodic innovator by George Herbert, whose "hieroglyphic" conception of poetic form enabled
him to achieve a full identification of thought and expression.[13]

The shift in the concept of form, like the shifts in dominant
genres, does not, of course, constitute a watershed between the
Renaissance and Baroque periods. The early decades of the seventeenth century, in England and elsewhere, present any number of minor poets, and some major ones, occupying themselves
with work in the established Renaissance genres, articulated in
a conventional Renaissance manner. But most of the more vital
new voices give utterance to something new, and even among
the conservative authors certain shifts of emphasis imply a major alteration in sensibility. In England such shifts of emphasis
are nowhere more clearly marked than in the work of the brothers Phineas and Giles Fletcher—apart from the towering figure
of Milton, the most distinguished of seventeenth-century heirs
of Spenser.

The Fletchers were attracted to the epic genre as well as to
the allegorical mode, and however short they fell of their master
in poetic genius, in sustained energy and moral seriousness they
were worthy disciples. Phineas Fletcher wrote two poems epic
in scope and manner: *The Apollyonists* (1627), an English version of *Locustae vel Pietas Jesuitica,* his Latin heroic poem on
the Gunpowder Plot (ca. 1611); and *The Purple Island* (1633),
a long and very grotesque poem in which the human body is
presented in terms of an extended geographical allegory. Giles
Fletcher, distinctly the finer poet, wrote *Christ's Victory and
Triumph* in 1610. The Fletcher poems are all written in variants
of the Spenserian stanza, all employ either consistent or occasional allegory, and all are distinguished by a sensuous texture

13. J. Summers, in *George Herbert* (Cambridge, Mass., 1954), pp.
123–46, supplies a good discussion of that poet's hieroglyphic form.

which recalls the Elizabethans. Despite the conservatism of their style, however, the works are clearly Baroque and in the High Baroque manner.

Both *The Apollyonists* and *Christ's Victory and Triumph,* like *The Faerie Queene,* dramatize the authors' convictions about moral and religious truth, but the Fletchers, unlike Spenser and like Crashaw, make a frontal assault on their material. *The Apollyonists,* presenting the Gunpowder Plot as a scheme hatched in hell by Satan and his fellow-devils, portrays scenes in hell in a manner which clearly anticipates *Paradise Lost,* and *Christ's Victory,* divided into cantos dealing with the Nativity, the temptation in the wilderness, the Crucifixion, and the Ascension, moves at will between earth and heaven. Both epics are characteristically Baroque in that they treat religious material directly, without the mediation of an adorned narrative set in a world of recognizable human experience. As a corollary, if we except the idiosyncratic *Purple Island,* allegory is for the Fletchers an aspect of texture, something localized, rather than being, as it is for Spenser, the principal element of structure.

The Fletchers show little of Spenser's superb narrative gift; story, in fact, is no more central to their epics than is allegory. There is something curiously static about both *The Apollyonists* and *Christ's Victory,* and the reader remembers from them not a continuous pattern of narrative or the effect of such a pattern but rather isolated moments of atmosphere or transport. As in Crashaw, so in the Fletchers the ingredients of human experience are disposed to construct not a representation of that experience but a highly colored fantasy of an unimaginable experience. The following stanza from the final canto of Giles Fletcher's *Christ's Victory* exemplifies the High Baroque style as definitively as does the work of Crashaw. It is an evocation of the bliss of the saints on greeting in heaven the ascended Christ:

Their sight drinkes lovely fires in at their eyes,
Their braine sweete incense with fine breath accloyes,
That on Gods sweating altar burning lies,
Their hungrie cares feede on their heav'nly noyse,
That Angels sing, to tell their untould joyes;
   Their understanding naked Truth, their wills
   The all, and selfe-sufficient Goodnesse fills,
That nothing here is wanting, but the want of ills.[14]

Despite the vivid, rather hectic quality of the imagery, the stanza is informed with the same distrust of mundane experience, the same internalization of the imagination, which we found in Donne and Crashaw. In its fanciful satisfaction of a thirst for the absolute, it may be contrasted with the great concluding stanzas of Spenser's Mutabilitie cantos, with their melancholy but sane and courageous recognition that, this side of Paradise, the mortal world is all we can know:

When I bethinke me on that speech whyleare
Of Mutability, and well it way,
Me seemes, that though she all unworthy were
Of the heav'ns rule, yet, very sooth to say,
In all things else she beares the greatest sway:
Which makes me loath this state of life so tickle,
And love of things so vaine to cast away;
Whose flowring pride, so fading and so fickle,
Short Time shall soon cut down with his consuming sickle.

Then gin I thinke on that which Nature sayd,
Of that same time when no more change shall be,
But stedfast rest of all things, firmly stayd
Upon the pillours of eternity,

14. Giles Fletcher, in Phineas and Giles Fletcher, *Poetical Works*, ed. F. S. Boas, 2 vols. (Cambridge, 1908–09), 1:83.

That is contrayr to Mutabilitie:
For all that moveth doth in change delight:
But thenceforth all shall rest eternally
With Him that is the God of Sabbaoth hight:
O that great Sabbaoth God graunt me that Sabbaoths sight! [15]

I have applied the adjective "sane" to these lines. There is perhaps something crazy in the art of the age which followed
Spenser's, the art of the Fletchers, Crashaw, Donne, and the
others. But its unique greatness is related to its extremeness of
aim and its extravagance of means, related perhaps to its very
craziness.

Literature on the European Continent followed a pattern very
similar to that which it followed in England, although, on the
whole, the concept of form, at least in lyric poetry, underwent
less radical transformations. Such masters of the devotional lyric
as Sponde and La Ceppède in France, Gryphius and Fleming in
Germany, Huygens in Holland, and Quevedo in Spain resemble
the English Metaphysicals in both attitude and technique: rejection of the phenomenal world, internalization of vision, and
creation of a dramatically realized persona create for them as
well styles which are typically Baroque. [16]

The two most influential lyric poets of the Continent, the Italian Giambattista Marino and the Spaniard Luis de Góngora,
differ from the poets just mentioned as they differ from the
English Metaphysicals—in the triviality of their subject matter,
in the implicit disillusionment of their approach to it, and in the
sensuous elaborateness of their styles. Triviality of nominal subject need not, however, limit poetic achievement: Marino is a
very good poet, and Góngora a great one. Of particular interest
in the context of this chapter is that the sensuous elaborateness

15. Spenser, *Works,* pp. 676–77.
16. See my *European Metaphysical Poetry,* passim.

of these poets, like that of Crashaw and Giles Fletcher, paradoxically implies a doubt as to the philosophical reality of the
sensuous world evoked. Marino's imagery, whether in his lyrics
or in his interminable epic *L'Adone,* presents through tireless wit
a sensuous phantasmagoria in which the elements of earthly
experience are so identified with each other as to become in
themselves meaningless. And Góngora's practice of a similar
technique is exemplified in the following sonnet, in which he
addresses a brook in which his beloved has just seen the reflection of her face:

> O claro honor del liquido elemento,
> Dulce arroyuelo de luziente plata,
> Cuya agua entre la yerva se dilata
> Con regalado son, con passo lento,
> Pues la por quien elar, y arder me siento,
> Mientras en ti se mira, Amor retrata
> De su rostro la nieve, y la escarlata
> En tu tranquilo y blando movimiento:
> Vete como te vas, no dexes floxa
> La ondosa rienda al cristalino freno,
> Con que goviernas tu veloz corriente:
> Que no es bien que confusamente acoxa
> Tanta belleza en su profundo seno
> El gran señor del humido tridente.[17]

The brook is evoked periphrastically, and the beauties of the beloved, reduced to abstraction, are located ambiguously in her
face, in the surface of the brook, and in the mind of the lover.
The whole structure of the poem contains a subtle suggestion of
the transience of those beauties: the central image is the same
as that of the French devotional poet Jean-Baptiste Chassignet's

17. Luis de Góngora y Argote, *Obras en verso del homero español,* ed. D.
Alonso (Madrid, 1963), p. 15, verso.

sonnet "Assies toy sur le bort d'une ondante riviere," a religious meditation on evanescence, and of the great passage on earthly beauty in Donne's "Second Anniversarie":

> Dost thou love
> Beauty? (And beauty worthy'st is to move)
> Poore cousened cousenor, *that* she, and *that* thou,
> Which did begin to love, are neither now;
> You are both fluid, chang'd since yesterday;
> Next day repaires, (but ill) last dayes decay.
> Nor are, (although the river keepe the name)
> Yesterdaies waters, and to daies the same.
> So flowes her face, and thine eyes, neither now
> That Saint, nor Pilgrime, which your loving vow
> Concern'd, remaines; but whil'st you thinke you bee
> Constant, you'are hourely in inconstancie.[18]

Whether in profound philosophical poetry or in the poetry of casual compliment, the spiritual preoccupations of Baroque poetry remain constant.

It is probably impossible to determine precise extraliterary causes for the development of the Baroque poetic styles, and it is at least arguable that such a determination is in no way neccessary. Literary history has its own internal development, not bound to the events of political or intellectual history, and it is possible that an age such as the Renaissance, fascinated by the phenomenal world and fond of mirroring it in loving and vivid images of the senses, is inevitably followed by an age such as the Baroque, dubious about the phenomenal and drawn obsessively by a desire for the unchanging One. But I would propose that extraliterary considerations have something to do with the *particular* preoccupations of the Baroque poets. Some of the great masters of Baroque prose, in both their leading ideas and the

18. Donne, 1:262.

dominant qualities of their styles, may help to bring the shared
preoccupations into focus and to indicate something about their
intellectual sources.

The cited poetic passages, with their emphasis upon flux and
transience, have an affinity with the themes of the earliest great
master of Baroque prose, Michel de Montaigne.[19] Montaigne's
skepticism, as typified in the "Apologie de Raymond de Se-
bonde," has at its root a systematic doubt in the validity of appearances or in the capacity of the human reason to penetrate
them to arrive at truth. The element of aspiration toward the
unattainable, evident in such different figures as Donne and
Crashaw, is not present in Montaigne; his way, like that of
Shakespeare or Cervantes, is rather to embrace the human condition with a full awareness of its contradictions, inadequacies,
and mysteries. What he shares with the Baroque poets mentioned is a concentration on the internality and individuality of
experience; his tireless investigation of his own nature derives
from the same impulse as the Metaphysical poet's creation of
a dramatic persona as lyric protagonist.

It would be tempting to view Montaigne's skepticism, individualism, and tolerance as reactions to the religious warfare which
raged in sixteenth-century France and in which the author was
deeply involved. There are difficulties in doing so however: the
sustained partisan fury which informs the epic poem of Montaigne's Huguenot contemporary Agrippa d'Aubigné is a response more typical of the age. Montaigne's attitude may more
plausibly be seen as the response of a reflective mind to the tensions of an age of great and absolute intellectual oppositions:
Catholicism versus Protestantism, humanism versus devotion,

19. Montaigne's prose is considered typical of the Baroque in Morris
Croll's seminal study "The Baroque Style in Prose," in Croll, *Style,
Rhetoric, and Rhythm,* ed. J. Max Patrick, et al. (Princeton, 1966), pp.
207–33, and also in I. Buffum, *Studies in the Baroque from Montaigne
to Rotrou* (New Haven, 1957).

reason versus faith. Like Donne, Montaigne was fascinated by the existence of alternative angles of thought.

But the novelty of Montaigne, like that of the Baroque poets, lies at least as much in his style as in his ideas. The rejection of the Ciceronian rhetoric and sentence structure which had practically defined the prose style of the earlier Renaissance, the substitution for it of an idiosyncratic, asymmetrical, colloquial prose style—these are the features which make Montaigne one of the first great voices of the Baroque, and they ally him to such varied later prose writers as Bacon, Burton, Browne, and Pascal. However different the attitudes and values of these writers, they employ prose styles which aim, like the Baroque poetic styles, at making manner and matter one: the ideal is not the smooth and persuasive oratorical refashioning of ideas already formed but rather the vital expression of ideas in the process of formation.[20]

The typical prose writers of the Baroque age were distinctly conscious of, even programmatic about, their departures from the Ciceronian ideal. Sometimes they spoke of the new style as "Attic," implying (incorrectly) that they were modeling themselves on Demosthenes rather than Cicero. Sometimes, with more accuracy, they spoke of it as "Senecan." Modern critics have adopted, to an increasing degree, the neutral term "Baroque."

Style, then, and a certain shared habit of mind, give to the Baroque prose writers a unity which has nothing to do with specific ideas, philosophies, or values. The consistent traits of the Baroque prose writers are: an emphasis on individual experience, an avowed concentration on matter rather than manner, and a conviction that appropriate expression derives naturally, almost organically, from the particularities of thought and substance rather than from the categories of convention and rhetoric. This formulation abounds in seeming paradoxes: the very

20. Cf. Croll, *Style*.

word "Baroque" conjures up the idea of ornate adornment; and one of the major stylistic tendencies of the Baroque age is, I have suggested, accurately evoked by the term "Mannerism." But, as in the case of Baroque poetry viewed as a whole, the paradoxes may be resolved. The anti-Ciceronian movement, which is the central phenomenon of Baroque prose style, began as a conscious attempt to substitute the accurate particularities of a personal vision for the ready-made generalities of an oratorical style. The aim, involving the exaltation of matter over manner, of "things" over "words," remained constant for the great Baroque masters, [21] but for many of the minor writers anti-Ciceronianism gave birth to a "hopping" style as affected, as "mannered" in the common sense of the word, as the most academic Ciceronianism of the sixteenth century (typical of this tendency are such English writers as Owen Felltham and John Earle). Furthermore, the intellectual ferment of the seventeenth century allowed no commonly received intellectual position, and hence no thoroughly unified style of expression, to rule unchallenged. The idiosyncracy, even the eccentricity, of so much Baroque prose is to be regarded as the product not of mannered posturing but of the dedicated attempt to find a manner answerable to the personal vision.

Many of the Baroque writers—Montaigne, Burton, Browne, and Pascal come readily to mind—fashion for themselves a dramatic persona as memorable as Donne's or Herbert's. Such a writer as Bacon does not; there is little that is dramatic, little that is even personal, in his work. But even in Bacon, so atypical of the Baroque in most respects, a Baroque point of departure is evident—not only in his anti-Ciceronianism but also in the fact that his obsession with the inductive method reveals that sense

    21. It is this feature which relates Bacon most clearly to the age in which he wrote. See Croll, *Style,* pp. 219–22.

of the exclusive reality of the inner and individual which I have proposed as one of the central impulses of the sensibility of the age.

One further aspect of seventeenth-century prose writing will perhaps make my point clear: despite countless divergences in attitude, scheme of value, and technique, the Baroque prose artists understand each other. Sir Francis Bacon and Sir Thomas Browne offer as neat a contrast in sensibility as one can find in seventeenth-century English literature—Bacon, the prophet of scientific method, master of a prose style which attempts to excise the unruly and unpredictable vagaries of the personality; Browne, the last great heir of the medieval symbolic habit of mind, for whom the whole universe is a trope and for whom style is a means of rephrasing the great poem of creation. Yet Bacon, like no man after him, could say: "I have taken all knowledge to be my province," uttering the traditional and doomed ideal of universal wisdom, and Browne was, in his own distinctive way, a Baconian, whose longest work, the *Pseudodoxia Epidemica,* was an attempt to carry out Bacon's recommendation that a book be written exposing the vulgar errors in accepted opinion.

In France an even more striking contrast exists between Montaigne at the beginning of the Baroque age and Pascal near its close. Montaigne is Pascal's great enemy precisely because Pascal understands him so well and finds in the earlier essayist's exploration of an enigmatic self isolated in an incomprehensible world a yielding to the flux of experience which the later writer longs to transcend. Pascal, allied to Bacon—and to Montaigne— by his reliance on experience, is more closely allied to Donne and Browne by his profound need for some absolute transcendence of that experience. What ultimately unites all these writers is the examination of an inner world placed against the de-

ceptive appearances of the outer world and the communication
of their findings in a language that is concrete, dramatic, and
personal in imagery, sentence structure, and rhythm.

The great prose writers to whom I have been referring are
distinguished further from their predecessors by the fact that
their works are generally devoted, at least nominally, to some
extraliterary purpose—scientific, devotional, philosophical, or
didactic. This tendency in itself is typical of the Baroque, an age
in which prose fiction and the prose of entertainment in general
went into a marked decline, and it should make us dubious about
the conception, sometimes encountered, of the Baroque as an
age of frivolous and decorative literature. The purposeful, often
somber, nature of much Baroque prose parallels developments
in other genres—the emergence of the devotional lyric all over
western Europe, for example, or the shift from narrative poetry
on romance themes to narrative poetry on overtly Christian
themes (as in the Fletchers, Cowley, Milton, Du Bartas, d'Aubigné, Marino, and Vondel).

Despite the contrasts among the leading Baroque prose writers, we have seen a common concern with the motif of the individual isolated in a world of deceptive appearances. Turning
to fiction and drama we find a comparable obsession with the
relations of appearance and reality. In Spain, for example, the
Baroque age is framed by Cervantes at the beginning, whose
Don Quijote is one of the few masterpieces of prose fiction offered by the Baroque, and Calderón at the close. Illusion and
disillusionment, *engaño* and *desengaño,* are the great themes of
these masters, as they are of the whole Spanish Baroque. The relation to the general Baroque sensibility is evident.[22]

22. Opinions differ as to whether Cervantes is justly classified as a
Baroque writer; Calderón, however, is almost universally regarded as
one of the major figures of the Baroque. Curtius (especially pp. 280–301)
sees Spain as having a particularly strong "mannerist" tradition, and
H. Hatzfeld, in "El predominio del espiritu español en las literaturas del

Calderón, whose *La vida es sueño* is such a striking example
of the Baroque theme of appearance versus reality, reminds us
further that the Baroque is one of the few supremely great ages
of drama in the history of world literature. It is the age in which,
by common consent, the theatre reached its finest flowering in
England, France, Spain, and Holland. A certain problem raises
itself when we consider this fact: Why should an age which
showed itself so obsessed with the question of appearance and
reality, and so uncertain of its answers to that question, have
created such an eminent body of literature in that genre which,
above all others, confronts an audience with the concrete representation of man in action? It would be wise to postpone consideration of this question until a later chapter, concerned more
centrally with the drama (see below, pp. 66–89), but at this
point one might recognize that the drama itself, primitive and
ritualistic in its origins, retains always something of the character of those origins: the ludic and agonistic elements which are
its essence—role-playing and contest—imply a conviction, no
less operative for being possibly below the level of consciousness,
that ultimate reality, never to be determined by the appearance
of things, has the shape of the conflict of opposites. It is worth
remembering that much of the lyric poetry which we have been
considering is remarkable for its "dramatic" quality.

The authority, complexity, and profundity of Shakespeare's
work make it perhaps unrewarding to examine that work under
the rubric of any particular historical style, Renaissance, Mannerist, Baroque, or anything else. Nevertheless, all his plays

siglo XVII," *Revista de Filología Hispánica* 3 (1941): 9–23, makes the
more extravagant claim that Spain is the source of the Baroque spirit in
all European literature. See also Hatzfeld, in *Estudios sobre el barroco,*
who maintains further that Cervantes is a major Baroque figure and
Calderón a "barroquista," or exponent of a late, decadent, "amanerado"
form of Baroque style (pp. 69–72).

were composed after the general European Renaissance had begun shading into the Baroque, and the great tragedies and later romances belong to a time at which Baroque features (variously manifested in Donne, Giles Fletcher, John Webster, and others) were clearly dominant in English literature. Without proposing that Shakespeare be definitively classified as a "Baroque" artist, we might still find it profitable to note, briefly, his treatment of the theme of appearance and reality so obsessive for the entire epoch in question.

Shakespeare's preoccupation with the theme is evident at the very beginning of his career. In the earliest of the comedies, *The Comedy of Errors,* a conventional plot of mistaken identity, derived from Plautus, is handled with an elaboration and, occasionally, a poetic intensity which generate an effect not only of comic confusion but also of metaphysical wonder. The play offers little in characterization to compare with Shakespeare's mature work, but in the reactions of Antipholus of Syracuse to his incomprehensible predicament there is something of the passive openness to the workings of metamorphosis which will distinguish many figures in later plays—Sebastian in *Twelfth Night,* Edgar in *King Lear,* Antony in his last few scenes in *Antony and Cleopatra.* Worth noting also is the prominence in the play of the image of the sea, later so important in *Twelfth Night, Hamlet, Othello, King Lear, Pericles,* and, above all, *The Tempest.* The sea in Shakespeare is generally an ambiguous symbol, suggestive of both death and rebirth, separation and reunion, and so it operates in the plot of *The Comedy of Errors.* The symbol does not receive in that play its full development as an agency of magical transformations and reconciliations, as in *Pericles* or *The Tempest,* but in at least one passage it is associated with love as the element in which the individual identity in its finite and limiting aspect is purged away. The passage is that in which Antipholus S. avows his love to Luciana (3. 2. 45–51):

> Oh, train me not, sweet mermaid, with thy note,
>> To drown me in thy sister's flood of tears.
> Sing, siren, for thyself, and I will dote.
>> Spread o'er the silver waves thy golden hairs,
> And as a bed I'll take them, and there lie,
>> And, in that glorious supposition, think
> He gains by death that hath such means to die.[23]

One is reminded not only of the "sea-change" in *The Tempest* but also of the conclusion of the speech with which Orsino opens *Twelfth Night:*

> O spirit of love, how quick and fresh art thou!
> That, notwithstanding thy capacity
> Receiveth as the sea, naught enters there,
> Of what validity and pitch soe'er,
> But falls into abatement and low price,
> Even in a minute! So full of shapes is fancy
> That it alone is high fantastical.

Shakespeare's world is populated by the most completely realized individual characters in literature, but many of the most receptive of those characters, those who are most open to emotional experience, undergo an imaginative loss of identity which becomes, paradoxically, the condition of their identity at a higher level of existence. Romeo and Juliet, like lovers from Donne's *Songs and Sonets,* exchange identities and in so doing both lose and gain (a complex experience which both Shakespeare and Donne figure forth in the image of "dying," with the familiar Renaissance secondary meaning of "sexual climax"). At the highest pitch of experience the individual, sensing the illusory quality shared by both his own individuality and the entire phenomenal world, perceives experience as a shifting

23. The source of this and of subsequent quotations from Shakespeare is G. B. Harrison's one-volume edition of the *Complete Works* (New York, 1952).

flux of phantasmagoria, perpetual metamorphoses, behind
which lies the single reality figured forth in such images of
assimilation as the sea, the night, love, and music. So it is that
Antony, at the point of recognition of his tragic destiny, finds
in the sky an analogy for earthly life:

> Sometime we see a cloud that's dragonish,
> A vapor sometime like a bear or lion,
> A towered citadel, a pendent rock,
> A forked mountain, or blue promontory
> With trees upon't that nod unto the world
> And mock our eyes with air. Thou hast seen these signs,
> They are black vesper's pageants ....
> That which is now a horse, even with a thought
> The rack dislimns and makes it indistinct
> As water is in water.
>
> [4.14.2–11]

The passage ties in with the imagery of the four elements which
dominates *Antony and Cleopatra* from beginning to end, implying both the reduction of the phenomenal world to its com-
ponent parts and the transcendence of that world through a
passionate experience which elevates its participants to a position symbolized by the higher elements of air and fire. Antony,
who has "used to conquer standing on the earth" (3.7.66), has,
at the beginning of the play, given up his Roman element of
earth for the Egyptian element of water, associated throughout
with Cleopatra and with the principle of metamorphosis:

> Let Rome in Tiber melt, and the wide arch
> Of the ranged empire fall! Here is my space.
> Kingdoms are clay. Our dungy earth alike
> Feeds beast as man. ...
>
> [1.1.33–35]

The great descriptive speech of Enobarbus (2.2.195–245) ad-
duces all four elements to create his picture of Cleopatra, and
the battles between Antony and Caesar are significantly shaped
by Antony's decision to fight by water. Later, after the successful engagement on land, as Antony prepares to meet Caesar in
the second and finally disastrous sea-fight, he boasts:

> I would they'd fight i' the fire or i' the air.
> We'd fight there too. . . .
>
> [4.10.3–4]

The absoluteness of his passionate experience has made him incapable of effective action in the practical world of solid-seem-
ing appearances, within which Caesar is master. One is prepared for the lines from Cleopatra's death speech.

> I am fire and air. My other elements
> I give to baser life. . . .
>
> [5.2.292–93]

It is not only the experience of love which enables Shakespeare's characters to recognize the unreality of the phenomenal
world and the ultimate reality of some all-embracing unity.
Richard II revolves around one question: Is kingly power derived from the reality of the king's "name," or is the king's name
derived from the reality of kingly power?[24] Nothing in the
whole massive tetralogy of which *Richard II* is the first movement gives a final answer. It is worth noting, however, that that
unimaginative monarch, Henry IV, has one moment of illumination in which he is obsessed by one of Shakespeare's favorite
images of assimilation, against which the glories of an earthly
crown are measured. The moment occurs in Henry's apostrophe
to sleep *(2 Henry IV* 3.1.18–30):

24. See E. La Guardia, "Ceremony and History: The Problem of
Symbol from *Richard II* to *Henry V,*" in W. F. McNeir and T. N. Green-
field, *Pacific Coast Studies in Shakespeare* (Eugene, Ore., 1966), pp. 68–88.

Wilt thou upon the high and giddy mast
Seal up the ship boy's eyes, and rock his brains
In cradle of the rude imperious surge
And in the visitation of the winds,
Who take the ruffian billows by the top,
Curling their monstrous heads and hanging them
With deafening clamor in the slippery clouds,
That, with the hurly, death itself awakes?
Canst thou, O partial Sleep, give thy repose
To the wet sea boy in an hour so rude,
And in the calmest and most stillest night,
With all appliances and means to boot,
Deny it to a king? ...

The familiar collocation of sea, sleep, and music evokes an un-utterable reality in comparison with which political struggle and intrigue are the merest illusions.[25]

In a very different context *Much Ado About Nothing* presents a detailed view of the relations of appearance and reality. The entire play is concerned with the problem of "noting" as perception, with punning relationships to the "nothing" of the title (pronounced "noting" in Elizabethan English) and the "noting" engaged in by the musician (see, for example, 2.3.56–59). The evidence of the senses cannot be equated with reality, and Claudio and Don Pedro are convinced of Hero's guilt by "ocular proof" as unreliable as that which causes the destruction of Othello. In the case of Leonato individual pride and self-centeredness distort perception and even threaten to strangle parental affection. The characters capable of true "noting" —Beatrice, Benedick, Friar Francis—hold that capacity by vir-

25. G. Wilson Knight, *The Crown of Life* (London, 1947), passim, has much to say about the related images of sea, tempest, sleep, birth, and music. See also N. Frye, *A Natural Perspective* (New York and London, 1965), esp. pp. 118–59.

tue of a certain intuitive understanding which has nothing to
do with ocular proof and relatively little to do with abstract
reason. It has much more to do with the potentiality for self-
transcending love and faith.[26]

The Baroque preoccupation with the relations of appearance and reality is only one of the countless aspects under
which Shakespeare's achievement may be viewed. It is, however, an important one, and one which is constant in his work.
His final statement of the theme, in *The Tempest,* is complete,
and it epitomizes an attitude which I believe to be central to the
Baroque sensibility. It occurs in the most famous of Prospero's
speeches:

> Our revels now are ended. These our actors,
> As I foretold you, were all spirits, and
> Are melted into air, into thin air.
> And, like the baseless fabric of this vision,
> The cloud-capped towers, the gorgeous palaces,
> The solemn temples, the great globe itself—
> Yea, all which it inherit—shall dissolve
> And, like this insubstantial pageant faded,
> Leave not a rack behind. We are such stuff
> As dreams are made on, and our little life
> Is rounded with a sleep....
>
> > [4.1.148–58]

26. J. R. Brown, *Shakespeare and His Comedies* (London, 1957), pp.
117–18, is among the many critics who have noted the hierarchy of
perception in the church scene of *Much Ado.*

3

The Experience of Contradiction

A mong the constants of the Baroque sensibility, then, are an obsessive concern with the relations of appearance and reality and a conviction, expressed in various ways, that ultimate reality is some kind of all-embracing unity, accessible to the human spirit, if at all, only in moments of intense passionate experience. For the Baroque writer this passionate experience is not simply a matter of lax emotional surrender: openness to transcendent experience depends upon lively intellectual activity, often exercised in a rigidly formal manner,[1] just as the desirable surpassing of the individual identity depends upon the precise and self-aware definition of that identity. Seventeenth-century literature derives much of its tension from these paradoxes. Shakespeare's incomparably realized characters, I have suggested, exist in a world in which recurrent images of assimilation point up the unreality of the phenomenal. Donne's poetry is obsessed with questions of identity and with the paradoxical theme of simultaneous loss and realization of that identity in union with the beloved; Herbert's poetry is shot through with images of nests and protective enclosures, as Crashaw's is with images of melting, burning, and fusing.

1. L. L. Martz, *The Poetry of Meditation*, rev. ed. (New Haven, 1962), supplies an indispensable examination of certain aspects of that intellectual activity.

The self has a reality not to be found in the world of sense experience, but that self in turn must lose itself in order to find itself. Sir Thomas Browne projects through all his work a brilliantly delineated individual personality, but *Urn-Burial,* that archeological treatise which is also a magnificent meditation on death and immortality, ends with an eloquent vision of assimilation into the infinite: "And if any have been so happy as truly to understand Christian annihilation, extasis, exolution, liquefaction, transformation, the kisse of the Spouse, gustation of God, and ingression into the divine shadow, they have already had an handsome anticipation of heaven; the glory of the world is surely over, and the earth is ashes unto them."[2]

The Baroque conception of reality as transcendent underlies two prominent features of seventeenth-century literature—the paradoxical and the phantasmagoric. Emphasis upon one or another of these features results in the poetic styles which I have labeled "Metaphysical" and "High Baroque," manifestations, respectively, of the Mannerist and High Baroque alternatives within the Baroque age. The reader of seventeenth-century poetry is often struck by the contrast between these two poetic styles, between Donne, for example, and Crashaw; this chapter will examine some examples of Baroque lyric poetry in order to determine whether the two styles have a degree of identity, and whether any poetry of the period demonstrates an interpenetration of the two styles.

The role of the phantasmagoric in Baroque poetry has elicited much attention from modern critics. The hallucinatory, nightmarish, theatrical, or playful effects favored by such poets as Marino, Góngora, d'Aubigné, Gryphius, Vondel, and Crashaw have been analyzed extensively, and historians of style have suggested the relation of these effects to such varied phenomena

2. Sir Thomas Browne, *Religio Medici and Other Writings,* ed. F. L. Huntley (New York, 1951), p. 184.

as the influence of the Counter-Reformation, the rise of the new science, the decadence of High Renaissance literature, and the general violence and uncertainty of an age of wars, revolutions, and innovations. Except for Crashaw, the poets I have mentioned are all Continental, and Crashaw is notoriously the most Italianate of English seventeenth-century poets. Like his Continental coevals, he creates a phantasmagoric effect through an imagery which, though appealing vividly to the senses, is so disposed as to present a series of powerful contradictions of normal sensuous experience. The tears of his Magdalen, in "The Weeper," flow upward in defiance of the laws of gravity, as well as undergoing extravagantly conceited metamorphoses into stars, seeds, cream, and many other things.[3] The typical structure of Crashaw's lyrics, associational rather than logical, works with his sensuous conceits to create a frankly imaginary world which insists on its difference from ordinary life, even while, at the same time, both utilizing the sense data of that life and claiming an ontological status superior to it.

Many modern critics, as we have seen, stress the differences between the High Baroque poetry of Crashaw, Giles Fletcher, and numerous Continental poets and the Metaphysical or Mannerist poetry more typical of the English Baroque (e.g. Donne, Herbert, Marvell).[4] It might be rewarding, however, to consider some of the ways in which the sensuous, phantasmagoric kind of poetry and the intellectualized, argumentative kind are similar, some of the ways, indeed, in which they imply one another. One might begin by examining a poem by Andrew Marvell entitled "The Unfortunate Lover." Although not one of Mar-

3. Richard Crashaw, *Poetical Works,* ed. L. C. Martin (Oxford, 1927), pp. 79–83.
4. See my *European Metaphysical Poetry* (New Haven, 1961), pp. 2–3 and passim, as well as O. de Mourgues, *Metaphysical, Baroque and Précieux Poetry* (Oxford, 1953), pp. 67–75.

vell's better-known poems, it is in several ways typical of his imposing and idiosyncratic genius. The opening stanza of the poem is shot through with "Metaphysical" ambiguity—more precisely, with that cool multisignificance that is peculiarly Marvell's own:

> Alas, how pleasant are their dayes
> With whom the infant Love yet playes!
> Sorted by pairs, they still are seen
> By Fountains cool, and Shadows green.
> But soon these Flames do lose their light,
> Like Meteors of a Summers night:
> Nor can they to that Region climb,
> To make impression upon Time.[5]

Clearly set apart from the rest of the poem, this introduction seems to prepare us subtly for the appearance of the heroic lover who is the protagonist of the poem. It does so by setting up a contrast, by establishing the norm of "romantic" love (the kind manifested in the experience of Donne's "dull, sublunary lovers") and suggesting the forces that modify the absoluteness of that experience. In the quoted stanza the lovers' days are pleasant because "the infant Love" (i.e. Cupid) is still ("yet") playing with them—that is to say, they are still vouchsafed the experience of love. At the same time, however, their days are pleasant because the love they enjoy is merely an infant and is, as "yet," merely "playing" with them. The doom anticipated by the "Alas" that begins the poem may have either of two shapes: the lovers are to be pitied because their love will die out in time *or* because it will lose its idyllic quality and become the destructive force evoked in the rest of the poem. The "Flames" either will become extinct or will lose their capacity for illumi-

5. Andrew Marvell, *Poems and Letters,* ed. H. M. Margoliouth, 2 vols. (Oxford, 1952), 1:27–29.

nating without losing their capacity for consuming. In any case, the idyllic love which locates the lovers appropriately "by Fountains cool, and Shadows green"—images associated throughout Marvell's lyric work with the ideal order of nature, which attracts man but of which he can only fleetingly be a part—cannot last in a human context. Love will dwindle into nothing, or it will become the destructive force which it is for the protagonist of the poem. The heroic love that the protagonist represents dominates existence—or it doesn't exist at all. Or both.

Stanzas 2 and 3 present the unfortunate lover, whose existence may either negate or exemplify the amorous experience evoked in the first stanza:

> 'Twas in a Shipwrack, when the Seas
> Rul'd, and the Winds did what they please,
> That my poor Lover floting lay,
> And, e're brought forth, was cast away:
> Till at the last the master-Wave
> Upon the Rock his Mother drave;
> And there she split against the Stone,
> In a *Cesarian Section.*
>
> The Sea him lent these bitter Tears
> Which at his Eyes he alwaies bears.
> And from the Winds the Sighs he bore,
> Which through his surging Breast do roar.
> No day he saw but that which breaks,
> Through frighted Clouds in forked streaks.
> While round the ratling Thunder hurl'd,
> As at the Fun'ral of the World.

[1.27–28]

One is struck here by the purposeful distortion of the universe through sensibility which Mme de Mourgues sees as definitive

for Baroque poetry and finds exemplified in such poets as
d'Aubigné, Saint-Amant, and Théophile de Viau. The spec-
tacular hyperboles are, as Pierre Legouis has contended, pushed
so far as to suggest parody, but nevertheless, as the Misses Bradbrook and Lloyd Thomas point out, the picture of the lover
projects a sense of elemental power strangely at variance with
the "heraldic stiffness" of the design of the poem.[6] The systematic violence of the imagery has something to do with the
fact that the burlesque overtones of the poem do not render
entirely ludicrous its emblematic picture of heroic passion. The
mythic scope of that imagery has something more to do with
it: quite consistently, throughout the poem, the sufferings of
the lover are identified with the elements of nature, as in stanza
3, or are placed on a level of significance which makes them, as
it were, competitive with the elements of nature, as in stanza 7:

> See how he nak'd and fierce does stand,
> Cuffing the Thunder with one hand;
> While with the other he does lock,
> And grapple, with the stubborn Rock:
> From which he with each Wave rebounds,
> Torn into Flames, and ragg'd with Wounds.
> And all he saies, a Lover drest
> In his own Blood does relish best.
>
> [1.28]

The poet makes exorbitant claims for his protagonist, but to
some extent he succeeds in justifying them.

In a way, however, the reader is prepared to accept the claims
of passion precisely *because* of the overtones of parody or

---

6. De Mourgues, *Metaphysical,* pp. 73–75; P. Legouis, *Andrew Mar-
vell* (Oxford, 1965), p. 32; M. C. Bradbrook and M. G. Lloyd Thomas,
Andrew Marvell (Cambridge, 1961), p. 29. See also A. Berthoff, *The
Resolved Soul* (Princeton, 1970), pp. 75–88.

burlesque, the consistent wit which plays over the poem and implies that the poet does not take his stupendous hero altogether solemnly or, indeed, at all seriously. The lines spoken by the lover at the end of stanza 7 are surely comic in their connotations, and the concluding stanza of the poem incorporates an ambiguity which makes a burlesque reading even more tempting:

> This is the only *Banneret*
> That ever Love created yet:
> Who though, by the Malignant Starrs,
> Forced to live in Storms and Warrs:
> Yet dying leaves a Perfume here,
> And Musick within every Ear:
> And he in Story only rules,
> In a field *Sable* a Lover *Gules.*
>
> [1:28–29]

Does *Story* here mean history or legend, fact or fiction? And how are we to interpret the modifier *only?* Does the lover *only,* that is, uniquely, rule in history, or does the lover rule *only* in legend, in fiction? At the end, as throughout, the tone of the poem is poised neatly between passionate declaration and elaborate spoof.

The qualities of ambiguity and irony, the urbane tone of playfulness, are, most critics would agree, associated with Metaphysical poetry of the sort written by Donne, Herbert, and Marvell more than with the violent, hallucinatory poetry of Crashaw and many poets of the Continental Baroque (though this is surely not to deny to a poet like Marino his share of sophisticated wit). And indeed, it seems to me that "The Unfortunate Lover" is a fair example of Metaphysical style. What I would contend is that the sensuous, hallucinatory manner and the witty, ironic

manner are rooted in the same habit of mind and the same conception of art. Such poems as this, in which the two manners appear simultaneously, make apparent the identity of the impulse
—which derives, I believe, from the preoccupations discussed in
chapter 2.

Marvell's poem distorts the ordinary techniques of statement,
poetic or otherwise, much as it distorts the sensuous world—and
with much the same effect. Just as his imagery, in a High Baroque manner, succeeds in creating a weird, hallucinatory world
which has all the compelling precision of a dream, so too his
witty way with diction and syntax creates a world where one
doesn't have to choose, where the exclusive logic of decision has
lost its applicability. The imaginative "otherness" of Baroque
poetic worlds resides most of all in their dramatization of the
experience of contradiction—not only through the disposition
of sensuous images in such a manner as to defy ordinary experience but also through the thoroughgoing subversion of logic.
Our reason tells us that if something is true only in fiction it cannot be true in fact. Our reason tells us that if love is by definition
a transitory experience, it cannot even pretend to the static
absoluteness embodied in the unfortunate lover's emblematic
poses. Confronted by a contradiction, we know from reason that
only one of its terms can have existential validity. But our emotional experience may tell us something different, and this emotional experience is the material of Marvell's poetry.

One quality of poetry like Marvell's is that it cannot be successfully paraphrased: "The Unfortunate Lover," like "The Garden," "Upon Appleton House," and "The Picture of Little T.C.
in a Prospect of Flowers," is not really a poem that conveys a
meaning; it is a poem that constitutes an experience—the imaginative experience of the validity of contradictory truths. As
such, it is something ideally to be performed rather than some-

thing definitively to be construed; it is something which exists, as it were, in the sphere of play, with all the connotations of jest, mask, and make-believe contained in that word.

Marvell, for all his urbanity, is one of the most idiosyncratic and elusive of poets, but his concern with the experience of contradiction is shared by a significant number of other poets of the Baroque age. John Donne, in his exploration of the related phenomena of erotic and religious experience, displays a similar interest. In Donne we find the theme of contradiction typically approached not through the creation of phantasmagoric world of sensuous experience but almost solely through a rigorously intellectual concentration on paradox. His "Lovers Infinitenesse," for example, begins with the statement of a metaphysical problem embodied in passionate experience:

> If yet I have not all thy love,
> Deare, I shall never have it all,
> I cannot breath one other sigh, to move,
> Nor can intreat one other teare to fall,
> And all my treasure, which should purchase thee,
> Sighs, teares, and oathes, and letters I have spent.
> Yet no more can be due to mee,
> Then at the bargaine made was ment,
> If then thy gift of love were partiall,
> That some to mee, some should to others fall,
>   Deare, I shall never have Thee All.
>
> Or if then thou gavest mee all,
> All was but All, which thou hadst then;
> But if in thy heart, since, there be or shall,
> New love created bee, by other men,
> Which have their stocks intire, and can in teares,
> In sighs, in oathes, and letters outbid mee,
> This new love may beget new feares,

For, this love was not vowed by thee.
And yet it was, thy gift being generall,
The ground, thy heart is mine, what ever shall
    Grow there, deare, I should have it all.[7]

As one of Donne's modern critics has observed, the basis of feeling in the poem is "the love of the finite for the infinite."[8] There is thus a specific contradiction between the aspiration forced upon the lover by his passion and the logically demonstrable impossibility of his achieving that aspiration. It is the business of the poem, of course, to achieve the aspiration nevertheless:

Yet I would not have all yet,
Hee that hath all can have no more,
And since my love doth every day admit
New growth, thou shouldst have new rewards in store;
Thou canst not every day give me thy heart,
If thou canst give it, then thou never gavest it:
Loves riddles are, that though thy heart depart,
It stayes at home, and thou with losing savest it:
But wee will have a way more liberall,
Then changing hearts to joyne them, so wee shall
    Be one, and one anothers All.[9]

The discrepancy between finite being and infinite desire is here further complicated by the paradox of the shared identity of lovers, one of Donne's favorites. Regarded as anything more substantial than a hyperbolic trope, the joining of the lovers' hearts is as logically impossible as the finite lover's thirst for in-

---

7. John Donne, *Poetical Works,* ed. H. J. C. Grierson, 2 vols. (Oxford, 1912), 1:17. See also my reading of the poem in the Introduction to my edition of *John Donne, Poetry and Prose* (New York, 1967), pp. xvii–xx.

8. A. Stein, *John Donne's Lyrics* (Minneapolis, 1962), p. 158.

9. Donne, 1:17–18. Another Donne lyric which treats similar material in a rimilar way is "Loves Growth" (1:33–34).

finity. Both the problem and its solution can exist only in the
"other" world of art, not in the "real" world. But since both
problem and solution refer validly to existing emotions, certain
questions are raised as to the nature of what is real. The experience of contradiction, whether sensuously or intellectually presented, is the major form assumed by the Baroque concern with
appearance and reality. It is not surprising that, in Donne's
poem, the problem is stated and resolved through wit, nor is it
surprising that the statement takes the form of imagery traditionally associated with man's redemption through Christ, while
the resolution becomes an adaptation of the great Christian paradox that the loss of life is the condition of eternal life.

Sexual love and religious devotion are the two great areas
in which the experience of contradiction forces its claim upon
the imagination most insistently. Appropriately, just as Donne
in "Lovers Infinitenesse" uses religious references in order to
express a desire rooted in sexuality, so in a good many of his
Divine Poems he resorts to sexual imagery in order to express
his religious desire. The fabric of contradiction is tightly woven
in Donne's poetry, the absolute of spirituality and the absolute
of sensuality repeatedly becoming identified with each other.
The familiar lines which close his great sonnet "Batter my heart,
three person'd God" will serve as well as any others to epitomize
the devotional application of Donne's particular version of the
Baroque manner:

> Yet dearely I love you, and would be loved faine,
> But am betroth'd unto your enemie:
> Divorce mee, untie, or breake that knot againe,
> Take mee to you, imprison mee, for I
> Except you enthrall mee, never shall be free,
> Nor ever chast, except you ravish mee.[10]

10. Donne, 1:328.

The use of sexual imagery in the expression of devotional impulses is altogether standard in the writings of the mystics: Crashaw's "Hymne to the Name and Honour of the Admirable Sainte Teresa" typifies the affinity between that mystic's erotic metaphors and the more decorative variety of Baroque poetic style:

> How kindly will thy gentle Heart
> Kisses the sweetly-killing Dart!
> And close in his embraces keep
> Those delicious Wounds, that weep
> Balsom to heal themselves with. Thus
> When These thy Deaths, so numerous,
> Shall all at last dy into one,
> And melt thy Soul's sweet mansion;
> Like a soft lump of incense, hasted
> By too hott a fire, & wasted
> Into perfuming clouds, so fast
> Shalt thou exhale to Heavn at last
> In a resolving Sigh...[11]

Here the contraries of pain and rapture, flesh and spirit, multiplicity and unity, are fused into a single experience of the imagination through the agency of a sensibility which utilizes the sense data of worldly experience but rearranges those data in such a way as to transcend them, creating a world in which the ordinary contradictions have lost their capacity for enforcing choice. Different as Donne's poem is, it operates as a similar resolution of opposites: intense religious experience (like intense amorous experience) enables its recipient to embrace the irreconcilable alternatives of ordinary—a more appropriate word than "real"—life. The work of art is, for the three Baroque poets I have been considering, the earnest of the reality behind the

11. Crashaw, *Poetical Works*, p. 320.

apparent fact of contradiction, and it becomes thus an object to be experienced rather than a text to be paraphrased or a message to be decoded.

The Continental literatures offer many examples of poetry which, like Crashaw's, operates as a sensuous phantasmagoria affirming the simultaneous validity of opposed experiences, or which, like Donne's or Marvell's, uses logic and argumentation to subvert the bases of logic and argumentation, establishing thus the validity of opposed propositions in the realm of thought itself. In the sacred and secular lyrics of the German Paul Fleming, the Dutchman Constantijn Huygens, and the Spaniard Francisco de Quevedo, to select only a few examples, the same conception of art and of the important relationship between the work of art and the contradictory phenomena of intense emotional experience makes itself felt, sometimes creating a sensuous phantasmagoria which adds its hallucinatory effects to the performance, sometimes exploiting formal paradox, verbal ambiguity, and pervasive irony to the same effect.

In this chapter my observations have concerned themselves quite strongly with poetic themes—themes which seem consistently to underlie the typical Baroque devices of paradox and irony, oxymoron and catachresis, conceit and hyperbole. Selection of theme is in itself significant: the fact that so many poets of the Baroque chose to contemplate the mystery of love rather than detailing the beauties of the beloved, like the fact that they chose to examine the mystery of man's relation to God rather than writing hymns in praise of His omnipotence, goes a certain distance toward defining the style of the age. But the suggestion of a direct connection between much Baroque poetry and intense emotional experience ought not to be taken as implying any sort of blurring of the distance between art and life, a distance which the Baroque poets recognized and observed with a degree of sophistication seldom achieved since. The Baroque poet, conscious of the exceptional quality inherent in the mysteries of love and religion, created his art as an analogy—something equally exceptional, equally true to the illogical realities, and equally far from the masquerades of *common* reality. Baroque poetry, whether as the vivid distortion of the senses or as the witty subversion of the intellect, is a kind of art at the farthest remove from the naïve imitation of observed reality, at the farthest remove, one is tempted to say, from nature. But one might think of the words of Sir Thomas Browne: "Nature hath made one World, and Art another. In brief, all things are artificial; for Nature is the Art of God."[12] Or to close again with Shakespeare, one might remember the words of Polixenes to Perdita in *The Winter's Tale:*

> ... This is an art
> Which does mend Nature—change it rather, but
> The art itself is Nature.[13]
>
> [4.4.95–97]

12. Browne, *Religio Medici,* p. 18.
13. William Shakespeare, *Complete Works,* ed. G. B. Harrison (New York, 1948), p. 1454.

The World as Theatre

Totus mundus agit histrionem—"All the world plays the actor." So ran the motto over the newly erected Globe Theatre in London in 1599. Shakespeare's *As You Like It* was one of the first plays presented in the new building, and it has been suggested[1] that the most famous set-piece of that play, Jaques's speech beginning "All the world's a stage," is a kind of elaboration of the motto. In any case, the ancient topos of the world as stage held a particular fascination for Shakespeare, as it did for the entire seventeenth century. One thinks readily of the play-within-a-play motif in *Hamlet,* of Prospero's "Our revels now are ended" speech in *The Tempest,* or of the lines of King Lear: "When we are born, we cry that we are come / To this great stage of fools."

Curtius has traced in detail the history of the world-as-stage topos, from Plato and St. Paul to John of Salisbury, whose *Polycraticus* (1159) he regards as the specific source for most sixteenth- and seventeenth-century occurrences, citing in support of his contention the frequent reprintings of that work during

---

1. G. B. Harrison, ed., *Shakespeare: Complete Works* (New York, 1948), p. 773. E. R. Curtius, *European Literature and the Latin Middle Ages,* trans. W. R. Trask (New York, 1953), p. 140. Cf. the motto composed by Vondel for the Amsterdam theatre in 1637: "De wereld is een speeltoneel, / Elk speelt zijn rol en krijgt zijn deel" (J. van den Vondel, *Werken,* ed. A. Verwey [Amsterdam, 1937], p. 951).

those centuries.[2] It seems likely, however, that the theatrical
metaphor enjoys its popularity during the Baroque age not only
because of the availability of one particular source but also because the metaphor expresses with great cogency the concern
with the illusory quality of experience which runs obsessively
through the literature of the first two-thirds of the seventeenth
century. Occurrences of the topos are more frequent after 1590
than before, and it may be significant that the reprintings of the
Polycraticus are concentrated most heavily between 1595 and
1677, in the very heart of the Baroque era.

   The theatrical metaphor itself may have something to do
with the great efflorescence of European drama during the Baroque age—the governing topos of the world as stage justifying,
as it were, the conception of the stage as world, and thus bestowing on the dramatist's art that status of reality without
which any art degenerates into mere entertainment or adornment. But the metaphor is by no means confined to expression
in dramatic literature. Gracián entitles one chapter of his *Criti-
cón* "El gran teatro del universo,"[3] and Robert Burton, in his
encyclopedic *Anatomy of Melancholy,* writes:

> For now, as Sarisburiensis said in his time, *totus mundus his-
> trionem agit,* the whole world plays the fool; we have a new
> theatre, a new scene, a new comedy of errors, a new company
> of personate actors, *volupiae sacra,* as Calcagninus wittily
> feigns in his Apologues, are celebrated all the world over,
> where all the actors were madmen and fools and every hour
> changed habits or took that which came next.[4]

More somberly, in his *Religio Medici,* Sir Thomas Browne vis-

2. Curtius, *European Literature,* pp. 139–41.
3. Ibid., p. 141.
4. Robert Burton, *The Anatomy of Melancholy (A Selection),* ed.
L. Babb (East Lansing, Mich., 1965), p. 36.

ualizes the Day of Judgment as the final scene in what has been
all along a play: "This is that one day, that shall include and
comprehend all that went before it; wherein, as in the last scene,
all the Actors must enter, to compleat and make up the Catas-
trophe of this great piece."[5] And, with a different emphasis, John
Donne writes in Sermon *XXIII* of the 1640 folio: "The whole
frame of the world is the theater, and every creature the stage,
the medium, the glass in which we may see God."[6]

Lyric poets too were fond of the topos, none more than Tommaso Campanella, whose sonnet "Nel teatro del mondo am-
mascherate ("Masked upon the theatre of the world")[7] alters
the emphasis of the Donne quotation by presenting God as a
combination dramatist and stage director, who derives satisfaction from observing the performance of His work by the beings
He has created. Campanella's treatment, however, has really
more in common with earlier versions of the topos than with
the fully Baroque versions. For him, as for Luther, Ronsard, Sir
Walter Ralegh, and Sir Henry Wotton, the idea of the world as
theatre operates purely as metaphor, as a moral insight to be
communicated through a clever but perhaps arbitrary analogy.
An English Renaissance poem, Ralegh's "What is Our Life?"
exemplifies the manner:

> What is our life? a play of passion,
> Our mirth the musicke of division,
> Our mothers wombes the tyring houses be,
> Where we are drest for this short Comedy,
> Heaven the Judicious sharpe spectator is,

5. Sir Thomas Browne, *Religio Medici and Other Writings*, ed. F. L.
Huntley (New York, 1951), p. 53.
6. *Seventeenth-Century Prose and Poetry*, ed. A. M. Witherspoon and
F. J. Warnke (New York, 1963), p. 80.
7. Tommaso Campanella, *Poesie*, ed. M. Vinciguerra (Bari, 1938),
pp. 23–24.

That sits and markes still who doth act amisse,
Our graves that hide us from the searching Sun,
Are like drawne curtaynes when the play is done,
Thus march we playing to our latest rest,
Onely we dye in earnest, that's no Jest.[8]

Ralegh's poem works on principles similar to those of allegory. Like his contemporary Spenser, Ralegh forms images
which stand for earthly experience without being organically
related to that experience, as we see from the brilliant but frag-
mentized quality of the analogies as well as from the significant
modulation into simile near the end of the poem. A later poet,
Andrew Marvell, is equally devoted to the theatre-topos, but his
handling of it is altogether Baroque. For Marvell it is more than
an instructive analogy: the theatre is, in its essential nature as
metamorphosis and conflict, an absolutely valid projection of
the inner reality of earthly experience. To see the world as a
theatre is to see it as it is—not because life, in its "dramatic" texture, sometimes *resembles* a stage spectacle, but because life,
recognized as a conflict of opposites and as a shifting phantasmagoria of appearances, is fully identifiable with a stage spectacle.

Any play implicitly tells us "the theatre is like the world,"
dramatic art itself being the imitation of an action. The traditional topos tells us, as in Ralegh, "the world is like the theatre,"
wittily noting the stagy quality life sometimes assumes. Tradition is fond of two minor variations or heightenings of the topos:
the local application in which a literary character (e.g. Richard
III in Shakespeare's play) says "I am playing a part," and the sophisticated device, at least as old as Plautus and often found in
Shakespeare, wherein a character remarks, in effect, "this play is
like a play." The characteristic Baroque handling of the topos

8. Sir Walter Ralegh, cited in H. Gardner, ed., *The Metaphysical Poets* (Oxford, 1957), p. 33.

differs from these: it consists rather of saying "the world is the theatre"—a reversible equation which means also "the theatre is the world." For the Baroque literary artist—Marvell, Burton, Browne, Gracián, Calderón, and, in much of his work, Shakespeare—the topos asserts not a similarity but an identity, and it thus becomes a major vehicle for expressing the radical Baroque conviction that the phenomenal world is illusion.

Marvell's "Dialogue between the Resolved Soul and Created Pleasure" does not develop, as does Ralegh's poem, a set of witty analogies between life and a play. What it does, rather, is to take on the very form of drama, the form of an agon—one which is witnessed as a pleasing spectacle by Heaven:

> Earth cannot shew so brave a Sight
> As when a single Soul does fence
> The Batteries of alluring Sense,
> And Heaven views it with delight.[9]

Similarly, of the protagonist of "The Unfortunate Lover," we are told:

> And now, when angry Heaven wou'd
> Behold a spectacle of Blood,
> Fortune and He are call'd to play
> At sharp before it all the day.
>
> [p. 28]

Marvell's lyrics often assume the dialogue form of drama, and they almost always derive their inner form from the conflict of diametrical opposites: the ideal emotion in "The Definition of Love" ". . . was begotten by despair / Upon Impossibility" (p. 36); and the "Dialogue between the Soul and Body" is

---

9. Andrew Marvell, *Poems and Letters,* ed. H. M. Margoliouth, 2d ed., 2 vols. (Oxford, 1952), 1:10. Subsequent references to Marvell in the text will be to this edition.

shaped by the fact that the interlocutors, pursuing mutually exclusive goals of pure, undifferentiated Spirit and pure, undifferentiated Nature, are paradoxically constrained by their human
union to argue in terms which imply the values of their opposites. In Marvell, more than in any other Metaphysical poet, one
is made aware of the links between the paradoxical vision and
the dramatic mode.

Nowhere is one more aware of these links than in "Upon
Appleton House," the longest of the poet's nonsatiric works, a
complex, curious, and ill-understood poem which is beginning
to assume its rightful place as one of the masterpieces of seventeenth-century English poetry. Starting as what seems an exercise in the familiar Renaissance genre of the complimentary
poem in praise of a patron's house, Marvell's work describes in
its opening stanzas the country house of the great Lord Fairfax,
to whose daughter Maria the poet was at the time acting as tutor.
The ideally suitable proportions of the house and the hospitality
of its master and mistress are among the traditional motifs developed. Before long, however, the poem changes into something
resembling a different genre altogether—the topographical
poem as given definition a decade earlier by Sir John Denham in
"Cooper's Hill." The resemblance to that proto-Augustan work
is merely superficial: the historical digression which the landscape inspires in Marvell is an occasion not for moral common-
places expressed in a general manner but for an exuberant mock-
heroic account of how an earlier Fairfax abducted his beloved
from a nunnery whose dishonest and flattering occupants had
enticed her thither. The episode is fraught with significance, relating as it does to the theme of fertility central to the poem, but
the tone of the account is unmistakably playful, in every sense of
that complex word.

After the historical digression the poem modulates into a
witty description of the Fairfax garden through military meta-

phors (the poem was composed shortly after the civil wars, in
which Fairfax had been a leader of the Parliamentary forces),
followed by a lengthy description of the mowing of the fields, a
section which is the key to the whole work:

> To See Men through this Meadow Dive,
> We wonder how they rise alive.
> As, under Water, none does know
> Whether he fall through it or go.
> But, as the Marriners that sound,
> And show upon their Lead the Ground,
> They bring up Flow'rs so to be seen,
> And prove they've at the Bottom been.
>
> [p. 70]

For Marvell, as for Shakespeare, the sea is the element of transformation and metamorphosis, and in these lines, as in the more
famous passage (ll.41–48) from "The Garden," it is identified
with the entire green world of nature, a world which operates on
principles of constant metamorphosis and agon. The association
with theatre becomes overt in the next stanza:

> No Scene that turns with Engines strange
> Does oftner then these Meadows change.
> For when the Sun the Grass hath vext,
> The tawny Mowers enter next;
> Who seem like *Israelites* to be,
> Walking on foot through a green Sea.
> To them the Grassy Deeps divide,
> And crowd a Lane to either Side.
>
> [p. 71]

The lines clearly refer to such Baroque theatrical spectacles as
the masque and the opera, with their reliance on elaborate and

rapidly changing stage effects.[10] But the development of the
scene turns it into more quintessential—and primitive—theatre:
the mowers become figures of conflict, the mown field resembles
"A Camp of Battail newly fought" (p. 72), and death enters with
the accidental slaying of a nesting bird. There is an air of savage
and joyful ritual about the whole thing—in the preparing and
eating of the bird and in the mowers' dance which concludes the
day's efforts. If the mowers' ritual has to do with death (and the
traditional emblem of Death the Mower figures in the passage),
it has to do with rebirth as well: it is an action of involvement in
the unending cycle of nature.[11] The mowing sequence constitutes an experience of the reality of nature and, as such, assumes
the shape of theatre, the shape of agon and metamorphosis:

> This *Scene* again withdrawing brings
> A new and empty Face of things;
> A levell'd space, as smooth and plain,
> As Clothes for *Lilly* stretcht to stain.
> The World when first created sure
> Was such a Table rase and pure.
> Or rather such is the *Toril*
> Ere the Bulls enter at Madril.
>
> [p. 72]

In the context of the continuing theatrical metaphor the annual
overflowing of the meadow by the river (an obvious fertility

10. J. Rousset, *La Littérature de l'âge baroque en France: Circé et le
paon* (Paris, 1954), examines the importance of stage spectacle in the
Baroque age. See esp. chaps. 1–3.
11. See my article "Sacred Play: Baroque Poetic Style," *Journal of
Aesthetics and Art Criticism* 22, no. 4 (Summer 1964): 455–64. For a
somewhat different interpretation of the poem, see D. C. Allen, *Image
and Meaning: Metaphoric Traditions in Renaissance Poetry* (Baltimore,
1960), pp. 115–53.

motif) becomes part of a series of "acts" in the technical theatrical sense of the word as well as in the general sense:

> Then, to conclude these pleasant Acts,
> *Denton* sets ope its *Cataracts;*
> And makes the Meadow truly be
> (What it but seem'd before) a Sea.
>
> [p. 73]

Metaphor has become metamorphosis, as it has a way of doing
in Marvell, and, with the life-giving element spreading over the
fields of Appelton House, the speaker of the poem withdraws to
the woods, where, in close communion with nature, he under-
goes his own metamorphoses—into a bird, a tree, and, finally,
"some great *Prelate of the Grove*" (p. 77). Later his priesthood
of the grove transforms itself into something curiously, if play-
fully, Christlike, and the ritual implications of the mowing
scene receive a bizarre heightening:

> Bind me ye *Woodbines* in your 'twines,
> Curle me about ye gadding *Vines,*
> And Oh so close your Circles lace,
> That I may never leave this Place:
> But, lest your fetters prove too weak,
> Ere I your Silken Bondage break,
> Do you, *O Brambles,* chain me too,
> And courteous Briars nail me through.
>
> [p. 78]

The poem concludes with the appearance of Maria, a version of
the female principle through whose agency the virtues of the
Fairfax family will be continued into future times. Participating
imaginatively in the cycle of nature manifested at Appleton
House, the speaker of the poem has been vouchsafed an experience of reality, an experience which, inevitably, assumes the

theatrical shape of agon, transformation, and play. The poem prominently employs the traditional theatre-topos to communicate its recognition that the world is theatre, as theatre is the world.

Probably no poet has ever been more obsessed by the conception of the world as theatre than has Shakespeare. Almost every one of his plays employs the topos to some extent, in one or another of its manifold forms.[12] A certain development, however, may be perceived. The earlier Shakespeare, the dramatist whose art (though never ultimately to be circumscribed by classification) participates most fully in Renaissance style, is fond of the topos in its most traditional and detachable form: "the world is like the theatre." It finds its normal expression in set-pieces wittily observing the analogy—Antonio's lines in *The Merchant of Venice:*

> I hold the world but as the world, Gratiano—
> A stage, where every man must play a part,
> And mine a sad one.[13]
>
> [1.1.77–79]

or, most notably, Jaques's speech in *As You Like It:*

> All the world's a stage,
> And all the men and women merely players.
> They have their exits and their entrances,
> And one man in his time plays many parts.
>
> [2.7.139–42]

and so on through the "seven ages of man." It is the mood of Ralegh's "What is Our Life?"—philosophical, moralistic, frank-

12. A. Righter, *Shakespeare and the Idea of the Play* (New York, 1962), examines in detail Shakespeare's use of the theatrical metaphor.

13. Shakespeare, *Complete Works,* ed. G. B. Harrison (New York, 1948), p. 584. Subsequent citations of Shakespeare in the text will be to this edition.

ly analogical. In essence, such speeches imply a play which is an imitation of a real world which is *not* a stage but which in some respects resembles one.

More complex are the implications of the motif of disguise so central to Shakespearean comedy. The inveterate habit of masking and role-playing displayed by the characters in *Love's Labor's Lost, Much Ado About Nothing, As You Like It,* and *Twelfth Night* suggests a world rather like Marvell's; it is a world in which the characters with the most vivid personal identities—Beatrice, Benedick, Rosalind, Viola, Feste—possess those identities partly by virtue of their cheerful willingness to compromise them by disguise. The conspicuous femaleness of Rosalind and Viola, one might note, is intensified rather than diminished by their assumption of male disguise, and Malvolio lays himself open to being "most notoriously abused" precisely because he is so injudicious as to contemplate his own identity with unquestioning self-assurance and complacency. The plays mentioned are all "festive comedies,"[14] deeply involved with the cycle of nature, and their ritual quality is nowhere more evident than in the consistency with which they insist on the motif of the transformation of the self—through disguise, through drink, through music, most of all, through love. By means of role-playing, the creatures of Shakespeare's comic world participate in the reality of nature, which manifests itself as the ceaseless masquerade of the seasonal year.

If metamorphosis is an element which relates Marvell's pastoral world and Shakespeare's comic world, so too is agon. Conflict of some sort is patently the essence of drama, but it is notable that, in Shakespeare's high comedies, the conflicts central to the plot are generally slighted in favor of sportive, exuberant play-conflicts at the periphery of plot. It is in such latter conflicts that the soul of comedy is to be found. The most

14. C. L. Barber, *Shakespeare's Festive Comedy* (Princeton, 1959), passim.

famous example, of course, is *Much Ado About Nothing,* in which the witty love-combat of Beatrice and Benedick steals the show completely from the conflict between Don John and his dupes, the conflict on which the plot is erected. But some such agon is the center also of *Love's Labor's Lost,* in which the lords of Navarre and the ladies of France line up against each other in a formal tournament of amorous wit, and *As You Like It,* in which the plot-conflict of usurper versus victim is virtually abandoned for the delineation of the disguised Rosalind's sweet needling of her lover. *Totus mundus agit histrionem:* Shakespeare's high comedies owe a large part of their artistic power to the fact that they present reality in its aspect as drama, as metamorphosis and agon. Their very mode of being is rooted in a profound perception, of which Jaques's sententious speech is merely an affected approximation.

Hamlet's first extended speech, expressing his tortured concern with the relations of appearance and reality, makes conspicuous use of theatrical metaphor:

> Seems, madam! Nay, it is. I know not "seems."
> 'Tis not alone my inky cloak, good Mother,
> Nor customary suits of solemn black,
> Nor windy suspiration of forced breath—
> No, nor the fruitful river in the eye,
> Nor the dejected havior of the visage,
> Together with all forms, moods, shapes of grief—
> That can denote me truly. These indeed seem,
> For they are actions that a man might play.
> But I have that within which passeth show,
> These but the trappings and the suits of woe.
>
> [1.2.76–86]

There has been an important shift in emphasis. "Role-playing," identified in the high comedies with such qualities as vitality, sympathy, and insight into nature, has here become identified with falsity, insincerity, and sterility. Hamlet is tormented by the suspicion that his grief for his dead father is a mere role-playing emotion, not rooted in his private self as is his anguish at his mother's betrayal and his consequent sense of defilement. His anguish is, of course, intensified unbearably shortly after that speech when he learns of the murder of his father and his obligation to avenge that murder. The role thrust upon him is one he should be able to play without any trace of theatricality; yet, for reasons he cannot understand, he cannot play it at all.

The great soliloquy "Oh, what a rogue and peasant slave am I!" (2.2.576–634) is permeated with theatrical imagery which proposes the contrast between reality and playing. Neverthe-less, the soliloquy attributes a degree of positive function to the theatre: the projected "mousetrap" will "catch the conscience of the King"; the performed fiction will have an effect on the real, nontheatrical world. Shortly before, Hamlet has com-mented on the positive function of the theatre when he refers to the players as "the abstract and brief chronicles of the time" (2.2.549–50). One notes here that the positive function is iden-tified with the capacity of the theatre for mimicking accurately the real world beyond the theatre: the attitude is paraphrase-able as "the theatre is like the world," not as "the theatre is the world; the world is the theatre." The tragic universe of *Hamlet*, unlike either the comic universe of the plays of the 1590s or the very different comic universe of the late romances, seems to have no place for the world-theatre topos in its full Baroque sense.

"Seems," that is, until Act 5, when Hamlet has returned from his sea-voyage with a mysteriously altered personality. The graveyard scene which opens the act is a definitive representa-tion of the Prince's melancholy, but an attentive reading will perhaps reveal that Hamlet's attitude has undergone significant changes in emphasis. The obsession with mortality remains as strong as ever, but the anguished bitterness of the earlier Hamlet has been replaced by a sad acceptance of human limitations. In Act 5, scene 2, his conversation with Horatio reveals the extent to which he is now capable of recognizing the unfathomable mystery of things, accepting the grim inscrutabilities and the chance graces of fate without believing, any longer, that it is possible to alter them through will or action. The earlier mood, epitomized in his cry "The time is out of joint. Oh, cursed spite / That ever I was born to set it right!" (1.5.189–90), has been replaced by the mood of "There's a divinity that shapes our ends, / Roughhew them how we will" (5.2.10–11), or "The interim is mine, / And a man's life's no more than to say 'One'" (5.2.73–74), or "The readiness is all" (5.2.233–34). In this context the reappearance of the theatrical metaphor in the course of Hamlet's narrative to Horatio about the thwarting of Rosencrantz and Guildenstern assumes considerable significance. "Ere I could make a prologue to my brains / They had begun the play" (5.2.30–31): Hamlet's rash, intuitive response to the situation is accurately described in terms of the theatre. *Hamlet* is, of course, all about the problem of "acting," but that word itself is thoroughly ambiguous, denoting simultaneously "performing action" and "playing a role."[15] Earlier in the play Hamlet has felt these meanings to be irrevocably opposed; in Act 5, as he assumes his full stature as tragic hero, he implicitly recognizes their mutual involvement. As he lies dying, his final utterance of the word "act' fuses both its meanings:

> You that look pale and tremble at this chance,
> That are but mutes or audience to this act,
> Had I but time—as this fell sergeant, Death,

15. My general reading of *Hamlet* is particularly indebted to: A. C. Bradley, *Shakespearean Tragedy* (New York: Meridian Books, 1955), pp. 71–143; Ernest Jones, *Hamlet and Oedipus* (New York: Anchor Books, 1955); and Maynard Mack, "The World of Hamlet," in *Tragic Themes in Western Literature,* ed. C. Brooks (New Haven, 1955), pp. 30–58.

> Is strict in his arrest—oh, I could tell you—
> But let it be. . . .

                                              [5.2.345–49]

At this point, as a modern critic has pointed out,[16] the surviving characters of the play are transformed into an audience for the individual drama of Hamlet himself, and thus they become identified with us as audience. The play of *Hamlet* becomes, as it were, itself a play within the larger play in which we are all actors. Fortinbras concludes the play with words which sustain the theatrical metaphor, though still ambiguously:

> Let four captains
> Bear Hamlet, like a soldier, to the stage.
> For he was likely, had he been put on,
> To have proved most royally. . . .

                                              [5.2.406–09]

A part of the peculiar greatness of *Hamlet* rests in the profundity with which it combines the seemingly opposed conceptions of "action" as contrary to role-playing and as identical with it. There is at least a suggestion, at the end of the play, that to understand the world as a theatre is to understand it as having a certain kind of reality. In the deeper gloom of some of the later tragedies, the concept of the world as theatre becomes synonymous with the perception of the world as wholly unreal. Iago, the master-actor, is so totally destructive and negative as to defy psychological analysis, although it may be worth noting that a possible explanation of his diabolic behavior is simply that he is fond of playing.[17] Lear speaks of "this great stage of fools." And Macbeth, employing the theatre-topos in the most negative sense conceivable, speaks lines which deny entirely

16. Righter, *Shakespeare*, p. 164.
17. For Iago as practical joker, see W. H. Auden, *The Dyer's Hand* (New York, 1962), pp. 246–72.

the implication of the high comedies—that "playing" is somehow involved with vitality, nature, and reality:

> ... Out, out, brief candle!
> Life's but a walking shadow, a poor player
> That struts and frets his hour upon the stage
> And then is heard no more. It is a tale
> Told by an idiot, full of sound and fury,
> Signifying nothing.
>
> [5.5.23–28]

The world is a stage; hence it has no meaning, indeed no reality.

In Shakespeare's last plays, the romances, the theatre-topos
assumes its most profound shift of implication. It acquires again
some of the positive connotations it possessed in the high comedies, but it permeates the romances in an even more radical
way than those earlier works. In *Pericles, Cymbeline, The Winter's Tale,* and *The Tempest* the life imitated by the action on
stage becomes in itself an action on the cosmic stage. Prospero's
most famous speech dismisses human life as illusion, and the
theatre-topos dominates his lines as it does the entire play. In
The Tempest, however, in contrast to *Macbeth,* to regard the
world as a stage is not to deny it all reality but rather to perceive
its nature as a provisional version of reality: "such stuff as
dreams are made on" is a fragile substance, but it has a tougher
weave than "a tale told by an idiot."

In *The Winter's Tale* what *seems* turns out quite consistently
to be what *is:* Perdita, the play-princess of the shearing feast, is
in fact the true princess; and the statue of Hermione, with
which "the life [is] as lively mocked as ever / Still sleep mocked
death" (5.3.19–20), turns out in fact to be the living Hermione.
Reality is merely something played, but at the same time the
something played is reality, in the only terms in which we can
understand it. The treatment of the theme of art in *The Winter's*

Tale—the motif of the living statue already referred to, and, in a more sweeping sense, the play's persistent habit of drawing attention to its own theatricality and artificiality[18]—suggests that, to the Baroque Shakespeare, the work of art has as valid a claim to the status of reality as any other of the deceptive phenomena of experience.

The seventeenth century is the great age of western European drama, but not all Baroque dramatic works embody the theatre-topos in its full sense as a metaphysical questioning of the ultimate reality of the phenomenal world. The classicistic drama of Ben Jonson, with its studious imitation of human types, does not operate in that dimension, nor, in general, does the drama of Corneille, with its insistence on the autonomy of the heroic individual and its glorification of the will.[19] The Baroque age presents us with two major types of drama: the classicistic, often satiric and didactic and consistently aiming at the faithful representation of character and custom; and the manneristic—illusionary, quasi-ritualistic, and consistently concerned with the dramatic mode as a form of experience rather than as a form of instruction. Both types are typically Baroque (Rousset has demonstrated the degree to which Corneille is obsessed by the theme of metamorphosis,[20] and imaginative excess is one of the striking features of Ben Jonson's imagery), but it is in the second type, in the dramas of Shakespeare, Webster, and

18. S. L. Bethell, *The Winter's Tale: A Study* (London, n.d.), pp. 47–67. See also G. Wilson Knight, *The Crown of Life*, rev. ed. (London, 1958), pp. 76–128.

19. But Rousset *(La Littérature de l'âge baroque*, pp. 210–17) finds in Corneille's creation of the hero of unalterable will the indication of an obsessive concern with the phenomena of change which in itself characterizes Corneille as Baroque. One should note also the central emphasis on the theatre–topos manifested by Corneille in his earlier works, especially *L'Illusion comique* (1636).

20. Rousset, *La Littérature de l'âge baroque*, pp. 205–13.

Middleton, of Routrou, Calderón, Vondel, and Gryphius, that the Baroque finds its definitive dramatic embodiment.

The action of John Webster's two great tragedies characteristically takes place "in a mist" (to apply the phrase spoken by both the dying Flamineo in *The White Divel* and the dying Bosola in *The Duchess of Malfy*); for all their extraordinary vigor, his characters inhabit a darkened and doomed world in which personal identity flickers desperately in its desires, then is extinguished. Bosola's dying speech appropriately links the mist image to the theatre-topos in one of its more sophisticated forms; he refers to his unintentional slaying of Antonio:

> In a mist: I know not how,
> Such a mistake, as I have often seene
> In a play...[21]

Thomas Middleton's tragic masterpiece, *The Changeling*, does not manifest, as do Webster's tragedies, a consistently dark and tortured poetry, but the dramatic situation which it presents displays a similar sense of the ironic commerce of appearance and reality. Beatrice-Joanna conceals behind her physical beauty and her superficial delicacy qualities of viciousness which approach the absolute: the doubleness of her name symbolizes the duplicity of her nature. Her instrument, the repulsive and aptly-named De Flores ("deflowers"), has always aroused her disgust, but after he has forced her to sleep with him as the price of the murder he has committed for her, one recognizes that De Flores has been from the beginning her alter ego. At the denouement of the play, Beatrice-Joanna and De Flores have been joined in a kind of hellish parody of marriage. The incomprehensible world is populated by changelings.

21. John Webster, *Complete Works*, ed. F. L. Lucas, 4 vols. (London, 1927), 2:124.

Continental drama in the Baroque age shows generally the same divisions as English. What I have called the classicistic drama appears in Corneille and, later and more definitively, in Racine and Molière; what I have called the manneristic drama appears in the work of Vondel in Holland, of Gryphius in Germany, and, most strikingly, of Rotrou in France and Calderón in Spain. To these names one might add that of Monteverdi, whose operas, particularly his *Orfeo* of 1607, show a relevant preoccupation with the motifs of transformation.

Lope de Vega in most of his dramatic work creates a type of theatre which cannot be accurately designated either classicistic or manneristic: its formal looseness conflicts with the ideals of seventeenth-century Classicism, and its vigorous, almost naturalistic presentation of observed life deflects it from the preoccupations of the illusionary stage. Nevertheless, the force of the Baroque obsession with the world-as-theatre leads him on occasion to go beyond the simple representation of human life to the full "representation of human experience in its relations to the universe" (the phrase is Curtius's).[22] The play in which Lope most impressively adapts the theatre-topos to such representation is his *Lo Fingido Verdadero* (ante 1618), concerned with the martyr Ginés, a Roman actor who, portraying a Christian for the amusement of the emperor Diocletian, is converted to the faith which he is portraying. Theatrical appearance, in short, turns out to be reality. The fascination which the theatre-topos held for the Baroque age is suggested by the fact that it appears even in Lope, a dramatist who does not as a regular practice use his stage to dramatize metaphysical mysteries. Significantly, even in *Lo Fingido Verdadero* the topos is far from being all-dominating: the play opens with an extended treatment of Diocletian's rise to power, goes on to a consideration of the unrequited amorous desires of the as-yet-unconverted

22. Curtius, *European Literature*, p. 142.

Ginés, and reaches its true theme only in the third and final act, with the unprefigured conversion. Thus, despite the hero's poetic exploitation of the theatre-topos, particularly in his dying speech, the work as a whole assumes clearly distinguished levels of reality and illusion.

A greater play inspired by Lope's—*Le Véritable Saint Genest* (1646), by Jean Rotrou[23]—demonstrates a more radical and more fully Baroque manipulation of the topos. Rotrou is concerned throughout with confounding the levels of appearance and reality, theatre and life, kept essentially separate by Lope. In the French play, in accordance with the dictates of a burgeoning Classicism, the action is confined to a few hours of a single day, on a single scene. It is thus centered exclusively on Genest (i.e. Ginés), who appears near the end of Act 1 to discuss the nature of theatre with Dioclétien and to accede to the emperor's request that he portray a zealous Christian martyr. Act 2 opens with Genest discussing the setting with the decorator; left alone, he rehearses a few lines of his part and almost immediately feels the motions of grace within him. He offers some resistance ("Il s'agit d'imiter et non de devenir"), but is encouraged by a celestial voice ("Poursuis, Genest, ton personage; /

23. *Lo fingido verdadero* was reprinted in *Obras de Lope de Vega publicadas por la Real Academia Española*, vol. 4 (Madrid, 1894). For *Le Véritable Saint Genest*, see the edition of R. W. Ladborough (Cambridge, 1954). Rousset, *La Littérature de l'âge baroque*, pp. 72–74, and I. Buffum, *Studies in the Baroque from Montaigne to Rotrou* (New Haven, 1957), pp. 212–39, supply studies of the latter play, as do W. Leiner, in *Das Französische Theater*, ed. J. von Stackelberg, 2 vols. (Düsseldorf, 1968), 1:37–53, and R. J. Nelson in *Play within a Play* (New Haven, 1958). E. M. Szarota, *Künstler, Grübler und Rebellen* (Bern and Munich, 1967), examines not only the plays of Lope and Rotrou but also two other plays dealing with the motif of the converted actor: Jacob Bidermann's neo-Latin *Philemon Martyr* and N. Desfontaines's *L'Illustre Comédien*. (See also Rousset, pp. 71–72.) It is interesting to note that Jean-Paul Sartre's recent study of the contemporary writer Jean Genet bears the title *Saint Genet* as a punning tribute to Rotrou's masterpiece.

Tu n'imiteras point en vain")[24] which he explains to himself as that of some joking colleague. The remainder of the act, together with Acts 3 and 4, is taken up largely with the performance by Genest and his troupe of the tragedy of Adrien, a Christian martyred a few years before on the orders of Maximin, who, as the betrothed of Dioclétien's daughter, is actually in the audience. In making of his play-within-a-play a fully developed drama in its own terms, Rotrou departs from the example of Lope, whose Ginés had portrayed simply an anonymous Christian at his moment of martyrdom. The effects are notable: the reader (and presumably the audience) of Rotrou's play is caught up by the drama of Adrien, even to the point of forgetting that it is merely a play-within-a-play. The effect is similar to what would happen if Hamlet's "mousetrap" were to dominate the middle three acts of his tragedy and were to be composed with as much stylistic conviction as the play within which it is an interlude. The breaking of the interior illusion in *Saint Genest*, as Dioclétien and his friends comment during the intermissions in the play of Adrien, draws one from the consideration of Genest-as-Adrien to the consideration of Genest-as-Genest. Moreover, the radical inducement of disillusion sets up a kind of chain reaction: the exposure of Adrien as a player (Genest) reminds us that Genest himself is a player (Monsieur X of Rotrou's company), and it ultimately questions the reality of our own experience, that is, our experience as spectators watching spectators watching actors. This purposeful confusion, a kind of inverted *Verfremdungseffekt*, is further heightened by the representation of a Maximin (who is, after all, played by an actor) watching a Maximin being played by an actor, as it is also heightened by the dramatist's dwelling on the technical details of theatre: Rotrou, following Lope, has one of Genest's company, puzzled by the actor's departure from the script, call

24. Rotrou, *Le Véritable Saint Genest*, p. 16.

for the prompter, only to be told by Genest that he is being prompted by an angel. One almost sympathizes with poor Dioclétien's perplexity when, near the end of Act 4, Genest changes his identity, observing:

> Ce monde périssable et sa gloire frivole
> Est une comédie où j'ignorais mon rôle.
> J'ignorais de quel feu mon cœur devait brûler;
> Le démon me dictait quand Dieu voulait parler;
> Mais, depuis que le soin d'un esprit angélique
> Me conduit, me redresse et m'apprend ma réplique,
> J'ai corrigé mon rôle, et le démon confus,
> M'en voyant mieux instruit, ne me suggère plus.
>
> [4.7.1303–10]

In the most complete way possible, all the world's a stage.

There remains, finally, one of the greatest of Baroque dramatists, Pedro Calderón de la Barca, whose profound and consistent deployment of the theatre-topos emphasizes its theological relevance with remarkable intensity.[25] The *auto sacramental*[26] *El gran teatro del mundo* is his most extended version of the metaphor, but the sense of the world as theatre permeates almost all his work. In his masterpiece, *La vida es sueño*, the metaphor is uttered twice, once by the hero, Segismundo, and once by his father, Basilio, and it does not become, as for Rotrou, an organic part of the play. Nevertheless, it serves as an expression of Calderón's philosophic theme—life as a dream—and in

---

25. See Curtius, pp. 141–44, 559–70. A recent volume in English, *Critical Essays on the Theatre of Calderón*, ed. B. W. Wardropper (New York, 1965), has considerable value; it includes, among other good studies, E. M. Wilson's indispensable essay on *La vida es sueño* (pp. 63–89).

26. The *auto sacramental* is a distinctively Spanish dramatic genre— an allegorical play on the mystery of the Eucharist, performed on the feast of Corpus Christi. Calderón is generally considered the greatest writer of *autos*.

so doing becomes not the witty observation of an analogy but the profound assertion of an identity. For Calderón, as for Shakespeare, "dream" and "theatre" almost always imply each other. In *La vida es sueño* the preoccupation with dream is obsessive, as a summary of the plot will indicate: Basilio, king of Poland, an adept at astrology, has ascertained that the fate of his son, Segismundo, is to become a bloody and unjust tyrant. To circumvent this destiny he has the prince imprisoned from infancy in a desolate tower in the wilderness under the supervision of Clotaldo, who is at once his jailer and teacher. In old age, tormented by an uneasy conscience, Basilio determines to give Segismundo an opportunity to demonstrate that the stars are wrong. Segismundo is drugged and transported to the palace, where he awakes to find himself king. His subsequent actions are senseless and violent: he throws a servant from the palace window, attempts to murder Clotaldo, speaks offensively to his father, insults one lady and offers rape to another—all this despite the warnings of Basilio and Clotaldo, who tell him that he may be dreaming. Basilio concludes that free will is powerless against destiny. Drugged again, Segismundo is removed to the tower, where he is told by Clotaldo that the entire palace experience was a dream. Act 2 ends with Segismundo's great soliloquy, the beginning of his redemption, in which he concludes that all of life is a dream and that, whatever the nature of one's dream, the only important thing is to do what is right:

> Qué toda la vida es sueño,
> Y los sueños, sueños son.[27]

In Act 3, when his fortunes bring him once again to power, Segismundo utilizes his new awareness to reject the dictates of

27. Pedro Calderón de la Barca, *La vida es sueño and El alcalde de Zalamea,* ed. S. E. Leavitt (New York, 1964), p. 90.

his baser nature, make amends for his past behavior, and, having defeated the king his father, submit to him. Basilio is shown the error and cruelty of his astrological determinism, and all ends in happiness and peace.

La vida es sueño has been criticized as philosophically inconsistent. It has been held, for example,[28] that the theological emphasis on free will and good works is flatly contradicted by the play's governing metaphor: if all life is a dream, then the will is not free and actions are neither good nor bad. More recent criticism has tended to defend the play, pointing out, for example, that Segismundo's great Act 2 soliloquy applies the term *sueño* "not to the fact that one *is,* but to *what* one is."[29] The reality and freedom of the soul are not questioned; what is questioned is the reality of the insubstantial stage on which that soul acts. The defense seems just and logical, and it draws our attention once more to Calderón's pervasive sense of the unreality of the phenomenal world. The profound conviction that life is a dream relates the Spanish dramatist not only to the later Shakespeare but also to the entire literary Baroque, whose cloud-capped towers, gorgeous palaces, and solemn temples always hint at their own insubstantiality, always suggest the existence of a transcendent reality in the light of which they will ultimately dissolve, leaving not a rack behind.

28. A. Farinelli, *La vita è un sogno, parte seconda* (Torino, 1916), pp. 283–85.
29. Wilson, in Wardropper, *Critical Essays,* pp. 63–89.

5

Art as Play

The preceding chapter has remarked on the Baroque pre-occupation with the idea of the world as a theatre and life as a play, an idea which is, as we have seen, an inversion of the more obvious perception of conventional mimesis, in terms of which the theatre is the world and the play is life. The topos "life is a play" is, it was suggested, one of the typical forms in which the Baroque vision of life is communicated, by essayist and lyric poet as well as by dramatist. It is to be expected that the world-view implied by a governing metaphor of such wide prevalence would give rise to a specific conception of art significantly different, at least in its emphases, from those of some other ages. In Sir Thomas Browne, as in Gracián and the other theorists of the conceit, the ancient idea of God as artist and the creation as work of art receives striking elaboration, and Calderón never tires of making use of the same idea.[1] The theatre-metaphor, one might say, is a special instance of the literally held ontological theory of creation as art.

That theory in itself, if it inspired little in the way of overt literary speculation, permeated a great deal of the creative litera-

1. See E. R. Curtius, *European Literature and the Latin Middle Ages,* trans. W. R. Trask (New York, 1953), pp. 544–70. Also J. A. Mazzeo, *Renaissance and Seventeenth-Century Studies* (New York, 1964), pp. 54–59; and cf. Sir Thomas Browne, "Religio Medici," in *Religio Medici and Other Writings,* ed. F. L. Huntley (New York, 1951), pp. 17–18.

ture of the Baroque age. It is difficult to respond as fully as is desirable to a great many characteristic Baroque works of literary
art if one has not developed a sense of the very mode of artistic
being of those works, a mode of being which has little to do
with simple didacticism and still less to do with simple mimesis.
It has, I believe, a great deal to do with the phenomenon of
play—that vast and crucial area of human activity of which *a*
play is a particular local division. If the entire creation is literally a work of art, then that creation has of its very nature something of that attractively and gently spurious quality which ad-
heres to any artifact as soon as it is consciously felt *as* artifact,
and much of that quality, that complex of jocosity, make-believe,
and ambivalence which makes up the concept of *play,* will
characterize creation at one remove, that is to say, the art of
man.

In *Homo Ludens,* his profound study of the play-element in
culture, Johan Huizinga defines his subject in the following
terms: "play is a voluntary activity or occupation executed
within certain fixed limits of time and place, according to rules
freely accepted but absolutely binding, having its aim in itself
and accompanied by a feeling of tension, joy and the consciousness that it is 'different' from 'ordinary life.' " In the course of his
study Huizinga attempts to establish the important connections
which he believes exist between this activity and the phenomena
of myth and ritual, those phenomena which embody man's attempt to understand—or, better, to participate in—the incomprehensible mystery of existence. To the mind of "the savage,
the child and the poet," reality presents itself as an "agonistic
structure," and the "processes in life and the cosmos are seen as
the eternal conflict of opposites which is the root-principle of
existence."[2] Such a confrontation of existence is perhaps the

2. J. Huizinga, *Homo Ludens,* Eng. trans. (Boston: Beacon Press,
1955), pp. 28, 116.

defining feature of all art which is truly successful as art; it is, I
think, surely the defining feature of the art of the Baroque age,
an age which, in spite of its utilitarian, didactic, and polemic concerns, lived in constant awareness of the specific qualities of art.
This awareness may supply a shadow of an answer to the questions posed at the end of chapter 1: How is it that typical Baroque literary works combine utilitarian purpose with mannered
and self-conscious style? How is it that they fuse, in a manner
astounding to modern naïveté, the presumably opposed qualities
of formality and individuality? How is it that they express, in
forms of the greatest sophistication, a life-experience which is
primitive in its intensity?

The sense of life as the conflict of opposites supplies a clear
spiritual basis for the seventeenth-century preoccupation with
the drama: on an unconscious level, presumably, the agon of
fictional characters reenacts, as did that of the ancient Greeks,
the universal agon of the cosmos. The all-embracing conflict of
opposites includes also a specific conflict which is central to the
theatre-topos examined in the preceding chapter, as well as to a
wide variety of other literary phenomena of the age. That is the
conflict between the self and the non-self, or, more precisely,
between the concept of the self as the self and the concept of
the self as other-than-the-self. One might consider in this connection John Donne's obsessive preoccupation with the conflict
in his *Songs and Sonets:*

> Loves riddles are, that though thy heart depart,
> It stayes at home, and thou with losing savest it:
> But wee will have a way more liberall,
> Then changing hearts, to joyne them, so wee shall
> Be one, and one anothers All.[3]

3. John Donne, *Poetical Works,* ed. H. J. C. Grierson, 2 vols. (Oxford, 1912), 1:18. Further citations of Donne in this chapter are to this
edition and will be given in the text.

But one might also consider a wide range of other manifestations—the creation of the self as a dramatic character in the
prose works of Montaigne, Burton, and Browne, and the central role played by dramatic projection of the self in formal
meditation and in the religious poetry related to such meditation.[4] Agon and make-believe, two of the constituents of the
play-attitude, lead inevitably to that experience of almost vertiginous levity, of extravagant release, which one associates
with the phenomenon of play. All three elements—agon, make-
believe, and levity—are conspicuously present in Baroque
literature. Their presence—and to a degree that perhaps war-
rants the overall conception of Baroque art as played art—
does not in any sense mean that Baroque literature is not serious.
It is intensely serious, profoundly in touch with the sacred, precisely because it *is* played.[5]

The efflorescence of the dramatic lyric in the Baroque age is
one of the most striking manifestations of the play-spirit in art,
and it is undoubtedly significant that a large number of those
dramatic lyrics are devotional in nature: one need only think of
Donne's *Divine Poems,* of Herbert's *The Temple,* and, on the
Continent, of the religious poems of Huygens and Fleming, of
La Ceppède and Quevedo. In such poems a concern with the
divine is by definition primary, but that concern expresses itself
neither through simple pious praise nor through formal exhorta-
tion but rather through the acting out of a tense dramatic situation, an agon in which the contestants may be God and the soul,
the soul and some personified abstraction, opposed aspects of
the soul, or some other dramatis personae projected outward

4. L. L. Martz, *The Poetry of Meditation,* rev. ed. (New Haven,
1962).
5. Huizinga, pp. 16–27; R. Caillois, *Man, Play, and Games,* trans.
M. Barash (New York, 1961); F. J. Warnke, "Sacred Play: Baroque
Poetic Style," *JAAC* 22, no. 4 (Summer 1964): 455–64, and "Play and
Metamorphosis in Marvell's Poetry," *SEL* 5, no. 1 (Winter 1965): 23–30.

from inner experience. Baroque devotional poetry is saturated with the spirit of play in a larger sense as well: the Victorian parsons who kept alive Herbert's modest reputation throughout the nineteenth century, excusing his "quaintness" for the sake of his piety, erred in the same direction as some modern critics who insist that we see the poet's wit solely as an instrument of sober spiritual vision. Neither recognizes just how funny much of the poetry is, and just how necessary an appreciation of its funniness is to an appreciation of its profound, personality-transforming seriousness.

"Funny" may be the wrong adjective, but some equally extreme element of the play-spirit hovers constantly over *The Temple.* "The Collar" has often, and justly, been praised for the intensity and gravity with which it gives voice to religious experience, and yet the poem operates on the basis of extravagant wit, extending from the multiple puns of the title ("collar" in general, clerical "collar," "caller," and "choler") through the Eucharistic imagery which persistently and ironically dominates the blasphemous language of the rebellious speaker, to the intentionally ludicrous peripeteia of the final line. The experience of a sympathetic reading of "The Collar" is a curiously ironic and strangely invigorating one: as the images of liberation accumulate, the reader, identifying with the rebellious speaker, feels not release but rather something like a progressive strangulation as the objects of material desire close in around him. With the final turn of the poem, submission is experienced as true liberation; the collar is revealed as the way to freedom.

> But as I rav'd and grew more fierce and wilde
>   At every word,
> Me thoughts I heard one calling, *Child!*
>   And I reply'd, *My Lord.*

The poem is, in part, an artistic rendering of the kind of experience Herbert refers to in the words which he spoke on his deathbed to his friend Mr. Duncon, describing the poems of *The Temple* as "a picture of the many spiritual Conflicts that have past betwixt God and my Soul, before I could subject mine to the will of Jesus my Master, in whose service I have now found perfect freedom."[6]

Relevant here is the connection between the experience of paradoxical liberation embodied in "The Collar" and the account of the play-spirit as we find it in Huizinga: "a voluntary activity . . . executed within certain fixed limits . . . according to rules freely accepted but absolutely binding, having its aim in itself and accompanied by a feeling of tension, joy and the consciousness that it is 'different' from 'ordinary life.' "[7] There is something theological-sounding about Huizinga's definition, as there is much playful about the experience of "The Collar"; one is reminded of the lines from a poem on childhood by Herbert's disciple Henry Vaughan: "Quickly would I make my path even, / And by meer playing go to Heaven."[8]

Intellectual play is the very essence of Herbert's formidable technique, not only in such obvious examples as his "shaped" or "pattern" poems, "The Altar" and "Easter Wings," but also, more subtly, in such poems as "Deniall," in which the breakdown of the speaker's contact with God reflects itself in the breakdown of the rhyme-scheme, "Trinitie Sunday," which is made up of three stanzas of three lines each, and "Paradise," in

6. George Herbert, *Works*, ed. F. E. Hutchinson (Oxford, 1941), pp. 153–54, xxxvii. Further citations from Herbert are to this edition and are given in the text.

7. *Homo Ludens*, p. 28.

8. Henry Vaughan, *Works*, ed. L. C. Martin, 2d ed. (Oxford, 1957), p. 520.

which the central metaphor of pruning is reinforced by lopping off letters progressively to form the rhyme-words:

> When thou dost greater judgements SPARE,
> And with thy knife but prune and PARE,
> Ev'n fruitfull trees more fruitfull ARE.

[p. 133]

"My God must have my best, ev'n all I had," writes Herbert in "The Forerunners" (pg. 176), the finest of the many poems on poetry scattered throughout *The Temple*. His best, the best of a Baroque poet, is his wit, his tricks with language; and his volume becomes, from one point of view, an offering like that of the jongleur of Notre Dame.

Herbert's devotional poetry, with its play-aesthetic behind it, is in no sense unique in the Baroque age. In England, in their various ways, the other devotional poets of the Metaphysical succession—Crashaw, Vaughan, and Traherne—display similar emphases, and Continental devotional poetry exhibits a similar fusion of intense religious emotion and intellectual play. The religious lyrics of the German Paul Fleming and the Dutchman Constantijn Huygens abound especially in examples of such fusion.[9] The Baroque devotional poets were often struck by the same divine jokes, and one can find numerous examples of identical witty motifs turning up all over Europe in the seventeenth century. One such motif is that which describes the good thief who was crucified beside Christ as having "stolen" his salvation: Giles Fletcher, in *Christ's Victory and Triumph*, writes: "And with him stood the happy theefe, that stole / By night his owne salvation . . . "[10] On the Continent, Jean de la Ceppède writes of the repentant thief "dont aujourd'huy l'invin-

9. See my *European Metaphysical Poetry* (New Haven, 1961).
10. Giles and Phineas Fletcher, *Poetical Works*, ed. F. S. Boas, 2 vols. (Cambridge, 1908), 1:71.

cible valeur, / Le Christ mesme a volé"; the Dutch poet Heiman
Dullaert observes that he "komt het Hemelryk tot roofgoet te
verrassen" ("he seizes Heaven as a robber's prey"); Giuseppe
Artale introduces the same jest; and both Quevedo and Lope de
Vega have poems based on it.[11] In every case the jest operates
as a mechanism of psychological release—both in the general
sense in which any jest effects a kind of release, and in the more
special religious sense in which the participant is released from
mundane life into a spiritual world dominated by norms of
value which are utterly different from the mundane (the paradoxes which occur so heavily in Donne's *Holy Sonnets* work
in much the same way).

Thus far, then, there are two respects in which the typical
Baroque devotional poem gives evidence of the play-element:
it is agonistic in mode, and it employs a kind of serious jocularity, expressed in witty metaphor, pun, and elaborate formalism,
with the final effect of achieving a breakthrough into a kind of
solemn lightheartedness, the result of a transcendence of or
liberation from the mundane and secular. (The mundane itself,
so prominent in the diction and imagery of Herbert and Donne,
is spiritually transformed by being viewed in the context of the
divine.)

If the contentions made early in this chapter have any
validity, the play-attitude should be noticeably present in types
of literature other than the devotional. Such is, I am convinced,
the case. To choose only two examples, such massive—and profoundly serious—prose works as *The Anatomy of Melancholy*
and the *Religio Medici* habitually joke with the reader, sometimes gravely, sometimes with an almost carnival-like abandon.
Even more consistently, both works operate through the projection of a persona, an image of the author's self which some
other aspect of the author regards with a curious combination

11. See my *European Metaphysical Poetry*, p. 64.

of delight, astonishment, trepidation, and bemused fascination. The splitting of the self characteristic of both Burton and Browne bestows on their masterpieces something of the agonistic quality already noted in the work of the devotional poets.

The *Anatomy* and the *Religio* are both simultaneously religious and scientific works. If we turn to Baroque works of an avowedly secular character, we shall find the play attitude expressed with comparable force and thoroughgoingness.

There is a lot of playing in the love lyrics of the seventeenth century—most obviously in the more lighthearted of Donne's *Songs and Sonets* and poems written under their influence by Thomas Carew, Sir John Suckling, and other English poets, and in several of the lyrics of Théophile de Viau, Marc-Antoine de Saint-Amant, and other of the French *libertins*. But play is also present in love poems which cannot be classified as merely jocular. In such passionate and profound utterances as "The Good-Morrow," "Lovers Infinitenesse," "The Anniversarie," and "The Extasie," Donne creates an atmosphere of play, almost of joke, without in the least degree compromising the seriousness of his statements, all of which, significantly, have as part of their subject the transcendence of the individual identity through participation in a mutual love. In Donne's love poetry as in his, or Herbert's, devotional poetry, the fact that the poem exists in the sphere of play relates at once to its dramatic and agonistic qualities, its powerful emotional effect, and its manifestation of the theme of transcendence.

The playfulness of Baroque love poetry shows itself in four distinct but related features: the imposition of a double view, through which the speaker simultaneously voices his personal passion and distances himself from it in a half-amused way; the formulation of the speaker's relation to the beloved in quasi-dramatic terms; the use of comic hyperbole; and the practice of insulting or showing aggression toward the beloved, with the consequent creation of a kind of amorous agon, or erotic flyting. Conspicuously present in Donne's love poetry, these features almost define the practice of many other important Baroque love poets both in England and on the Continent. Distancing, usually jocular and frequently dramatic, is as characteristic of Carew, Suckling, and Lovelace as it is of Donne. In Suckling's "I prithee send me back my heart," or Carew's "Mediocrity in Love Rejected," the speaker's passion, protested to his beloved in direct address, is coupled with an attitude of levity conveyed through extravagant wit and a tone which might be described as tenderly jesting. Much of Suckling's work takes the form of unequivocal joke, as in the familiar songs "Why so pale and wan, fond lover" and "Out upon it, I have loved," but he is equally capable of the typically Baroque combination of the playful and the passionate.

The combination continues throughout the period. John Cleveland's hyperbolic spoofs are not devoid of a certain intense, however paradoxical, emotional involvement, and Dryden's songs, composed when the Baroque style was moribund, still operate on a basis of combined passion and levity which recalls both Carew and Ben Jonson. Many of the Continental poets project their amorous avowals to the accompaniment of the same kind of ironic distancing—Paul Fleming and Hofmann von Hofmannswaldau in Germany, Constantijn Huygens in Holland, Marino in Italy, and Etienne Durand, Théophile de Viau, and Marc-Antoine de Saint-Amant in France. The accompaniment seems obligatory in such French lyrists as Jean Bertaut and Pierre Motin. The latter is particularly fond of erotic jokes which depend on religious associations, as in one sonnet in which he begs his lady's favor on the grounds that faith without "good works" is insufficient to salvation, or another in which he points out to a certain Mademoiselle La Croix that her name implies more mercy than she has hitherto shown her frustrated lover.[12] More trivial than Donne's, Motin's lyrics nevertheless demonstrate the same compulsion to transfer both amorous and devotional materials to the realm of play, a realm in which, strangely, the seriousness of those materials is ratified rather than compromised.

The devices of comic hyperbole and amorous agon are sufficiently important to demand separate consideration. Comic hyperbole constitutes one special form of ironic distancing, but its relation to the play-spirit is not limited to such distancing, or, rather, the distancing which it induces relates not only to the irony of obvious exaggeration but also to more mysterious potentialities for transformation inherent in the figure of hyperbole itself. There is nothing inevitably comic or playful in extreme hyperbole of the sort that marks the Petrarchan tradition, as one may see by turning to Petrarch himself: the desperate exaggeration and tormented ingenuity of his metaphors operate as fully accurate correlatives for the lover's psychological condition, and it is on that condition that our attention, with sympathy and fascination, is centered. Typical Baroque hyperbole, even among the heirs of Petrarch, operates rather differently. One type, frequently encountered in Marino, Herrick, Carew, and Cleveland, is frankly and obviously playful. In poems employing such hyperbole, it is clear that the poet-speaker in no sense intends his protestations to be taken seriously—even as indications, on the psychological level, of the speaker's passion (one might note, for example, Cleveland's "Fuscara; or, the Bee Errant" and "Upon Phyllis").

Another type of Baroque hyperbole is more complex in its effects, more serious, one might say, in its playfulness. In Donne's "The Canonization," for example, the burlesque of conventional Petrarchan hyperbole functions simultaneously as a

12. Ibid., pp. 122–25.

humorous parody, a modest affirmation of the truth of the
speaker's emotion, and a highly sophisticated placing of that
emotion in a context of recognition of the world outside his
amorous sufferings. By virtue of conceding that his sorrows do
not affect the external world, the speaker at once admits the
existence of that world and asserts the substantial, if limited,
validity of his amorous protestations:

> Alas, alas, who's injur'd by my love?
> What merchants ships have my sighs drown'd?
> Who saies my teares have overflow'd his ground?
> When did my colds a forward spring remove?
> When did the heats which my veines fill
> Adde one more to the plaguie Bill?
> Soldiers finde warres, and Lawyers finde out still
> Litigious men, which quarrels move,
> Though she and I do love.
>
> [1:14]

"The Canonization" depends for a part of its effect on the
reader's awareness of the tension between the convention of
Petrarchan hyperbole and the poet's simultaneous burlesque
and rehabilitation of that convention. There is another variety
of Baroque hyperbole which operates on principles radically
different from those inherited from Petrarch. In the lyrics of
Góngora, typically, images drawn from nature are applied to
the speaker's beloved with a hyperbolic stress on the superiority
of the girl's beauties to those of nature. There is nothing seemingly novel or distinctive about this device: such hyperbolic
comparisons are as old as amorous poetry itself. What distinguishes Góngora's practice as characteristically Baroque is his
emphasis on the vehicle of the hyperbole to the virtual exclusion of the tenor—a paradoxical exclusion, in view of his
ostensible motive. In his sonnet "Mientras por competir con tu

cabello," for example, the speaker declares that his mistress's charms excel the beauty of the sun, the lily, the pink, and the crystal water.[13] But the reader's attention is directed not, as it would be by Petrarch or the Elizabethans, toward a visualization of the girl's beauty, but rather toward a visualization of natural beauties in themselves. Moreover, those natural beauties are presented in a manner not representational or picturesque but quasi-abstract. We are aware not of the pictorially presented sun, lily, pink, and water, but of gold, white, red, and crystal as qualities in themselves, abstracted from the objects in which they have their being. The sonnet concludes with the poet's reminder to the beloved that her beauties will ultimately dissolve into earth, smoke, dust, shade, nothing: "En tierra, en humo, en polvo, en sombra, en nada." As in Donne and Andreas Gryphius, the *carpe diem* theme, with its conventional reminder that beauty will age, die, and decay, is heightened to an assertion that beauty will turn to nothing at all. Góngora's hyperboles express the obsessive Baroque concern with the illusoriness of the phenomenal and the transitoriness of all earthly experience.

Another sonnet, "O claro honor del liquido elemento," manifests the same concentration on the hyperbolic vehicle and the same tendency toward abstraction.[14] Although the poem hyperbolically places the beloved in a position of superiority to the river, the superfluous admonition to the river that it continue to flow reminds us of the inexorable passage of time which will destroy the lady's beauty. The effect of the poem is surely not comic, but both its evocation of metamorphosis and its strangely dispassionate awareness of illusion relate it generally to the phenomenon of play.

13. Luis de Góngora y Argote, *Obras en verso del Homero español,* ed. D. Alonso (Madrid, 1963), p. 12, recto.
14. Ibid., p. 15, verso. See above, pp. 38–39.

The Italian Marino's exaltation of female beauty above the
beauty of landscape works with a more simple playfulness, as
in "La bella schiava," in which the beauty of a lovely Negress
is presented as surpassing that of the sun—with incidental puns
on the various meanings of "sole" in Italian:

> La 've più ardi, o Sol, sol per tuo scorno
> un sole è nato; un Sol, che nel bel volto
> porta la notte ed ha negli occhi il giorno.[15]

In "Vergänglichkeit der Schönheit," a sonnet by the German
Marinist Christian Hofmann von Hofmannswaldau, a fusion
of Marino's lightheartedness and Góngora's somber thought-
fulness occurs: the beauties of the beloved, analogized to the
beauties of nature, will ultimately turn to complete nothingness—except for her heart, which, being as hard as diamond,
will endure forever:

> Dein Herze kann allein zu aller Zeit bestehen,
> Dieweil es die Natur aus Diamant gemacht.[16]

The lover's sufferings do not dampen his sense of humor.

A final type of comic hyperbole might be perceived in some
of the amorous poems of Góngora's countryman Don Francisco de Quevedo, several of whose sonnets go beyond the traditional Petrarchan exaggeration of the lover's suffering to
achieve something like the grotesque: the speaker becomes
ludicrous, even if his emotion does not, and the poems establish a tension between his real and painful emotion and his
self-conscious perception of the state to which he has been reduced.

Donne, Góngora, Marino, Hofmannswaldau, and Quevedo
thus demonstrate some of the more complex uses of hyperbole.

15. G. B. Marino, *Poesie Varie*, ed. B. Croce (Bari, 1913), p. 105.
16. My *European Metaphysical Poetry*, pp. 188–89.

What unites the various uses is a recognition that hyperbole, through its arbitrarily and absolutely aesthetic mode of existence, can enable the poet simultaneously to give utterance to intense passion and to stand outside that passion as an observer. Baroque hyperbole, in short, tends toward the sphere of play and toward the curious transcendence of normal concerns and values which typically occurs within that sphere.

Another stock device of Petrarchan poetry retained and strikingly elaborated by the Baroque amorous poets is the assumption of a state of enmity between lover and beloved. Petrarchan poetry abounds in *dolci nemiche*—"dear enemies" and "sweet warriors"—the lady's obligatory rigor causing her lover such pain that he must regard her as his enemy. The conventional attitude assumes some bizarre twists in the Baroque age. In the insolent banter of many of Suckling's anti-Petrarchan lyrics, as in the aggressive arrogance of some of Carew's poems, the pose of hostility has been transformed from one signifying abject complaint to one signifying the cheerful acceptance of combat with an hereditary enemy. Donne, whose *Songs and Sonets* constitute a compendium of Baroque amorous attitudes, exemplifies the pose of agonistic insult in such poems as "Womans Constancy," "The Indifferent," and "The Apparition." The consistent implication, for these seventeenth-century poets, is that woman is the "sweet enemy" not simply because of her rigor toward her suitor but rather because she is man's opposite—necessary and desirable, but nevertheless (or perhaps therefore) opposite. The mood of these agonistic poems, and of even more extreme examples provided by such French *libertin* poets as Théophile de Viau and Marc-Antoine de Saint-Amant, is that of much amorous comedy, the mood of the flytings between Beatrice and Benedick in *Much Ado About Nothing,* between Rosalind and Orlando in *As You Like It,* and between Millamant and Mirabell in *The Way of the*

World (not for nothing is "natural, easy Suckling" Millamant's favorite poet). The condition of playful sexual agon, so emphasized by the Baroque love poets and so underplayed by most of their Renaissance predecessors, is a recurrent psychological constant. It underlies the Saturnalian and Fescennine rites of the ancients, as it underlies in our own day the convention of initial antipathy between boy and girl which turns up in so much popular fiction and theatre, the primitive quality of which is suggested by the forms it sometimes assumes—the comic-strip cliché of the wife armed with a rolling pin, and the Hollywood comedy cliché of the girl who receives a spanking from her irate suitor. What is involved, and stressed particularly in the Baroque version of the constant, is the celebration of "the eternal conflict of opposites which is the root principle of existence," which Huizinga sees as central to the play-element in culture.[17]

Agonistic insult as a convention in Baroque love poetry ranges from playful but still basically Petrarchan complaint in such a poem as Hofmannswaldau's "Vergänglichkeit der Schönheit," through the bantering but often tender animosities of Donne, Carew, and Suckling, to the outright slanders of Saint-Amant. Implicit in all versions of the attitude is the quasi-mythic sense of the playful agon as a participation in reality—another instance of the curious Baroque tendency to incorporate into forms of great elegance and sophistication a profoundly primitive sense of nature and of man's place in it. The feeling for nature in Baroque amorous poetry seldom issues as a sense of the picturesque. Donne shows almost no interest in nature as picture, Marino's confections have more to do finally with the poet's wit than with his senses, and Góngora's use of landscape, as we have seen, breaks natural imagery down analytically into its abstract constituents. Nevertheless, the

17. Huizinga, *Homo Ludens,* p. 116.

amorous agon often takes place in a setting of nature, with a consequently implied identification of human sexuality with the processes of the earth.

Saint-Amant's long erotic poem "La Jouissance" opens with the careful staging of a natural scene against the background of which the protagonist and his mistress consummate their love. The evocation of the landscape, though relatively detailed and specific, is not mere descriptive ornament, for it is clear that in the ecstasy of love the participants become a part of the land-scape: their bodies stretched out on the earth become in a sense a part of that earth (as they do also in Théophile's "La Soli-tude"). Possessed by nature, the lovers in Saint-Amant possess nature in turn, and the French poet makes use of one of Donne's favorite tropes: that in owning each other the lovers own more than all the kings of earth. Shortly thereafter, as Saint-Amant celebrates the consummation of love, he introduces the agon-motif in one of its most playful and paradoxical forms:

> La langue, estant de la partie,
> Sitost qu'un baiser l'assiégeait,
> Au bord des lèvres se rangeait,
> Afin de faire une sortie;
> L'ennemy, recevant ses coups,
> Souffrait un martyre si doux,
> Qu'il en bénissait les atteintes;
> Et mille longs soupirs, servant en mesme temps
>   De chants de victoire et de plaintes,
> Montraient que les vaincus estoient les plus contents.[18]

The inherent association among the theme of love, the motif of agon, and the setting in nature is suggested by the fact that

18. Marc-Antoine de Saint-Amant, *Oeuvres Poétiques*, ed. L. Vérane (Paris, 1930), p. 44.

even John Donne, Londoner and scorner of the country, provides both a landscape and a muted version of the agon-motif
for his most profound exploration of the metaphysics of love,
"The Extasie":

> Where, like a pillow on a bed,
>> A Pregnant banke swel'd up, to rest
> The violets reclining head,
>> Sat we two, one anothers best.
>
> [1:51]

A few stanzas later the rapt lovers are presented as adversaries:

> As 'twixt two equall Armies, Fate
>> Suspends uncertaine victorie,
> Our soules, (which to advance their state,
>> Were gone out,) hung 'twixt her, and mee.
> And whil'st our soules negotiate there,
>> Wee like sepulchrall statues lay;
> All day, the same our postures were,
>> And wee said nothing, all the day.
>
> [1:51–52]

In these Baroque love poems, ironic distancing, dramatic
form, comic hyperbole, and jocular aggression, either separate-
ly or in combination, enable the lover-protagonist to experience sexual passion as simultaneously the transcendence of his
individual identity and the condition of existence of that identity
at its highest and truest level. In Donne and in the German
Paul Fleming the lover finds his heart only through losing it.
In such poems as "La Jouissance," "La Solitude," and Herrick's
"Corinna's Going a-Maying," nature and sexual love are assimilated to each other, and the self is asserted by virtue of the
fact that it is provisionally annihilated in contact with the
totality of nature. The pattern suggested here reminds one of

some aspects of Shakespeare's comedies: disguise, particularly disguise of sex, as a symbolic expression of the capacity for metamorphosis, for the loss of self, which is in turn the indispensable condition and infallible sign of a self of the truest and most fully differentiated sort.

It reminds one also of the uses made of the themes of withdrawal and engagement in much Baroque poetry. In such poems as "La Solitude" or Marvell's "The Garden" and "Upon Appleton House" withdrawal into nature constitutes a quasi-mystical loss of the sense of individual identity—not, however, in the manner of Romantic nature poetry, largely because of the invariable presence of the play-element. The seventeenth-century gentleman's encounter with nature leads not to a state of permanent pantheistic trance but rather to a witty recognition of a temporary state in which the identity, by being compromised, is paradoxically affirmed. The basic pattern is one of alternating withdrawal and engagement—withdrawal from social and passionate life and engagement with nature, followed by withdrawal from nature and reengagement with society and passion. The pattern appears at its clearest and most complete in the poems of Marvell, but it underlies poems by Saint-Amant, Théophile, Lovelace, and Herrick as well.

No Baroque lyric poet explores the themes of nature, love, and metamorphosis more cogently than does Andrew Marvell, and no poet is more committed to the devices of play. An examination of his work in the love lyric may bring more clarity to a consideration of play as a central mode in such poetry. Comic hyperbole is the principal feature of "The Unfortunate Lover"; and "The Gallery" and "The Fair Singer" supply amusing examples of neo-Petrarchan love-agon with a new twist. "The Gallery" presents tableaux of the speaker's mistress in the various contradictory poses she assumes in his mind—as

murderess and Aurora, as witch and Venus. All versions of the
lady are accurate, for her nature as the erotic focus identifies her
with the metamorphic principle of nature, as the poem's last
picture makes clear. All the transformations of which she is
capable have their origin in her role as Shepherdess:

> But, of these Pictures and the rest,
> That at the Entrance likes me best:
> Where the same Posture, and the Look
> Remains, with which I first was took.
> A tender Shepherdess, whose Hair
> Hangs loosely playing in the Air,
> Transplanting Flow'rs from the green Hill,
> To crown her Head and Bosome fill.[19]

"The Fair Singer" has fun with the Petrarchan trope of the
sweet enemy by the simple expedient of turning the amorous
agon into a full-scale military campaign:

> To make a final conquest of all me.
> Love did compose so sweet an Enemy,
> In whom both Beauties to my death agree,
> Joyning themselves in fatal Harmony;
> That while she with her Eyes my Heart does bind,
> She with her Voice might captivate my Mind.
>
> I could have fled from One but singly fair:
> My dis-intangled Soul it self might save,
> Breaking the curled trammels of her hair.
> But How should I avoid to be her Slave,
> Whose subtile Art invisibly can wreath
> My fetters of the very Air I breath?

19. Andrew Marvell, *Poems and Letters,* ed. H. M. Margoliouth, 2
vols., 2d ed. (Oxford, 1952), 1:26. Further citations are to this edition
and are given in the text.

> It had been easie fighting in some plain,
> Where Victory might hang in equal choice,
> But all resistance against her is vain,
> Who has th' advantage both of Eyes and Voice,
> And all my Forces needs must be undone,
> She having gained both the Wind and Sun.
>
> [1:31]

Other poets of the age, notably Herrick, Carew, and Lovelace in England, and Joost van den Vondel in Holland, were fond of the situation celebrated here—the singing of a beautiful woman—but Marvell's stress on the agonistic and jocular potentialities exemplifies very completely the Baroque tendency to make of the play-attitude an instrument for controlling and understanding emotion without losing or disarming it.

One could cite many other occurrences of the play-attitude in Marvell—"The Picture of Little T.C. in a Prospect of Flowers," for example, or "Ametas and Thestylis Making Hay-Ropes," in which love's dependence on mutual opposition is debated in a formal agon. But the most familiar and celebrated of Marvell's love lyrics—"To His Coy Mistress"—embodies effectively all the devices of play thus far isolated: ironic distancing, dramatic form, hyperbole, and agon. And, like some of the poems referred to earlier, it effects an association between the speaker's passion and the processes of nature.

Shaped as a dramatic address to a clearly implied interlocutor, the poem begins with a blaze of hyperbole comic not only in its extremeness but also in its quizzical recognition that the hyperbole is valid only in the realm of impossible hypothesis:

> Had we but World enough, and Time,
> This coyness Lady were no crime.
> We would sit down, and think which way
> To walk, and pass our long Loves Day.

> Thou by the Indian Ganges side
> Should'st Rubies find: I by the Tide
> Of Humber would complain. I would
> Love you ten years before the Flood:
> And you should if you please refuse
> Till the Conversion of the Jews.
> My vegetable Love should grow
> Vaster then Empires, and more slow.
> An hundred years should go to praise
> Thine Eyes, and on thy Forehead Gaze.
> Two hundred to adore each Breast:
> But thirty thousand to the rest.
> An Age at least to every part,
> And the last Age should show your Heart.
> For Lady you deserve this State;
> Nor would I love at lower rate.

One senses the agonistic stratum which underlies the elaborate compliment: the entire poem, after all, constitutes one stage in a continuing dispute, and as a subtle reinforcement to his witty plea the speaker suggests that the lady's defense of her chastity bears some resemblance to the haggling of a merchant eager for the largest possible profit. The undertone of affectionate but insolent insult continues through the chilling reminders of death which make up the second movement, reminders which typify, in their combination of the lurid and the urbane, the phenomenon of ironic distancing already noted in other lyric poets of the Baroque age:

> But at my back I alwaies hear
> Times winged Charriot hurrying near:
> And yonder all before us lye
> Desarts of vast Eternity.
> Thy Beauty shall no more be found;

Nor, in thy marble Vault, shall sound
My ecchoing Song: then Worms shall try
That long preserv'd Virginity:
And your quaint Honour turn to dust;
And into ashes all my Lust.
The Grave's a fine and private place,
But none I think do there embrace.

[1:26]

The conventional *carpe diem* poem refers to the lover's goal under such delicate metaphors as the flower of Waller's "Go, lovely rose." Marvell's poem employs images which quite bluntly suggest the female genitalia to which the speaker hopes to get access: the formidable image of the worms turns "Virginity" from an abstraction into a metonymy, and in context the adjective "quaint" in the next line comes to suggest the Middle English noun "queynte" (i.e. "cunt"). The directness of the poet's imagery, in a context of gallant elegance, constitutes if not an insult then surely an aggression, a prefiguration of the agonistic imagery which dominates the final movement of the poem and brings the whole passionate syllogism to a close:

Now therefore, while the youthful hew
Sits on thy skin like morning dew,
And while thy willing Soul transpires
At every pore with instant Fires,
Now let us sport us while we may;
And now, like am'rous birds of prey,
Rather at once our Time devour,
Than languish in his slow-chapt pow'r.
Let us roll all our Strength, and all
Our sweetness, up into one Ball:
And tear our Pleasures with rough strife,
Thorough the Iron gates of Life.

> Thus, though we cannot make our Sun
> Stand still, yet we will make him run.
>
> [1:27]

The lovers, in the speaker's apostrophe, are caught up in a pattern of dynamic nature which contrasts with the unnatural stasis of the impossibly hypothetical world in which time stands still.

In "Damon the Mower" and "The Mower's Song' we are presented with a protagonist whose activity resembles that of the mowers in "Upon Appleton House" (see above, pp. 71–75), with the addition of a yet deeper ambiguity. Initially, we are made aware, Damon's mowing has been an action which manifests his union with nature: his "depopulation" of the ground has been an act of creative participation (like that of the Appleton House mowers) which in no sense prevents him from seeing in the meadows the reflection of his own hopes or from finding fellowship amid the grass ("The Mower's Song," 1:45). In Damon's earlier state his mowing is simply an aspect of the vital cycle of nature. After he falls in love with Juliana, however, the same action becomes an aggression. His mowing takes on revenge as a motive, and he aspires to bring flowers, grass, and himself to a "common Ruine" ("The Mower's Song," 1:45). The nature of that ruin is made specific in "Damon the Mower" when the speaker carelessly strikes his scythe into his own ankle, prefiguring the action of Death the Mower (1:44). Man in nature, as long as he is free of the goad of sexual love, is in a state of communion with a kind of ideal order. Sexual love disrupts that order, renders impossible the experience of withdrawal, and reminds him poignantly of the mortality which separates him from the ideal order of nature.[20]

---

20. Harold E. Toliver, *Marvell's Ironic Vision* (New Haven, 1965), pp. 103–09, seems to me to exaggerate the element of asceticism in the poem, though his basic point is well taken.

Many of Marvell's poems imply a balanced scheme of dualism: an ideal world of pure Spirit toward which Soul is drawn, and an ideal world of pure, undifferentiated Nature (the "green world" investigated in his nature poems) toward which Body is drawn. Each constitutes an ideal order in itself, but man can finally rest in neither—at least as long as he lives.[21] Until Juliana comes to remind him of his humanity and his mortality, Damon has existed in a state of unity with green nature, of whose precariousness he is ignorant. His paradise, like all paradises, must be lost, and it can be regained only in brief experiences of life-giving withdrawal.

The Mower poems are not playful in the openly comic manner of "The Gallery" or "The Fair Singer," but in their irony as in their strongly agonistic nature they have a connection to the phenomenon of play. The two poems in which Marvell celebrates the experience of withdrawal most specifically—"The Garden" and "Upon Appleton House"—operate through a dazzling display of play motifs. The speaker in "The Garden" begins by asserting that the condition of repose in nature is preferable to any and all states of social involvement:

> How vainly men themselves amaze
> To win the Palm, the Oke, or Bayes;
> And their uncessant Labours see
> Crown'd from some single Herb or Tree,
> Whose short and narrow verged Shade
> Does prudently their Toyles upbraid;
> While all Flow'rs and all Trees do close
> To weave the Garlands of repose.[22]

[1:48]

21. The pattern emerges most clearly in "A Dialogue between the Soul and Body." See my article "Play and Metamorphosis in Marvell's Poetry."

22. Among the more important analyses of "The Garden" may be cited the following: W. Empson, *Some Versions of Pastoral* (London, 1950); L. W. Hyman, "Marvell's 'Garden,'" *ELH* 25 (1958): 13–22;

The graceful metonymies of the second line inspire a playful misunderstanding on the part of the speaker: with deliberate dull-wittedness, he interprets the symbols of achievement as being in themselves the incentives to social activities, military ("Palm"), civic ("Oke"), and artistic ("Bayes"). If it's foliage you want, he points out, you can get a whole forest for no expenditure of effort at all. After a stanza in elaboration of the praise of solitude, he proceeds, in stanza 3, to a specific rejection of the conventionally erotic:

> No white nor red was ever seen
> So am'rous as this lovely green.
> Fond Lovers, cruel as their Flame,
> Cut in these Trees their Mistress name.
> Little, Alas, they know, or heed,
> How far these Beauties Hers exceed!
> Fair Trees! where s'eer your barkes I wound,
> No Name shall but your own be found.
>
> [1:48]

In a manner reminiscent of Góngora he reduces female beauty to the abstract colors of which it is conventionally composed, and opposes to them his favorite color, also abstracted from its embodiment in trees, grass, and the like. As he closes in on the experience of the garden, he delicately stresses through the jocular tautology of lines 23–24 the self-contained quality of the order of nature to which he is gaining access. Stanza 4 takes up again the playful device of the deliberate misunderstanding, as the speaker blandly attributes a passion for trees to the girl-chasing deities to whom he alludes:

F. Kermode, "The Argument of Marvell's 'Garden,'" *Essays in Criticism* 2 (1952): 225–41; S. Stewart, *The Enclosed Garden* (Madison, 1966), pp. 150–83.

> When we have run our Passions heat,
> Love hither makes his best retreat.
> The *Gods,* that mortal Beauty chase,
> Still in a Tree did end their race.
> *Apollo* hunted *Daphne* so,
> Only that She might Laurel grow.
> And *Pan* did after *Syrinx* speed,
> Not as a Nymph, but for a Reed.
>
> [1:48]

A further element of complexity, essentially playful in its operation, is present in the opening lines of the stanza: Is the withdrawal to nature and solitude possible only *after* one has experienced the heat of sexual passion (like that experienced by Damon in "Damon the Mower")? Or is the initial conjunction to
be taken without that much force, as a casual indicator of time
without indication of causality? As so often in this poem, an unequivocal answer is not to be found.

Stanza 5 brings us into the garden and to the first phase of
the experience of withdrawal as undergone simultaneously by
the body, the mind, and the soul:

> What wond'rous Life in this I lead!
> Ripe Apples drop about my head;
> The Luscious Clusters of the Vine
> Upon my Mouth do crush their Wine;
> The Nectaren, and curious Peach,
> Into my hands themselves do reach;
> Stumbling on Melons, as I pass,
> Insnar'd with Flow'rs, I fall on Grass.
>
> [1:49]

It is impossible to miss the strongly erotic note of this stanza:
the paradise into which the speaker has withdrawn supplies in
an absolute degree all the charms which he has rejected in its
favor. It is also difficult to miss the implicit reference to Eden

made by the imagery: within our tradition, a narrative in which
someone walks in a garden, eats fruit, and falls can scarcely fail
to summon up associations with Genesis. These associations have
often been noted by critics, but frequently with a sobriety hardly
warranted by the tone of the stanza.[23] The point, it seems to
me, is not that the experience of stanza 5 recapitulates or symbolizes the primal fall but rather that it constitutes a played
equivalent, wholly guiltless, of that fall. The garden of withdrawal is a world of pure play, where nothing is possible but
innocence—for as long as the protagonist can remain withdrawn.

Stanza 6 presents the experience of the mind, and it is shot
through with the intellectual play of ambiguity:

> Mean while the Mind, from pleasure less,
> Withdraws into its happiness:
> The Mind, that Ocean where each kind
> Does streight its own resemblance find;
> Yet it creates, transcending these,
> Far other Worlds, and other Seas;
> Annihilating all that's made
> To a green Thought in a green Shade.[24]
>
> [1:49]

Marvell's modern editor, Margoliouth, points out one of the
more complex ambiguities of this stanza: the fact that the last
couplet may be taken as saying either that the mind is "reducing
the whole material world to nothing material" or that it is
"considering the whole material world as of no value compared
to a green thought."[25] But there are further ambiguities. The el-
liptical syntax of the first couplet says simultaneously that: the
mind withdraws from the lesser pleasure to the presumably

---

23. See, for example, Hyman, "Marvell's 'Garden.' "
24. Empson, in *Pastoral,* supplies a provocative reading of this stanza.
25. Marvell, *Poems and Letters,* 1:226.

greater pleasure (i.e. "*its* happiness"); the mind, reduced (made
"less"), by pleasure, is no longer limited by its narrowly discursive functions and is thus made capable of its own kind of
withdrawal; and the mind, as a result of its not deriving pleasure
from charms which appeal to the body, withdraws into its own
kind of happiness. All three meanings are surely present, and all
three contribute to the description of the mind's function in a
state of transport, in which its capacity for reflecting or contain-
ing the objects of the sensible world is abandoned for its specifically imaginative or creative capacity.

The mind, in this poem, occupies a kind of middle ground
between the body and the soul: the body, in stanza 5 sinks into
complete union with the ideal, self-sufficient order of nature,
while simultaneously, in stanza 6, the mind sinks into a reflective
consideration of its own creativity. What it shares with the body
at the moment of transport is a liberation from bondage to separate, plural objects: what is jointly experienced is unity.

The soul's experience, by definition, cannot be so complete.
Its position during the moment of transport is one of attendance
rather than consummation:

> Here at the Fountains sliding foot,
> Or at some Fruit-trees mossy root,
> Casting the Bodies Vest aside,
> My Soul into the boughs does glide:
> There like a Bird it sits, and sings,
> Then whets, and combs its silver Wings;
> And, till prepar'd for longer flight,
> Waves in its Plumes the various Light.[26]

[1:49]

26. Stewart *(Enclosed Garden,* pp. 177–80) errs, I believe, in seeing
this stanza as an expression of fulfilled contemplation. The playful mode
of the poem in a sense modifies the experience in the direction of the
aesthetic as opposed to the devotional.

The moment of communion with reality is brief, and stanza 8, with the breaking in of the past and conditional tenses, initiates the withdrawal from the garden:

> Such was that happy Garden-state,
> While Man there walk'd without a Mate:
> After a Place so pure, and sweet,
> What other Help could yet be meet!
> But 'twas beyond a Mortal's share
> To wander solitary there:
> Two Paradises 'twere in one
> To live in Paradise alone.
>
> [1:49]

Many commentators have found in this passage an overt statement of the misogyny which they feel to be present throughout the poem, but surely Marvell's emphasis here falls more on the idea of solitude than on that of freedom from woman in particular.[27] In order for the body to achieve union with the order of nature, and in order for the soul to be able to attend with equanimity its union with the order of spirit, a state of separation from society is necessary, and such a state is impossible except in rare moments of imaginative concentration.

Yet the inevitable withdrawal from the garden is not, as it might be for a Romantic poet, an occasion for dejection on the poet's part. The final stanza, though it notes implicitly the speaker's withdrawal, recognizes with a kind of cheerful security the continued existence of the garden, free from chronological time and under the benign influence of a well-disposed creator:

> How well the skilful Gardner drew
> Of flow'rs and herbes this Dial new;
> Where from above the milder Sun

27. On this question I agree with Stewart, *Enclosed Garden*, p. 164.

> Does through a fragrant Zodiack run;
> And, as it works, th'industrious Bee
> Computes its time as well as we.
> How could such sweet and wholsome Hours
> Be reckon'd but with herbs and flow'rs!
>
> [1:50]

Although it is a much longer poem than "The Garden," and although it deals with a wider range of thematic material, "Upon Appleton House" finally conveys an experience very similar to that of the shorter poem. As has already been noted, "Upon Appleton House" makes considerable use of the topos of the theatre and also of other varieties of play-device. The opening compliments to Lord Fairfax's house abound in lighthearted and extravagant conceits, the narrative digression on the storming of the nunnery is broadly comic, and the whole mowing scene constitutes a kind of ritual agon. The theme of withdrawal and engagement is equally conspicuous, both in the relation of the poem to Fairfax's retirement from public life[28] and in the speaker's retirement to the grove at the time of the overflowing of the fields. Quasi-mystical and semi-Christian as that retirement is, it has a hedonistic side which reminds us that it is a withdrawal into that world of play which is, for Marvell, as real as the world of social involvements.

When young Maria, the presiding genius of the poem, makes her appearance near its conclusion (1:79), she finds her tutor engaged in the idle pastime of angling. With a touch of another traditional topos—the world turned upside down[29]—the tutor reprimands himself for showing such frivolity before the grave eyes of his pupil:

---

28. See D. C. Allen, *Image and Meaning* (Baltimore, 1960), pp. 115–53.

29. See Curtius, *European Literature*, pp. 94–98.

> But now away my Hooks, my Quills,
> And Angles, idle Utensils.
> The *young Maria* walks to night:
> Hide trifling Youth thy Pleasures slight.
> "Twere shame that such judicious Eyes
> Should with such Toyes a Man surprize;
> *She* that already is the *Law*
> Of all her *Sex,* her Ages Aw.
>
> [1:79]

The whole treatment of Maria is elaborately playful: like "little
T.C.," she is a female child who is also a giant intellect and a
goddess of beauty and chastity. She is, furthermore, destined to
continue the virtuous Fairfax dynasty. Deification of woman is
a motif frequently encountered in Renaissance and Baroque
poetry, the most conspicuous example being the treatment of
Elizabeth Drury in Donne's "Anniversaries." But Maria's age
and her position as Marvell's pupil lend a distinct jocularity to
the adulation expressed in the following stanza:

> 'Tis *She* that to these Gardens gave
> That wondrous Beauty which they have;
> *She* streightness on the Woods bestows;
> To *Her* the Meadow sweetness owes;
> Nothing could make the River be
> So Chrystal-pure but only *She;*
> *She* yet more Pure, Sweet, Streight, and Fair,
> Then Gardens, Woods, Meads, Rivers are.
>
> [1:80]

At the risk of belaboring a point, I should like to suggest again
that playfulness does not necessarily mean lack of seriousness: in
a sense Marvell means everything he says in this stanza, recognizing as he does that Maria contains *in potentia* both the mature virtues of the Fairfax family and the regenerative power

which the mythic imagination ascribes to woman. His seriousness is validated rather than undercut by the affectionate gaiety
with which he sees his girl-student superimposed on her own
intense symbolic value. Similarly, in the penultimate stanza of
the poem, he is being at once gay and sober, serious and jocular,
when he sees his Appleton House as a simulacrum of the paradise which has been lost:

> 'Tis not, what once it was, the *World*;
> But a rude heap together hurl'd;
> All negligently overthrown,
> Gulfes, Deserts, Precipices, Stone.
> Your lesser *World* contains the same.
> But in more decent Order tame;
> *You Heaven's Center, Nature's Lap.*
> *And Paradice's only Map.*
>
> [1:82]

There ought to be a better word than *play* to denote the cast
of mind underlying the work of Marvell and so many other
Baroque figures, but our language does not seem to have one.
One might, to try to delineate it further, suggest that this cast
of mind has something to do with a radical sense of the power
of an aesthetic conception to hold in solution all manner of opposed conceptions which are, however opposed, mutually valid.
Such a sense informs the conceits, paradoxes, and ironies of the
Metaphysical poets, but it informs also much of the work of
John Milton, a poet who is, despite the occasional grim humor
of *Paradise Lost,* scarcely to be thought of as playful. Nevertheless, the play-spirit, with its dynamic potentiality for synthesis,
fills "L'Allegro" and "Il Penseroso," and, though it would require a perverse love of paradox to classify "Lycidas" as a "playful" poem, there is a sense in which that great elegy operates
through an awareness of the power of an aesthetic conception

to achieve resolutions which neither faith nor philosophy can reach.

Those critics are probably all extinct who once taught that Milton really had more sympathy with his thoughtful man than with his joyful man, as proven by the fact that "Il Penseroso" is some twenty-four lines longer than "L'Allegro." The absurdity of such an approach is obvious; what is less obvious, perhaps, is that any approach to these poems which aims at the sober determination of "meanings" or "attitudes" is doomed to founder. Both poems (or, more accurately, both movements of the single poem) remain with flawless tact on the aesthetic surface of things—appropriately enough, since their concern is with the aesthetic surface of things and with the re-creation of a specifically aesthetic joy.[30]

The connection between this aesthetic joy and the spirit of play should be made clear by the gusty humor of the opening of "L'Allegro," with its burlesque diction, its comic hyperbole, and its amusingly inappropriate heaviness of tone:

> Hence loathed Melancholy
>> Of *Cerberus,* and blackest midnight born,
> In *Stygian* Cave forlorn
> 'Mongst horrid shapes, and shreiks, and sights unholy,
> Find out some uncouth cell,
>> Wher brooding darknes spreads his jealous wings,
> And the night-Raven sings;
>> There under *Ebon* shades, and low-brow'd Rocks,
> As ragged as thy Locks,
>> In dark *Cimmerian* desert ever dwell.[31]

30. The central thesis of Susan Sontag's essay "Against Interpretation" (in her *Against Interpretation* [New York, 1965]) is, though somewhat overstated, basically just. It is a healthy corrective to the conception of criticism as translation or paraphrase which afflicts so many different critical schools.

31. John Milton, *Poetical Works,* ed. H. Darbishire (London, 1958), p. 420. Further citations are to this edition and are given in the text.

The mood of "Il Penseroso" renders its parallel opening dismissal of "vain deluding joyes" less obvious in its playfulness, but it is impossible to read much gravity into the lines[32] if we recognize that the thoughtful man is having every bit as much fun in his activities as is the joyful man, and that he is quite as hedonistically single-minded in his pursuit of pleasure, even at the end of the poem when the speaker, with a kind of luxuriant sentimentality, pictures his old age:

> And may at last my weary age
> Find out the peacefull hermitage,
> The Hairy Gown and Mossy Cell,
> Where I may sit and rightly spell,
> Of every Star that Heav'n doth shew,
> And every Herb that sips the dew;
> Till old experience do attain
> To somthing like Prophetic strain.
>
> [p. 428]

The careful way in which the activities of the two men (or the two moods) are balanced reminds us consistently that both poems are about pleasure: the difference finally is no more than the difference between enjoying tragedy and enjoying comedy— two different kinds of play. Structural balance also has the effect of modulating the tone, preventing it from ever becoming so intense as to exceed the purely aesthetic. The matched references to the myth of Orpheus (always one of Milton's favorites) supply an example of such modulation. In "L'Allegro," near the very end of that joyful poem, the reference is to the myth in its most pathetic aspect: the epithet in the last line of the ensuing passage renders that pathos with great poignancy:

32. For a discussion of the comic aspects of these openings, see E. M. W. Tillyard, *The Miltonic Setting* (Cambridge, 1938), pp. 1–28.

> Untwisting all the chains that ty
> The hidden soul of harmony.
> That *Orpheus* self may heave his head
> From golden slumber on a bed
> Of heapt *Elysian* flowres, and hear
> Such streins as would have won the ear
> Of *Pluto,* to have quite set free
> His half regain'd Eurydice.
>
> [p. 424]

In the melancholy context of "Il Penseroso," on the other hand, the poet chooses a very different moment in the myth, the moment at which, however precariously, love has triumphed over death:

> But, O sad Virgin, that thy power
> Might raise *Musaeus* from his bower,
> Or bid the soul of *Orpheus* sing
> Such notes as warbled to the string,
> Drew Iron tears down *Pluto's* cheek,
> And made Hell grant what Love did seek.
>
> [p. 426]

In each case the tension between the mood of the poem and the mood of the reference prevents the overall mood from becoming either exclusively cheerful or exclusively melancholy, and the effect is to keep both poems within the realm of the aesthetic, another word, perhaps, for the realm of play within which the poems have their being. Hence, though the emotions they evoke are exquisitely moving, those emotions are always aesthetic.

To describe "L'Allegro" and "Il Penseroso" as "purely aesthetic" works is, in a sense, to describe them as impersonal, or rather suprapersonal, works. Such works expose themselves to the charge of insincerity as their opposites, confessional works, expose themselves to the charge of sentimentality. Insincerity is the charge historically brought against "Lycidas." The charge, whether it presents itself in its classicistic or its romantic form,[33] is almost automatically refuted by a consideration of literary traditions and systems of decorum larger than those of Dr. Johnson or of the nineteenth century, and such were, of course, the traditions and systems from within which Milton wrote. The death by drowning of Milton's classmate Edward King is as clearly an "occasion" for an artistic work as is the untimely death of Elizabeth Drury (Donne's "Anniversaries"), and the work which it occasions is a pastoral elegy—by definition a kind of poem in which a distinct aesthetic distancing occurs, a variety of material is encompassed, and a certain psychological pattern, wider than the strictly individual, is accomplished.[34]

Pastoral elegiac tradition itself also refutes the charge of diffuseness which has been leveled against the poem. The alleged "digressions" on fame and on the corrupt clergy are not only conventional for the Renaissance pastoralist; they are firmly integrated into the poem by the fact that they have reference to the two symbolic functions of the shepherd-figure for the Christian humanist: the shepherd as poet and the shepherd as priest.[35] If the poem presents problems of interpretation, they derive not from any supposed lack of unity or sincerity but from complex ambiguities which lie at its very heart. One might ex-

---

33. The definitive version of the classicistic charge is leveled by Dr. Johnson in his "Life of Milton" (1778), in *Lives of the English Poets,* ed. L. Archer-Hind, 2 vols. (London, 1925), 1:95–96. The romantic charge may be encountered in the response of the average untutored modern reader.

34. J. H. Hanford, "The Pastoral Elegy and Milton's *Lycidas,*" *PMLA* 25 (1910): 403–47, gives perhaps the best account of Milton's relation to the tradition from which "Lycidas" derives. See also, N. Frye, "Literature as Context: Milton's *Lycidas,*" in his *Fables of Identity* (New York, 1963), pp. 119–29.

35. M. H. Nicolson, *John Milton: A Reader's Guide to His Poetry* (New York, 1963), pp. 87–111.

amine, for example, the question of where Lycidas is at the climax of the poem, in the passages immediately preceding and constituting the consolation experienced by the speaker. At the conclusion of the great flower catalog, the speaker recognizes with pain that even the consolation of decorating the poet's corpse is denied his mourners by the fact that the corpse has been lost at sea. The recognition leads at once to the lowest spiritual point of the poem, but that point is immediately transcended, illogically and mysteriously, in the apostrophe to St. Michael and the dolphins:

> Ay me! Whilst thee the shores, and sounding Seas
> Wash far away, where ere thy bones are hurld,
> Whether beyond the stormy *Hebrides,*
> Where thou perhaps under the whelming tide
> Visit'st the bottom of the monstrous world;
> Or whether thou to our moist vows deny'd,
> Sleep'st by the fable of *Bellerus* old,
> Where the great vision of the guarded Mount
> Looks toward *Namancos* and *Bayona's* hold;
> Look homeward Angel now, and melt with ruth,
> And, O ye *Dolphins,* waft the haples youth.
>
> [p. 451]

The puzzling swiftness of the consolation is intensified by the lines which follow:

> Weep no more, woful Shepherds, weep no more,
> For *Lycidas* your sorrow is not dead,
> Sunk though he be beneath the watry floar,
> So sinks the day-star in the Ocean bed,
> And yet anon repairs his drooping head,
> And tricks his beams, and with new spangled Ore,
> Flames in the forehead of the morning sky:
> So *Lycidas* sunk low, but mounted high,

Through the dear might of him that walk'd the waves;
Where other groves, and other streams along,
With *Nectar* pure his oozy Locks he laves,
And hears the unexpressive nuptiall Song,
In the blest Kingdoms meek of joy and love.
There entertain him all the Saints above,
In solemn troops, and sweet Societies
That sing, and singing in their glory move,
And wipe the tears for ever from his eyes.
Now *Lycidas* the Shepherds weep no more;
Henceforth thou art the Genius of the shore,
In thy large recompense, and shalt be good
To all that wander in that perilous flood.

[p. 451]

We are told that Lycidas has been carried away by the ocean
tides, that he is among the blessed in heaven, and that he has
been appointed the genius of the shore of the sea in which he
was drowned. The mutual opposition of the assertions is per-
plexing, even if we regard the first assertion as one which is
retracted by the other two (and, in view of the forceful conviction of the lines, it is difficult to do so with much confidence).
The point is, I think, that the multiplicity of assertions as to the
whereabouts of Lycidas constitutes in itself the consolation.
Liberated from the restrictions of his finiteness, the dead poet
can now be simultaneously absorbed into the element of his
death, alive forever in heaven, and present as a guardian spirit
by the shores of the Irish Sea.

The abruptness of the speaker's reversal from dejection to
joy is also justified by the ambiguity of the water-symbol itself.
In the course of the vision of the lost corpse, the weight of the
symbolic meaning shifts from water-as-death to water-as-re-
birth.[36] For Milton, as for so many poets before and after him,

36. Ibid.

water as symbol inevitably carries both associations, and so it is
that what we thought was the low point of the poem is revealed,
at the moment of the appeal to the archangel, as the high
point. Water imagery has, of course, been conspicuously present since the beginning of the poem—in the invocation to the
"Sisters of the sacred well," in the reference to the head of
Orpheus sent "Down the swift *Hebrus*," in the apostrophes to
"Fountain *Arethuse*" and "Smooth-sliding *Mincius*," in the
appearances of Camus and St. Peter ("The Pilot of the *Galilean*
lake"), and elsewhere—and it is supremely appropriate that
at the climax of the poem, after Lycidas's death has been revealed as his life, Christ should make his appearance as he
"that walk'd the waves."[37]

The point I am making, of course, is that the effective resolution of "Lycidas" derives not from religious doctrine or philosophical conviction per se but rather from the recapitulation
of a mythic pattern of death and rebirth; and such mythic patterns, one might suggest, are the ultimate source of all literary
conventions. The resolution of "Lycidas" derives from its
literary form: the basis of the speaker's consolation may be
Christian faith, but that faith operates within the poem under
a larger, nonspecific aspect—one which is mythic, conventional, literary, artistic.

"Lycidas" is not a playful poem in the sense of "The Garden"
or "Upon Appleton House," but it is in a sense a "played" poem.
Perhaps it would have been more accurate to entitle this chapter "art as art," for the eminence of the art of the seventeenth
century rests upon the artist's radical awareness of the authority which his art by its very nature possesses, as a form of
knowledge and a variety of spiritual achievement.

37. Nicolson, *John Milton,* p. 102. For a consideration of "Lycidas" as
a Baroque poem on rather different grounds, see L. Nelson, *Baroque
Lyric Poetry* (New Haven, 1961), pp. 64–76, 138–52.

6

Metaphysical and Meditative Devotion

The conspicuous presence of the play-element in the literature of the Baroque does not imply the dominance of a spirit of frivolity or gaiety. Indeed, the dramatic, agonistic, and jocular features of that literature sometimes articulate and sometimes mask widespread tendencies toward pessimism and melancholy—epitomized in the mature tragedies of Shakespeare, in the death-obsessed lyrics of Sponde, Gryphius, Quevedo, and Donne (in his *Holy Sonnets*), in the prose works of Burton, Browne, and Jeremy Taylor, and in the revival of formal satire in the western European literatures.

Douglas Bush is surely right in arguing against the popular concept of an all-embracing "Jacobean pessimism" in England,[1] but one must, nevertheless, note the prevailing sobriety of seventeenth-century European literature, its almost ever-present concern with religious truth. The major manifestation of that concern is the remarkable efflorescence of religious lyric poetry which manifested itself all over western Europe between 1580 and 1680.

The religious lyric of the Baroque may be more narrowly defined as *devotional:* the poem, that is, does not, characteristically, engage in either simple praise of the deity or simple ex-

---

1. D. Bush, *English Literature in the Earlier Seventeenth Century* (Oxford, 1945), pp. 3–4.

hortation of the faithful; it attempts, rather, to achieve and express a personal and intense relationship between the protagonist of the poem and God. The devotional lyric is hence private rather than public in its manner, intimate rather than formal in its tone, dramatic rather than discursive in its structure. "Wilt thou meet arms with man, that thou dost stretch / A crumme of dust from heav'n to hell?" asks George Herbert in "The Temper" I,[2] suggesting in the query the dominant impulse of devotional poetry toward an impossible aspiration—the confrontation of the infinite by the finite on terms of the greatest intimacy and immediacy.

The impossibility of the task which such poetry attempts—and sometimes achieves—may account for the curious complexity of tone and craftiness of strategy which distinguish it. It may account, for example, for the coexistence of levity and seriousness, playfulness and sobriety, which has already been noted in reference to Herbert's art. If incongruity, or disproportion, is indeed one of the sources of the comic, from one point of view Baroque devotional poetry constitutes, in the vivid discrepancies it projects, a kind of breathtaking and perilous cosmic joke. Early in *The Temple,* in "The Thanksgiving," Herbert's protagonist attempts to "meet arms"—and to "measure weapons"[3]—with the crucified Christ. Overwhelmed with gratitude for the gift of grace, the finite speaker desires to repay his God in kind, only to recognize at the end of the poem the gaping impossibility of that desire:

> Nay, I will reade thy book, and never move
>   Till I have found therein thy love,
>   Thy art of love, which I'le turn back on thee:

2. George Herbert, *Works,* ed. F. E. Hutchinson (Oxford, 1941), p. 55. Further citations are to this edition.
3. Hutchinson, in Herbert, *Works,* p. 494.

O my deare Savior, Victorie!
Then for thy passion—I will do for that—
Alas, my God, I know not what.

[p. 36]

The ill-matched agon has been, of course, a total defeat for the
speaker, but his very defeat has been the occasion for a kind
of success: he has been enabled to feel the presence of God
the infinite in a direct and immediate way. "The Reprisall,"
which immediately follows "The Thanksgiving" and is its
sequel, applies the achievement of the earlier poem to the
formulation of an overt paradox in which finite and infinite are
united:

Yet by confession will I come
Into thy conquest: though I can do nought
Against thee, in thee I will overcome
The man, who once against thee fought.

[p. 37]

Similarly, in Lope de Vega's exquisite religious sonnet
"Pastor que con tus silvos amorosos," the sacrificed Christ, as
loving shepherd, is identified with the amorous shepherd of
pastoral convention and is seen as standing outside the speaker's window in hopeful expectation. Infinite mercy is made the
object of immediate experience through an agile leap of wit.
Lope links the transcendent and the mundane yet more firmly
through a series of puns at the end of the sonnet:

Espera pues, y escucha mis cuidados,
¿pero cómo te digo que me esperes,
si estás para esperar los pies clavados?

The verb esperar, meaning both "to wait" and "to hope," conveys great richness of meaning; even more significantly, the
phrase los pies clavados ("the feet nailed") operates on both

levels of the poem's fiction: literally, it refers to the feet of the crucified Christ, while colloquially, it has simply the meaning of the English "rooted to the spot."[4]

Lope's sonnet is an example of what Martz has called "sacred parody" and has discussed in the work of Herbert and Southwell.[5] Such parody is found extensively in the religious poetry of Baroque Europe. The German Paul Fleming is particularly addicted to devotional lyrics in which he deploys amorous paradoxes similar to those prominent in Donne's secular poetry. His "Andacht," for example, after piling up a series of familiar Christian paradoxes, concludes with the very Donnesque paradox of the interchange of identities between lover and beloved. Elsewhere, as in "Also hat Gott die Welt geliebet," he introduces the Petrarchan clichés of fire and ice and beloved enemy —with a witty reversal of the latter, Christ being the faithful suitor who returns love for scornful hate.

Paradox of one sort or another is central to the genre of devotional poetry. In addition to the fusions of finite and infinite, profane and sacred, mundane and transcendent, which occur so frequently in Donne and Herbert and their Continental contemporaries, a whole vocabulary of logical contradiction marks the religious poetry of the Baroque age. In Donne's *Holy Sonnets* the paradoxical element is so intense and all-pervasive as finally to leave the reader with the impression that there are, for Donne, two opposed orders of truth: the earthly, founded on experience, and the heavenly, which systematically and unfailingly reverses or defies the findings of experience and logic and, in so doing, surpasses them. In "Batter my heart, three person'd God," imagery of rape and imprisonment signifies

4. See E. M. Wilson, "Spanish and English Religious Poetry of the Seventeenth Century," *Journ. Eccl. Hist.* 9 (1958): 38–53.

5. L. L. Martz, *The Poetry of Meditation,* rev. ed. (New Haven, 1962), pp. 184–93 and passim.

chastity and liberation; in "Show me deare Christ, thy spouse,"
the traditional symbolism of the church as the bride and Christ as
the bridegroom is wittily exploited to the point at which Christ
becomes a willing and cooperative cuckold. Sense imagery
itself is purposefully subverted in "Oh my blacke Soule" and "I
am a little world made cunningly." In the former the essential
qualities of colors are reversed:

> Oh make thy selfe with holy mourning blacke,
> And red with blushing, as thou art with sinne;
> Or wash thee in Christs blood, which hath this might
> That being red, it dyes red soules to white.[6]

In the latter one kind of supernatural fire paradoxically counter-
acts the infernal fire which is the punishment due the speaker's
sinful fire:

> But oh it [the speaker as microcosm] must be burnt! alas the fire
> Of lust and envie have burnt it heretofore,
> And made it fouler; Let their flames retire,
> And burne me ô Lord, with a fiery zeale
> Of thee and thy house, which doth in eating heale.
>
> [1:324]

The *Heilighe Daghen* of the Dutch poet Constantijn Huygens
make a comparable exploitation of the pyrotechnics of paradox.
Sometimes, as in "Nieuwe Jaer" ("New Year's"), Huygens fuses
the spiritual and the mundane, presenting the concept of a spiritual rebirth under the metaphor of a new suit of clothes. In
"Sondagh" ("Sunday") he engages in a more strictly verbal kind
of wit, employing the pun on "sun" and "Son" beloved by English, Dutch, and German devotional poets, but elaborating it to
unprecedented lengths through further wordplay. "Sunday" is
"Son-day," but it is also "Soen-dagh" (Reconciliation-Day"),

6. John Donne, *Poetical Works,* ed. H. J. C. Grierson, 2 vols.
(Oxford, 1912). Further citations are to this edition.

and fallen man has a tendency to make it "Sond-dagh" ("Sin-
day"). Huygen's extravagance of verbal wit allies him closely
with Herbert, Fleming, and his own countryman Jacob Revius.

In "Paeschen" ("Easter") Huygens recalls the Donne of the
Holy Sonnets in the complex way in which he investigates the
image of blood—the symbol simultaneously of human lust, of
the mortal punishment due to sin, and (as Christ's blood) of the
redemption of mankind from inevitable damnation. In the final
couplet the blood of the paschal lamb which marked the houses
of the Israelites in Egypt as exempt from destruction is equated
with the blood shed by Christ, who is at once the lion of Judah
and the lamb of God:

> Merckt onser herten deur, o Leeuw van Judas Stamm,
> En leert ons tydelijk verschricken voor een Lam.[7]

The device of scriptural prefiguration employed here is frequent
in Baroque devotional poetry: Fleming, in "An meinen Erlöser,"
utilizes the same association of the blood of Christ with the
paschal blood—"Auch dein Blut, Oster-Lam, hat meine Thür
erröhtet"[8]—and the *Théorèmes spirituels* of La Ceppède and the
Preparatory Meditations of the New England Puritan Edward
Taylor are both based on the passionate application to individual
life of a typological analogy drawn between an episode in the
Old Testament and its fulfillment in the New.[9] Prefiguration
thus becomes yet another means of expanding the significance
of the poem beyond the limits of merely individual experience
without losing any of the concrete immediacy of such experience.

Baroque devotional poetry consistently achieves an expansion
of the limits of personal experience through a paradoxical fusion

7. F. J. Warnke, *European Metaphysical Poetry* (New Haven, 1961),
p. 236.
    8. Ibid., p. 180.
    9. L. L. Martz, "Forword" to Edward Taylor, *Poems,* ed. D. E. Stan-
ford (New Haven, 1960), pp. xxi–xxii.

of apparent opposites—the playful and the serious, the mundane and the transcendent, the finite and the infinite, the melancholy and the elated (as in the religious poems of La Ceppède and Gryphius, in which contemplations of the most somber or distressing sort are likely to conclude in an almost vertiginous awareness of the infiniteness of God's mercy or the absolute liberation to be expected from death). Such expansion of experience seems to involve a yet deeper paradox—a liberation from the self which nevertheless constitutes, on one level, a realization of the true self which could not otherwise occur: "Loves riddles are, that though thy heart depart, / It stayes at home, and thou with losing savest it."[10] The Baroque liberation from the self operates through three major preoccupations which usually imply one another—the dramatic, the metaphysical, and the meditative.

The specifically dramatic quality of most Baroque religious poetry is readily apparent. There is almost invariably a protagonist in the poem, a speaker whose diction, imagery, and syntax characterize him with a good degree of precision and vividness. A careful reading of such poets as Donne, Herbert, Huygens, and Quevedo will demonstrate further that the poet consistently employs the protagonist as a persona, a mask which projects aspects of the poet's own personality, but aspects which are artfully selected and combined for effect within a given context. Thus the protagonist in *The Temple* shares many traits with the man George Herbert—aristocratic tastes, worldly ambition, love of music, a fondness for fine clothes—but the poet George Herbert always has him firmly in artistic focus, combining, recombining, emphasizing, and choosing traits which will delineate a character appropriate to the themes and spiritual concerns of

10. The fact that the quoted passage occurs in an amorous poem ("Lovers' Infinitenesse") suggests the unity which characterizes Donne's poems whatever their subject.

each individual poem. The speaker in a typical Baroque devotional poem is finally a fictional character, as much as is a character in a novel or a play.

Furthermore, Baroque devotional poetry almost always supplies the reader with the sense of a specific setting and an implied audience within the poem. Much lyric poetry of other periods, including much poetry religious in subject, addresses its readers directly as audience. We are told about the glory of God or we are exhorted to a life of virtue and faith, or we are told a story about the religious experiences of the speaker.[11] In religious poetry of the seventeenth century we do not so much hear a communication as overhear it: the communication itself is directed at God or at some aspect of the speaker's self. The relation of reader to poem, then, is precisely that of audience to drama. Other features contribute to the dramatic effect of Baroque poetic devotion: the fact that it is typically offered in the present tense, not as something that has happened, but as something that is happening, and the fact that it is projected in a vitally engaged idiom—abrupt, exclamatory, and colloquial.

But drama cannot be had merely for the asking, and the dramatic lyric, like the drama itself, is born only from spiritual circumstances of a rather special sort. Those circumstances, it might be suggested, have much to do with the ability to modify one's identity—the same ability which Shakespeare, bestowing on some of his most attractive comic characters, seems himself to have possessed in the highest degree.[12] The "confessional" poet, as some literary phenomena of our own day remind us, is a bit uncertain of his identity and as a result constantly busies himself with getting that identity on paper—and getting it right, truth-

---

11. Cf., for example, Francis Thompson's "The Hound of Heaven."
12. See above, pp. 107–08. Relevant in this context is Keats's famous concept of "negative capability." On "detachment" and related questions in devotional poetry, see A. Stein, *George Herbert's Lyrics* (Baltimore, 1968), esp. pp. 88–97.

fully. The Baroque literary artist, whether dramatist or lyric poet, is so serenely sure of his identity that he can play tricks with it—splitting himself into aspects of his own personality; distancing himself from the aspirations and desires most immediate to himself, and achieving simultaneously the expression of the force of those desires and an ironic liberation from them; taking on, Viola-like, a person that is not and yet in some strange way is his own. The modification of the self is, in a sense, the precondition of the dramatist's art: it is, of course, an attitude of "play," incorporating the sense of reality as conflict, the knowledge that to play a role is to participate in realities beyond the private, and the feeling of vertiginous liberation that issues from an attitude of disrespectful levity toward all that does not transcend the earthly.

Still, the precondition cannot be willed, and it would be indefensibly mystical to assume that the great writers of the Baroque possessed magical powers which have since been lost to the human race. The quality of "committed detachment" which I find at the root of Baroque drama and Baroque devotional verse is nurtured, I think, by two phenomena of peculiar force in the age—philosophical sophistication and spiritual discipline. These qualities, finally, explain the Baroque poet's extraordinary capacity for speaking with personal immediacy about things which transcend human sense.

It has been suggested that Metaphysical poetry as a whole derives its typical features from a habit of viewing emotional experience in terms of its implicit metaphysical and theological mysteries, "problems either deriving from, or closely resembling in the nature of their difficulty, the problem of the Many and the One."[13] The work of the devotional poets, with its passionately personal involvement in the insoluble contradictions of the infinite and the eternal, illustrates the thesis admirably. A concern

13. J. Smith, "On Metaphysical Poetry," *Scrutiny* 2, no. 3 (1933): 228.

with metaphysical speculation obviously engages the ratiocina-
tive powers profoundly, and any poetry of a devotional character
engages the emotions with an equal intensity. From the simultaneous presence of these two varieties of engagement emerges
that strongly marked feature of Metaphysical poetry which has
been variously labeled "passionate ratiocination" and "unified
sensibility."[14]

And yet a capacity for expressing simultaneously individual
emotion and complex thought, that capacity being regarded as
fundamental to the dramatic thrust of the devotional poem, cannot be willed. Perhaps the Baroque tradition of spiritual discipline can provide some clues as to how both the dramatic and
the metaphysical operate in the kind of poetry under discussion.
Formal meditation is the principal instrument of spiritual discipline in the later sixteenth and seventeenth centuries. Meditation, as Louis L. Martz describes it, consists of a series of rigorous
intellectual actions having as their aim the right ordering of
memory, understanding, and will so as to accomplish a successful experience of religious devotion.[15] Not to be confused with
the contemplation engaged in by the mystic, meditation issues
not in the beatific vision (though it may, for those gifted with
special grace), but rather in effective prayer. Meditation and its
fruits are thus available to any Christian who is willing to follow
the steps laid down by St. Ignatius and other adepts of the discipline.

The process of meditation is complex. After a number of
preparatory exercises, the meditator enters the "composition," or
first stage of his exercise. Here, with the greatest possible sensuous vividness and detail, he pictures to himself some scene

---

14. H. J. C. Grierson, "Introduction" to *Metaphysical Lyrics and
Poems of the Seventeenth Century* (Oxford, 1921), p. xxxiv; T. S. Eliot,
"The Metaphysical Poets," in his *Selected Essays* (New York, 1950), p.
248.

15. Martz, *The Poetry of Meditation*, esp. pp. 25–70.

from the life of Christ or of the saints, some imaginary scene relating to himself (e.g. his own deathbed scene), or some illustrative similitude. The faculty of memory having been brought into play (for even scenes of fantasy depend on past experience), the meditator moves into the second phase, in which the faculty of understanding engages in an analysis of the significance of the scene which the imagination has staged. The image-making capacity of the mind is inseparable from this process of analysis. In a successful meditation, as Martz describes it, "gradually the will takes fire and the appropriate affections arise."[16] When the affections have arisen, the meditator is in a position to let the will, or third faculty of the soul, come into play in a "colloquy," or emotionally immediate discourse with God or with some aspect of himself.

Martz has convincingly demonstrated the specific influence on seventeenth-century poetry of this mode of spiritual discipline as well as its general relevance to the intellectual life of the period. He has proven, furthermore, the degree to which this originally Roman Catholic practice infiltrated Protestant spirituality. Most significantly, he has pointed out the ways in which the practice of meditation, which "begins in the understanding, endeth in the affection" (the quotation is from Joseph Hall), may lead to the kind of poetry in which feeling and thought are fused—in short, to Metaphysical poetry.[17] For our particular purposes here, we might note the specifically dramatic form assumed by the meditation, and the fact that its progression depends on the meditator's creation of the self as a kind of dramatic character on an inner stage: "The essential process of all true meditative poetry depends upon the interaction between a projected, dramatized

16. L. L. Martz, ed., *The Meditative Poem* (Garden City, 1963), p. xxii.
17. Martz, *The Poetry of Meditation.* The relevance of formal meditation to Metaphysical poetry has also been demonstrated by Helen Gardner in her edition of Donne's *Divine Poems* (Oxford, 1952) and by Wilson in "Spanish and English Religious Poetry."

part of the self, and the whole mind of the meditative man."[18]
Meditation, thus, relates to both the dramatic and the transcendent qualities of devotional poetry by providing a means through which the self is at once distanced and realized and is so brought into meaningful relation with absolute and infinite truths which transcend the powers of ordinary experience to recognize. It domesticates the inconceivable.

The full relationship of the meditative process to dramatic formulation may be observed in such poems as Donne's *Holy Sonnets,* Herbert's "Man" (among many others in *The Temple*), La Ceppède's *Théorèmes spirituels,* Quevedo's *Lágrimas de un penitente,* and Lope de Vega's "Pastor que con tus silvos amorosos." Sometimes, as in Henry Vaughan's "I walkt the other day (to spend my hour)," a Baroque devotional poem will incorporate the complete structure of a formal meditation, with composition of place, analysis, and colloquy standing in the same tight psychological relationship that obtains under the Ignatian scheme. In all these cases it is worth noting that the poem is charged with dramatic realization, depending in part on the characterization of a protagonist, and that the strong emotion which emerges from the dramatic realization coexists with intellectual activity of the most restless and probing sort. The dramatization of the self results not in a theatrical falsity but in what Martz, appropriating the phrase from W. B. Yeats, calls "unity of being."[19]

Until halfway through the seventeenth century, the intellectual fuel which feeds the great blaze of Baroque devotional poetry is the inherited complex of traditional beliefs concerning the structure of the universe and man's place within it. A poem like Herbert's "Man" is based on the ancient theory of correspondences which saw a set of universal analogies relating the

18. L. L. Martz, *The Poem of the Mind* (New York, 1966), p. 7.
19. Martz, *The Poetry of Meditation,* pp. 64–67, 321–30.

microcosm man to the macrocosm of the universe, these analogies in turn providing a basis for political, medical, and scientific thought as well as for philosophical speculation in general.[20] Such a passage as the following, from Donne's *Devotions upon Emergent Occasions,* will typify the degree to which orthodox Renaissance scientific thought permeated Baroque meditation:

> It is too little to call *Man* a *little World*; except *God,* Man is a *diminutive* to nothing. Man consistes of more pieces, more parts, than the world; than the world doeth, nay than the world is. And if those pieces were extended and stretched out in Man, as they are in the world, Man would bee the *Gyant,* and the Worlde the *Dwarfe,* the World but the *Map,* and the Man the *World.* If all the *Veines* in our bodies, were extended to *Rivers,* and all the *Sinewes,* to *Vaines of Mines,* and all the *Muscles,* that lye upon one another, to *Hilles,* and all the *Bones* to *Quarries* of stones, and all the other pieces, to the proportion of those which correspond to them in the world, the *Aire* would be too litle for the *Orbe* of Man to move in, the firmament would bee but enough for this *Starre;* for, as the whole world hath nothing, to which something in man doth not answere, so hath man many pieces, of which the whole world hath no representation.[21]

The artist's fancy here revises and modifies the accepted doctrine of the microcosm-macrocosm correspondence, but the modification itself depends on assuming the orthodox doctrine as a point of departure. The dramatized meditator, thoroughly en-

20. Among those who have examined such connections, one might particularly note M. H. Nicolson, *The Breaking of the Circle,* rev. ed. (New York, 1960), and J. A. Mazzeo, *Renaissance and Seventeenth-Century Studies* (New York, 1964), chaps. 2–3.
21. John Donne, *Poetry and Prose,* ed. F. J. Warnke (New York, 1967), pp. 312–13.

gaged in both emotion and intellect, seizes and reworks accepted
cosmological belief until he is in a position to regard the great
paradoxes at the heart of his relationship to absolute reality.
Thus is the self expanded without ceasing to be a self, and thus
is the Baroque artist in a psychological and spiritual position
which enables him to create devotional poetry and prose.

From the point of view of general intellectual history, the
most important happening of the first half of the seventeenth
century was the gradual shift from the assumptions of the traditional cosmology—geocentric, theological, based on the theory
of correspondences—to the adoption of the new cosmology deriving from Copernicus, Kepler, and Galileo—heliocentric, secularized, and liberated from the metaphors of universal analogy.[22] Whatever the benefits accruing thereby to science and
technology and human life as a whole, the discovery of a world-
picture more nearly in accord with fact had a disturbing effect
on poetry in general and a destructive effect on devotional poetry
in particular. What one might call a poetry of total statement,
giving utterance simultaneously to a highly personal consciousness and a sense of the relatedness of that consciousness to the
absolute and transcendent, was rendered all but impossible by a
cosmology which placed the individual at an incalculably great
imaginative distance from the root of all being.

The impulse toward the creation of such poetry did not, however, die out as soon as the intellectual circumstances which
made it possible ceased to exist. The second generation of Metaphysical poets, active during the second half of the seventeenth
century, attempted, very often with success, to write devotional
poetry, a poetry of total statement, intensely personal and yet
directed toward an immediate awareness of the presence of God.

22. See Nicolson, *Breaking of the Circle*. See also E. M. W. Tillyard,
The Elizabethan World Picture (New York, 1944), and B. Willey, *The
Seventeenth Century Background* (London, 1934).

Deprived of the traditional cosmology and its related "poetic of correspondence,"[23] such poets as Marvell, Vaughan, and Traherne in England, Quirinus Kuhlmann and Catherina Regina von Greiffenberg in Germany, and Jan Luyken in Holland were obliged to formulate a new basis for this kind of poetry. Three elements, often found in combination, seem to be the constituents of the new basis: wit and irony of a more personally radical sort than that found in the older poetry, the mystical apprehension of external nature, and the reliance on esoteric or arcane doctrines.

Only a few of Andrew Marvell's poems may be regarded as devotional, and it is interesting to observe that such poems as "On a Drop of Dew" and "Eyes and Tears" operate more in a descriptive mode than in the strongly dramatic mode of Donne and Herbert. Marvell's truest devotional poem, "The Coronet," is the wittiest and most ironic of his overtly religious poems. In it, through the bizarre expedient of admitting the inevitability of failure in the attempt at devotional verse, he achieves a brilliant success:

> When for the Thorns with which I long, too long,
>   With many a piercing wound,
>   My Saviours head have crown'd,
> I seek with Garlands to redress that Wrong:
>   Through every Garden, every Mead,
> I gather flow'rs (my fruits are only flow'rs)
>   Dismantling all the fragrant Towers
> That once adorn'd my Shepherdesses head.
> And now when I have summ'd up all my store,
>   Thinking (so I my self deceive)
>   So rich a Chaplet thence to weave
> As never yet the king of Glory wore:

23. Mazzeo, *Renaissance*, pp. 44–59.

Alas I find the Serpent old
That, twining in his speckled breast,
About the flow'rs disguis'd does fold,
With wreaths of Fame and Interest.
Ah, foolish Man, that would'st debase with them,
And mortal Glory, Heavens Diadem!
But thou who only could'st the Serpent tame,
Either his slipp'ry knots at once untie,
And disintangle all his winding Snare:
Or shatter too with him my curious frame:
And let these wither, so that he may die,
Though set with Skill and chosen out with Care.
That they, while Thou on both their Spoils dost tread,
May crown thy Feet, that could not crown thy Head.[24]

The poet begins with what amounts to the "composition of place" traditional in formal meditation.[25] In the course of that composition he admits that the devotional action he proposes has the form of sacred parody: the flowers with which he once constructed ornate headdresses for his "shepherdesses" are now to be drafted into the service of the "king of Glory." The reader is reminded of George Herbert and of the satisfaction that poet derived from applying the ornaments of poetry not to profane mistresses but to God, the only proper recipient of all praise. Marvell seems less persuaded of the suitability or the acceptability of his tribute—not only because of the profane taint of the materials which will make up the coronet but more significantly because of the "wreaths of Fame and Interest" which Satan hides under the flowers: the poet's necessary concern with his craft and with the consequent fulfillment of his ego-demands renders cor-

24. Andrew Marvell, *Poems and Letters,* ed. H. M. Margoliouth, 2 vols., 2d ed. (Oxford, 1952), pp. 14–15. Subsequent citations are to this edition.
25. H. E. Toliver, *Marvell's Ironic Vision* (New Haven, 1965), p. 97.

rupt the work designed as offering. What I have elsewhere referred to as the poetic of the jongleur, so operative in the work of Herbert (cf. "The Forerunners") seems to have lost its validity for Marvell. The issue, then, is failure: the best the poet can hope for is that God, unreachable through the corrupt instrument of the individual poetic sensibility, will accept the unworthy offering by trampling on it. The "curious frame" of line 22 is nicely ambiguous, referring to both the poet's ornate artifact and his own person, and in the latter connection the prayer for the abolition of the artifact becomes in a sense a prayer for the abolition of the self. It is in these terms, in the context of admitted failure, that the speaker becomes capable of direct colloquy with God, hence capable of successful devotion. The "Spoils" of line 25, as Toliver has pointed out, constitute "the spoils of victory as well as a spoiled wreath."[26] They constitute also, one might note, a spoiled serpent.

A little more than a century after Marvell wrote his lyrics, Dr. Johnson delivered himself of some opinions concerning devotional poetry:

> Let no pious ear be offended if I advance, in opposition to many authorities, that poetical devotion cannot often please. The doctrines of religion may indeed be defended in a didactic poem; and he who has the happy power of arguing in verse will not lose it because his subject is sacred . . . Contemplative piety, or the intercourse between God and the human soul, cannot be poetical. Man, admitted to implore the mercy of his Creator, and plead the merits of his Redeemer, is already in a higher state than poetry can confer . . . From poetry the reader justly expects, and from good poetry always obtains, the enlargement of his comprehension and elevation of his fancy; but this is rarely to be hoped by Christians from

26. Ibid., p. 97.

metrical devotion. Whatever is great, desirable, or tremendous, is comprised in the name of the Supreme Being. Omnipotence cannot be exalted; Infinity cannot be amplified; Perfection cannot be improved. The employments of pious meditation are faith, thanksgiving, repentance, and supplication. Faith, invariably uniform, cannot be invested by fancy with decorations. Thanksgiving, the most joyful of all holy effusions, yet addressed to a Being without passions, is confined to a few modes, and is to be felt rather than expressed. Repentance, trembling in the presence of the judge, is not at leisure for cadences and epithets. Supplication of man to man may diffuse itself through many topics of persuasion; but supplication to God can only cry for mercy.[27]

Several conceptions should be noted in this extended passage: art is decorated instruction; decoration can add nothing to the simple truths of Christian doctrine or the sublime reality of the Christian God; the majesty of God cannot be even suggested by the instruments of art; and the literary artist who applies his art to matter so much beyond its reach convicts himself of presumptuousness and, by implication, insincerity. Wellek has commented on Johnson's ultimate unwillingness to recognize the claims of art, as such, as a serious instrument of spiritual vision, his "incomprehension of the centrally metaphorical character of poetry,"[28] and such limitations surely underlie his rejection of a whole important poetic genre. But, more specifically, the passage in the "Life of Waller" indicates the degree to which Johnson, and with him the whole eighteenth century, had lost touch with the older modes of thought, in which a universe which in itself possessed poetic unity made possible the impingement of

27. Samuel Johnson, "Life of Waller," in *Lives of the English Poets* (1779–81), ed. L. Archer Hind, 2 vols. (London, 1925), 1:173–74.
28. R. Wellek, *A History of Modern Criticism,* 5 vols. (New Haven, 1955–   ), 1:99.

the characterized finite individual on the infinite and the absolute—without in any way diminishing the latter.[29]

In "The Coronet" 's confession of failure Marvell gives evidence of the weakening of those modes of thought in the second
half of the seventeenth century, particularly when he finds that
his own practice of art in the praise of God leads him to fear that
he is being insincere. But although the old picture of the world
can no longer, for Marvell, support the impulse toward poetic
devotion, the inherited—and extraordinarily sophisticated—conception of art makes it possible for him, at least in this one poem,
to realize that impulse. With a self-deprecating irony which
verges on the joking, he distances himself from himself, speaking with the full humility of the sincere worshiper as he offers
for destruction the wreath which the craftsman has fashioned.
For this moment in his career as poet, Marvell has found his way
back to the poetic of George Herbert.

Wit of a very radical sort is the defining feature of all Marvell's poetry, and in much of that poetry the wit appears in association with a quasi-mystical apprehension of nature. But one
of the aspects of Marvell's uniqueness in his age is the fact that,
although he finds in nature kinds of experience which transport
him beyond the limits of his finite self, those kinds of experience
seldom relate directly to Christian doctrine or myth. The soul of
the speaker in "The Garden" glides into a tree to wait "till pre-
par'd for longer flight," and that flight has the Christian heaven
as its presumable destination; similarly, the setting of the poem
is a version of the Garden of Eden. But the Christian Heaven is
not overtly referred to, and the speaker stumbles and falls in a
landscape which is, if a version of Eden, an ironic and innocuous
one (see above, pp. 116–17). In "The Garden," as in the
"Mower" poems and "Upon Appleton House," a kind of secular

29. Nicolson, *Breaking of the Circle,* pp. xiii–xviii.

mysticism (if the term is not too perversely paradoxical) is at issue: the protagonist is placed in relation not with the Christian
God but with the self-sufficient, all-embracing green order of
nature. Such poetry resembles devotional poetry in its mode of
operation as in the kind of experience it celebrates. But it is not
devotional poetry, and the experience is not Christian.

In Marvell's contemporary Henry Vaughan, as in Jan Luyken
in Holland, we encounter the full application to Christian experience of external nature mystically perceived. The result is a
highly personal, often eccentric devotional poetry, different in
many respects from the strongly individual and yet ultimately
tradition-oriented poetry of Donne and Herbert. Landscape and
natural object in Vaughan are treated with distinct concreteness
and particularity as compared with such phenomena in Herbert,
but a reading which would see Vaughan's approach to nature as
being in any significant sense proto-Romantic would be faulty.[30]
Nature plays a larger and more affecting role in Vaughan than
in the earlier Metaphysicals not because it is presented in a vividly descriptive manner but because it is charged with religious
significance and saturated with the emotions of the poet.

One of Vaughan's countless borrowings from an older poet
may provide an illuminating comparison. In "The Flower,"
George Herbert compares the effect of the favor of God upon his
heart to that of the coming of spring upon the flower. Although
the poem begins in the mode of simile, from the second stanza
on it displays a sensuous immediacy and a sympathetic identification with a natural object which are both rare in Herbert:

> Who could have thought my shrivel'd heart
> Could have recover'd greennesse? It was gone
> Quite under ground; as flowers depart

30. R. A. Durr, *On the Mystical Poetry of Henry Vaughan* (Cambridge, Mass., 1962), summarizes, with appropriate criticisms, the history
of the Vaughan-Wordsworth analogy.

To see their mother-root, when they have blown;
    Where they together
    All the hard weather,
Dead to the world, keep house unknown.

[p. 166]

If we turn to Vaughan's "Unprofitableness," we are struck by the greater intensity of the poet's identification with the natural object as well as by the fact that the flower has a significance in its own right, as distinct from the arbitrary and emblematic significance of Herbert's flower:

How rich, O Lord! how fresh thy visits are!
'Twas but Just now my bleak leaves hopeles hung
    Sullyed with dust and mud;
Each snarling blast shot through me, and did share
Their Youth, and beauty, Cold showres nipt, and wrung
    Their spiciness, and bloud;
But since thou didst in one sweet glance survey
Their sad decays, I flourish, and once more
    Breath all perfumes, and spice;
I smell a dew like *Myrrh,* and all the day
Wear in my bosome a full Sun; such store
    Hath one beame from thy Eys.
But, ah, my God! what fruit hast thou of this?
What one poor leaf did ever I yet fall
    To wait upon thy wreath?
Thus thou all day a thankless weed doest dress,
And when th'hast done, a stench, or fog is all
    The odour I bequeath.[31]

The difference, centrally, is that, whereas Herbert chooses the flower as a means for telling us something, Vaughan experiences

31. Henry Vaughan, *Works,* ed. L. C. Martin, 2d ed. (Oxford, 1957), p. 441.

the flower as something that Divine Wisdom has chosen in
order to tell him something. His implied reliance on a kind of
intuition of divinity acting directly but darkly through nature
contrasts with Herbert's selection of a natural object as an emblem drawn from the ordered and comprehensible universe.

Nature is continually telling things to Vaughan, and plant
life seems to be one of the most consistently articulate of the
elements of nature, as in the untitled poem beginning "And do
they so? have they a Sense," in which even inanimate nature
gives him example by joining with flowers and birds to praise
the Creator, or in the beautifully executed "meditation on the
creatures" which begins, "I walkt the other day (to spend my
hour)." In the latter poem the speaker, grieving at the death of
a friend, wanders in a winter landscape and on impulse digs up
the root of a flower which he remembers to have grown there.[32]
He intuits from this experience the assurance of immortality and
is thereby enabled to engage in colloquy with God. The poem
involves a kind of mystical application of seed-imagery[33] strikingly similar to that found in a poem of rather later date by Jan
Luyken—"De Ziele in aendacht over de nieuwe Creatuer" ("The
Soul in Devotion at the Birth of Life"). In Luyken's poem the
speaker notes the life-death-rebirth cycle manifested in the experiences of the seed and longs to become identified with the
seed and to be transformed into a blossom in a wreath on
Christ's head[34] (the recurrence of this idea in Marvell, Vaughan,
Luyken, and other Metaphysical poets of the second generation
is suggestive of the more active role forced upon observed nature
as an agency of spiritual enlightenment).

32. H. C. White, *The Metaphysical Poets* (New York, 1936), p. 250,
follows Paul Elmer More in identifying the friend as the poet's brother
William.

33. Durr, *Vaughan*, p. 31.

34. See my *European Metaphysical Poetry*, pp. 250–51; see also my
"Jan Luyken: A Dutch Metaphysical Poet," *Comp. Lit.* 10, no. 1 (Winter
1958): 45–54.

In such poems as these by Vaughan and Luyken the perception of external nature interacts with another of the characteristic concerns of the later Metaphysicals—esoteric doctrine as a means of regaining both the security and the articulateness called in question by the dissolution of the traditional world-view. The Hermetic philosophy, with its magical pretensions; the theosophical teachings of Jacob Böhme and other mystics; the more bizarre manifestations of Alexandrian and Florentine Neoplatonism—doctrines derived from these and similar sources inform the poetry of Vaughan and Luyken as they do later that of Quirinus Kuhlmann.[35] A plausible reason for this fact is not far to seek: the traditional world-view was constructed of rationally plausible guesses as to the structure implied by what the earth and the skies presented to the senses; it made no claim to a special divine insight which exempted it from criticism or correction at such time as shrewder and more sophisticated guesses might reveal a cosmos less tidily and reassuringly structured. Resistance to the new science during the Baroque age was occasioned not by a conviction that the old cosmology was in itself sacrosanct but by the reluctance of established ecclesiastical and civil authorities to admit the possibility of a cosmos which threatened the bases of their authority and by the emotional resistance of individuals to a menacing and chaotic world-view.

Among the older Metaphysical poets, Donne and Herbert show distress and uncertainty at the implications of the new science, but they manage ultimately, if precariously, to hold on

35. For Vaughan, see esp. Durr, White, and E. Holmes, *Henry Vaughan and the Hermetic Philosophy;* for Luyken, see A. C. M. Meeuwesse, *Jan Luyken als Dichter van de Duytse Lier* (Groningen, 1952), and my two pieces cited in n. 34; for Kuhlmann, see C. V. Bock, *Quirinus Kuhlmann als Dichter* (Basel, 1957), and my *European Metaphysical Poetry.*

to the old unitary conceptions.[36] (Gryphius, who found the
Copernican hypothesis enormously stimulating, is a signal ex-
ception, anticipating the responses of Kuhlmann and Traherne.)
Vaughan and Luyken are unable to sustain a belief in the old
cosmology, and yet the poetic impulse they share—toward devotional poetry, one of the chief varieties of what I have called
"the poetry of total statement"—requires a unitary conception
of the sort built into the old view of the world. Hence, perhaps,
their utilization of symbolic systems which make a suprarational
claim to a certainty and authority not subject to challenge and
verification and imbued with an unshakable sense of the unity
of all things. In Hermeticism, with its doctrines of universal
correspondences obtaining among all created things and active
commerce between heaven and earth, as in Böhme, with his
stress on opposition and the reconciliation of opposites, they
found an extreme restatement of the older unitary conceptions,
and it proved, for a while at least, a solid basis for a new poetic
of devotion.[37] The psychological dynamics involved bear, I
think, a significant analogy to those which may be perceived in
several of the chief poets of our own century—Yeats and Rilke,
most notably—who have found the formulation of special intellectual systems of a quasi-magical character a necessary precondition for the writing of the kind of poetry they are compelled to write—a poetry which is, in its own right, one of total
statement, with strong similarities to the poetry influenced in the
seventeenth century by the techniques of formal meditation.[38]

The importance of arcane doctrines for such poets as Vaughan

36. Donne's "Anniversaries" ultimately demonstrate such a holding
on, despite the doubts expressed in the "First Anniversarie." Earlier, for
the poets of the Renaissance, such doubts do not exist.
37. See White, pp. 271, 344. L. L. Martz, *The Paradise Within* (New
Haven, 1964), p. 37, relates the collapse of traditional institutions to the
revival of Platonic thought at the middle of the seventeenth century.
38. See Martz, *The Poetry of Meditation*, pp. 321–30.

and Luyken relates also to another feature of their lyric work: it is not nature itself which is the material of that work but rather the ineffable and divine reality to which nature points. In this respect they anticipate later formulations of the poet's task, formulations which have been central to the theory and practice of the art from the Romantic period until our own age. Blake, Wordsworth, Keats, Hölderlin, Leopardi, in their widely differing ways, sought a manner of seeing—through private myth or heroic personal aestheticism—which would enable them to find verbal equivalents for total reality. Such a manner of seeing can be found neither through minutely detailed description, however sensuously vivid, nor through immediate and unmodified personal outcry, however sincere. A few hours reading in contemporary journals of poetry will suggest the poverty of the first approach (despite the imagists) and the bankruptcy of the second (despite Whitman). The most considerable poets of our century—Yeats, Eliot, Stevens, Auden, Rilke, Valéry, Montale, Lorca, and a few others—work out their individual solutions in terms that imply a formulation of the problem similar to that effected by the devotional poets of the later seventeenth century —hence, perhaps, the prominence in their work of such elements as esoteric doctrine, mysticism as theme, metaphysical paradox, and the creation of the self as dramatic character.[39]

But the continuing attempts to create devotional poetry in the latter half of the seventeenth century anticipate modern poetry in yet another respect. If Marvell, Vaughan, and Luyken anticipate ironic, ingenious, and indirect ways of achieving a personal lyricism which is not trivial, Thomas Traherne represents an at-

39. Ibid. See also R. Tuve, *Elizabethan and Metaphysical Imagery* (Chicago, 1947), pp. 79–109, for an illuminating discussion of the functions of imagery and of the very minor role which "sensuous immediacy" has traditionally played in the operation of poetic images.

tempt, perhaps the first, to arrive via radical individualism at a lyric voice at once personal and cosmic. Despite his curious free-verse *Thanksgivings,* it would be erroneous to see Traherne as a kind of proto-Whitman. Traherne's is still a Christian world-view, but in the conviction—found alike in the poems, the *Thanksgivings,* and the prose *Centuries of Meditations*—that God and reality are found only within the individual personality, he anticipates developments not only in Romanticism but also in our own time.

Traherne's work is wholly devoid of the dramatic tension so characteristic of the earlier Metaphysicals, and, rather than creating personae as a device for transcending the self, he expands the sense of the self until it includes, as it were, the entire universe. The texture of his poetry and prose is hence distinguished not by wit and irony but rather by an almost overpowering syntax of exclamation and vision, as the content is distinguished by a highly individual and unorthodox theology. Even the sense of poetic form appears to have undergone significant transforma-tion: although the lyrics display the intricate stanzaic patterns familiar from Herbert and Vaughan, those patterns have little organic relevance to the poetic utterances. There is something casual to the point of irresponsibility about Traherne's poetic forms, and this is probably the chief reason for the preference many readers have shown for the prose *Centuries.*[40]

The eccentric German poet and mystic Quirinus Kuhlmann (1651–89) shows certain points of similarity to Traherne—enough at least to suggest a kind of unity in the devotional poetry created during the latter half of the seventeenth century and a common source of that unity in the breakdown of the tra-ditional world-picture. Even more exclamatory than his English

40. D. Bush, *English Literature in the Earlier Seventeenth Century* (Oxford, 1945), p. 148.

contemporary, even more extravagant in his doctrines of individualism, Kuhlmann remains extraordinarily articulate, and his lyrics, for all their breathless intensity of vision, demonstrate a sharper sense of form and function than do Traherne's. Kuhlmann's poems are sparks struck off from a life remarkable for its dedication to a personal quest. Convinced that his role was to found a new religion, the poet all but deified his own sensibility. His evangelical wanderings all over Europe led him finally to Moscow, where he was put to the torture and burned at the stake on the orders of the Patriarch.[41]

It is difficult to say which of these two curious poets departs more strikingly from tradition and orthodoxy. At first reading, one would say Kuhlmann, who was as surely mad as Traherne was surely sane. His madness issues partly as a conviction of his own divinity, but that conviction strangely coexists with an awareness of his sinfulness and with a passionate gratitude to Christ for the sacrifice on the cross. The presence of Christ in the poetry of the German enthusiast is as conspicuous as is His absence from the poetry of the priest of the Church of England. (Christ is mentioned more often in the *Centuries*.) Doctrinally, Traherne feels that his personal glorification comes from the atonement offered by Christ, but in his poetry we are aware primarily of an individual consciousness of the power and indwelling presentness of a God who is virtually identified with the universe. Accordingly, the central doctrine of original sin, accepted and emphasized by Kuhlmann, is on occasion specifically denied by Traherne (see, for example, his "Innocence"). What unites Traherne and Kuhlmann is their theological individualism, together with their sharp awareness of the cosmology of infiniteness. What they share further is a capacity, on the dizzying edge of failure, for creating a poetry which celebrates

41. C. von Faber du Faur, *German Baroque Literature* (New Haven, 1958), pp. 334–35; Bock, *Kuhlmann*, pp. 74–76.

union with God without sacrificing the sense of the individual
personality. Alienated from both the old metaphysics and the
old techniques of formal meditation, they nevertheless give
voice, for the last time, to the metaphysical and meditative devotion which is one of the distinguishing marks of the Baroque
age.

7

The Baroque Epic

The literary Baroque finds its most characteristic expressions in lyric poetry, nonfictional prose, and drama. All three genres exhibit traits of extravagance, irregularity, and asymmetry; all three show a tendency toward the blurring of generic distinctions. Thus in lyric poetry the English move away from fixed forms such as the sonnet toward unique, highly individualized forms, while the Italians compose *madrigali* and *canzoni* which counterfeit the effects of music (even as such a Baroque composer as Monteverdi creates music which approaches the condition of lyric poetry). Prose fiction withers away throughout the first half of the seventeenth century, but in Donne, Burton, and Browne, as earlier in Montaigne, nonfictional genres assume the thrust and vitality, sometimes even the techniques, of narrative.[1] While the spirit of drama comes to permeate lyric and discursive modes, the drama itself rises to supreme heights and, as it does so, formulates new genres such as tragi-comedy, in which classical generic distinctions are slurred over. In all three dominant genres formal uniqueness, dramatic individuality, and the weakening of traditional concepts of category suggest a pervasive skepticism about inherited artistic conceptions concerning the valid mimesis of unquestioned realities, physical and metaphysical.

1. This phenomenon is noted in an unpublished Ph.D. dissertation by Reinhard Friederich, University of Washington, 1971.

158

As previously noted, however, Baroque writers were generally unaware of how radically their literary assumptions and activities departed from those of their Renaissance predecessors. Literary theory and criticism remained primarily classicistic. The hierarchy of genres, with epic and tragedy ranked highest, remained unchallenged, and the European poet continued to regard the achievement of heroic narrative as his most exalted ambition. But such achievement was alien to the Baroque temperament, one deficient not only in the long breath necessary to narrative but also in the epic prerequisites of objectivity, fictive inventiveness, and mythopoeic facility. The discrepancy between the ambitions of the Baroque epic poet and what his sensibility equipped him to do bequeathed to literary history a large body of narrative poetry with epic pretensions, a body of poetry which includes ambitious failures (Davenant's *Gondibert*), bizarre hybrids (Marino's *Adone*), and works of quasi-epic power which diverge radically from the conventions of previous epic (d'Aubigné's *Les Tragiques*). The Baroque age also includes, as a salutary warning to the literary historian who believes in the prescriptive power of *Zeitgeist,* one triumphant example of epic poetry of the truest and highest sort: Milton's *Paradise Lost.*

Before attempting to trace some of the devious paths pursued by the epic impulse during the later sixteenth and the seventeenth centuries, it would be useful to isolate some of the options which had been available to the epic poet of the Renaissance and were, presumably, available to his counterpart of the Baroque. The Renaissance knew, with due veneration, the epics of Homer and Virgil, and were thus familiar with the two main types of epic recognized by later scholarship—the primary epic, which is, like the *Iliad* and the *Odyssey,* the inevitable expression of a primitive society; and the derived epic, which, like the *Aeneid,* exists because the primary epic once existed.[2] (Needless to say, the Renaissance did not make the distinction with the absoluteness imposed by a later sense of history.) Renaissance poets and critics also knew—although without much veneration—indigenous examples of the primary epic: the *Chanson de Roland,* the *Cantar de mío Cid, Beowulf,* the Arthurian stories, and others. If the discrimination between primary and derived epic had little force for the Renaissance poet, the discrimination between classical and vulgar materials did, and thus, between the fourteenth and sixteenth centuries, we find epic poets fairly neatly divided between those who strictly follow the ancients and take themselves seriously and those who mingle classical treatment with indigenous narrative material and take themselves only semiseriously. The strictest kind of emulation of the ancients is found in a work like Petrarch's *Africa,* in which the poet carries his imitation to the point of writing in Latin, but such works as Trissino's *Italia liberata dai Goti* (1547) and Ronsard's *Franciade* (1572) are, though written in the vernacular, comparably Virgilian in their ethical sobriety and their patriotic fervor. Unfortunately, they resemble the *Africa* rather than the *Aeneid* in their stiffness of technique and their lack of narrative vitality.

The Muse has an irresponsible way, often enough, of granting her favors to frivolous suitors while scorning those who approach her with piety and solemnity. The epics of Petrarch, Trissino, and Ronsard are forced and lifeless; those of Boiardo and Pulci overflow with poetic vitality, and Ariosto's *Orlando*

2. Among many significant studies of the epic may be mentioned: C. M. Bowra, *From Virgil to Milton* (London, 1945) and *Heroic Poetry* (London, 1952); T. M. Greene, *The Descent from Heaven* (New Haven, 1963); A. B. Lord, *The Singer of Tales* (Cambridge, Mass., 1960); and E. M. W. Tillyard, *The English Epic and Its Background* (New York, 1954). W. P. Ker, *Epic and Romance,* 2d ed. (London, 1908), retains its special value.

furioso, which derives from them, is one of the glories of epic literature. These latter works, based upon medieval romance and making no sustained claim to classical correctness, are often termed "romance" or "romantic" epics. The terms are perhaps misleading, the former connoting a linguistic distinction and the latter a confusion with the phenomenon of Romanticism. One might press into service the Italian word *romanzesco* as a nonambiguous designation for this central development in Renaissance literature.

Luigi Pulci and Matteo Maria Boiardo submitted to epic or quasi-epic treatment the stories of Orlando (i.e. Roland) and the other paladins of Charlemagne, stories which the humble *cantastorie* of the Italian villages had over the centuries stripped of their original martial power and turned into vulgar tales of the marvelous. Writing for an audience of Ferrarese aristocrats, Boiardo treated his material with consistent sobriety but with a purely aesthetic sense of the unreality of that material that leaves ultimately a sense of quiet irony. Pulci, invincibly bourgeois and irreverently comic, exploited a more boisterous irony.[3] From Pulci's *Morgante maggiore* Ariosto inherited his comic sense, which his immensely greater poetic powers refined and rendered entrancingly equivocal; from Boiardo's *Orlando innamorato* he inherited his plot and his characters, which he elevated into the model for Renaissance epic poetry. The plot situation which Ariosto derived from Boiardo was of incalculable importance for European literature: Boiardo's major achievement had been to strike on the idea of making Orlando fall in love, thus fusing the martial material of the Carolingian cycle with the amorous material of the Arthurian. Ariosto's major achievement was to turn the mixture into high art.

After Ariosto the poets of the high Renaissance brewed the

3. For Pulci and Boiardo, see F. De Sanctis, *Storia della letteratura italiana* (1870–71), ed. L. Russo, 5 vols. (Milan, 1950), 3:138–46.

same mixture—whether in *romanzesco* epics like Spenser's *Faerie Queene* (1590, 1596) or Tasso's *Gerusalemme liberata* (1576) or in historical-nationalistic epics like Camoẽs's *Os Lusíadas* (1572). In the *romanzesco* epic, with its combination of martial and erotic motifs, its structure as an infinitely varied and intricately intertwined series of adventures, and its stanzaic principles of composition, the Renaissance had found an art form which expressed to perfection its own inner nature.[4]

Beside the strict derivative epic and the *romanzesco* epic, including the historical-nationalistic variation, one must take note of two other subgenres of importance during the Renaissance— the burlesque epic, typified by Folengo's *Maccaroneae* (1517– 21) and, of much greater importance, the Christian epic, taking its material either from the Bible or from the lives of the saints. This latter subgenre, best represented in the high Renaissance by two neo-Latin works, Sannazaro's *De Partu Virginis* (1527) and Vida's *Christias* (1535, 1550), was destined to assume major importance during the Baroque age.

All the epic options formulated by the Renaissance were to appear in Baroque manifestations: the derived epic in Latin (e.g. Phineas Fletcher's *Locustae vel Pietas Jesuitica*), the vernacular epic of the strict variety (e.g. the Swedish poet Georg Stiernhielm's *Hercules*), the *romanzesco* epic (e.g. Lope de Vega's *La Hermosura de Angélica*), the burlesque epic (e.g. Alessandro Tassoni's *La Secchia rapita*), and the Christian epic (e.g. *Paradise Lost*, Hojeda's *La Christiada*, d'Aubigné's *Les Tragiques*, Cowley's *Davideis*, Saint-Amant's *Moïse sauvé*, and Vondel's *Joannes de Boetgezant*). On the whole, the Baroque shows a weakening of the epic impulse which had distinguished the Renaissance: one notes, in addition to a decline in narrative

4. See De Sanctis, vols. 3–4, passim. See also Greene, *Descent*, and A. B. Giamatti, *The Earthly Paradise and the Renaissance Epic* (Princeton, 1966).

thrust, inventiveness, and objectivity, an increased emphasis on the descriptive, the pathetic, and the elegiac which weakens the attempted heroic effect. This weakening seems especially to affect the attempts to carry on the *romanzesco* tradition. Lope's *Hermosura de Angélica* (1602) tries to emulate Ariosto, but without the Italian master's flawless gift for conducting complex multiple narratives and without his all-embracing aestheticism and comic verve. The attenuated sentimentality of the *Hermosura* marks also the English Baroque attempts at *romanzesco* epic, among which may be mentioned Sir William Davenant's *Gondibert* (1651) and William Chamberlayne's *Pharonnida* (1659). Although both are in the romance tradition, Davenant's poem moves toward a Neoclassical rationalism and abstractness which weaken its epic pretensions further. Davenant's theory of epic poetry reveals, in its suggestion that the structure of the epic should parallel that of the five-act play, a typical breakdown of the Renaissance feeling for genre.[5]

Epic poetry, as given definitive form in the Renaissance by Ariosto, Spenser, and other masters, had succeeded, despite the equivocal merriment of the former and the allegorical earnestness of the latter, in reaffirming the heroic. At its best, the *romanzesco* epic creates an irresistibly plausible dream-world— plausible precisely because it does have the lineaments of dream —and populates it with characters without character, figures who, never realistic, are always real. Angelica, Bradamante, Alcina, and the other female identities of the *Furioso* are not mimeses of individually imagined feminine characters; they are projections from an unconscious that we share with Ariosto, differing versions of the *Ewig-Weibliche* which operates as the anima within the male psyche. Orlando, Rinaldo, Ruggiero,

5. Sir William Davenant, *Discourse upon Gondibert,* reprinted in J. E. Spingarn, ed., *Critical Essays of the Seventeenth Century,* 3 vols. (Oxford, 1908–09).

and the other heroes are comparable psychological emanations with a comparable force and validity. The *Furioso* narrates to us a common human destiny, imagined in terms of nonrealistic, archetypal figures. *The Faerie Queene* does the same sort of thing, and thus, although Spenser's allegory is a part of the meaning of his great poem, it is not all of it.[6]

The Renaissance epics reflect a real world of experience, but in a manner which is appropriate to epic art—the real world in all its immediacy, but suffused with psychological meaning through the operation of the mythic imagination. The *romanzesco* epic loses this kind of meaning during the Baroque age: the sentimentality of the *Hermosura* and the rationalistic didacticism of *Gondibert* imply, despite the obvious differences between the poems, worlds which are imagined without faith in their artistic existence and characters who are imagined not in terms of what they are (as in Ariosto and Spenser) but in terms of what they can be willed to mean.[7]

Marino's *Adone* (1623), the most widely read epic of the Baroque, belongs not to the *romanzesco* tradition but to that of mythological narrative. Several of its features typify what happened to epic poetry on secular subjects during the Baroque age: its overt motive is neither ethical, as in Spenser, nor purely aesthetic, as in Ariosto, but frankly and cynically sensual (as Greene points out,[8] the claim it makes toward allegorical and moral

6. The assumptions underlying this paragraph derive, of course, from the thought of C. G. Jung. See esp. his *Spirit in Man, Art, and Literature*, trans. R. F. C. Hull (New York, 1966), pp. 65–105. My reading of Spenser in general is indebted to A. C. Hamilton, *The Structure of Allegory in The Faerie Queene* (Oxford, 1961), and H. Berger, Jr., *The Allegorical Temper* (New Haven, 1957).

7. Spenser's characters are, of course, allegorical but their allegorical significance does not exhaust their meaning. They have a fictional existence which includes but goes beyond any mental abstraction imposed on them by either the poet or the reader. This is not true of Davenant's one-dimensional, or perhaps nondimensional, creations.

8. Greene, *Descent*, pp. 239–40.

significance is transparently hypocritical); its material is drawn neither from ancient epic nor from indigenous legend, but from Ovid, a source which, for the Renaissance, had lacked the potential for epic dignity; its style, distinguished above all else by radical metaphor, conceit, and wordplay, evokes not an imagined world of palpable entities but a shifting, phantasmagoric pseudo-world in which the only principle is perpetual metamorphosis; and it often slights narrative as such in favor of recurrent displays of encyclopedic erudition which recall the French "scientific" poetry of the later sixteenth century.[9] Renaissance poetry on Ovidian themes—Marlowe's *Hero and Leander* and Shakespeare's *Venus and Adonis,* for example—had made no pretense to epic status, nor did the greatest of Baroque Ovidian poems, Góngora's *Fábula de Polifemo y Galatea.* Marino's apparent conviction that an erotic extravaganza, decorated with festoons of wit and learning, could present itself as an epic poem indicates the degree to which the "prince of the century" had lost touch with the traditional sense of the heroic.

For all its determined and accomplished sensuality, the world of the *Adone* is in a constant state of dissolution and flux. The images of that world, lacking the solidity and contour of Ariosto's or Spenser's, habitually melt into each other, in a manner familiar to the reader of Góngora or Crashaw. Marino's epic, then, suggests the familiar Baroque doubt as to the validity of the phenomenal world, and that doubt issues as an indifference toward the act of storytelling itself. Such an attitude may give

9. For scientific poetry see O. de Mourgues, *Metaphysical, Baroque and Précieux Poetry* (Oxford, 1953), pp. 26–46. Traditional hostile accounts of Marino may be found in De Sanctis, *Storia,* 5:31–45, and in B. Croce, *Storia dell' età barocca in Italia* (Bari, 1929). Greene, in *Descent,* has a chapter on the *Adone;* J. V. Mirollo, *The Poet of the Marvelous, Giambattista Marino* (New York, 1963), has devoted a book to the poet; and H. M. Priest, *Adonis* (Ithaca, 1967), has translated substantial portions of the epic into English verse, accompanied by a penetrating and largely sympathetic introductory essay.

birth to great poetry, as the Baroque lyric accomplishment reminds us, but it can hardly create epic poetry of true worth. That is, it can hardly create epic poetry on the secular subjects, amorous and military, dear to the poets of the Renaissance. In the subgenre of the Christian epic the Baroque poets produced a large amount of idiosyncratic but impressive work—the subject matter, as it were, liberating them from the inhibitions which the Baroque doubt placed upon secular narrative.

Before confronting the Christian epic proper, however, one is obliged to take up the question of Torquato Tasso's *Gerusalemme liberata,* the great epic poem which stands between Renaissance and Baroque both in its style and in its narrative preoccupations. Tasso's poem occupies a unique position in the history of the literary term *Baroque:* when Wölfflin first suggested the literary application of the term, he exemplified its validity by pointing to the stylistic contrasts between the *Orlando furioso* and the *Gerusalemme* (see above, p. 14n.). In the latter poem (1576) an overriding concern with atmosphere *(Stimmung)* and with images coalescing to form a unity replaces the clear visual imagination *(Anschauung)* of Ariosto's poem (1516), and this replacement parallels the development from Renaissance to Baroque in architecture and the plastic arts.[10] One could note, beyond Wölfflin, further contrasts between Ariosto and Tasso: although the *Gerusalemme* is a definitive example of the *romanzesco* epic, it employs the devices of the regular classical epic far more frequently and purposefully than does the *Furioso;* it gives prominence to didactic and religious motifs virtually absent from the *Furioso;* it shows a predilection for absolute metaphor in place of the neo-Homeric similes characteristic of Ariosto's work, and in so doing moves toward the imagery of metamorphosis typical of Baroque poetry as a whole;

10. See R. Wellek, *Concepts of Criticism* (New Haven, 1963), pp. 69–80.

it demonstrates what amounts to a naturalization, almost a do-
mestication, of many of the heroic and mythical elements of
Ariosto (e.g. Armida, Tasso's temptress, is not, like Ariosto's
Alcina, an effectively demonic being not subject to the condi-
tions of mortality, but, rather, a nice human girl gone wrong);
as a derivation from the preceding feature, there is in Tasso
a consistent emphasis on pathos almost never found in Ariosto
(e.g. the whole treatment of Armida, the episode of Sofronia and
Olindo, the combat of Tancredi and Clorinda and the death of
the latter); Tasso habitually modulates into lyric and elegiac passages which have almost no counterparts in Ariosto (e.g. the
Sultan's lament over the fall of Jerusalem);[11] although the
Gerusalemme does not abound in naked girls as does the Furioso,
and although their charms are not as lovingly and carefully
described, Tasso's poem is permeated with a heady and rather
disturbing eroticism not found in Ariosto's: the Furioso observes
always a distance between action and audience which preserves
the aesthetic purity of the work; the Gerusalemme plunges its
audience into a murky involvement which moves not only toward the Baroque but also toward the modern.[12]

Nevertheless, in several important respects the Gerusalemme
liberata remains a Renaissance epic—in its unflagging narrative
drive, in its linear construction, in its tireless invention of episode, in the final solidity and discreteness of its images. Tasso is
concerned with atmosphere and effect, but never to the extent
of implying, in the Baroque manner (cf. Marino, Crashaw, and
others), that atmosphere and effect are capable of evoking a
transcendent reality without the mediation of a real world out

11. See Greene, Descent, pp. 218–19.
12. Relevant in this context is Schiller's important distinction between
naïve and sentimental poetry, the "sentimental" in his sense being
virtually synonymous with the "modern." "Über Naïve und Sentimen-
talische Dichtung" (1795), in Friederich Schiller, Werke, 2 vols. (Munich,
1962), 2:642–710.

there somewhere—a world of which the poet's creation is a responsible mimesis.[13] The great episode of the fall of Jerusalem with which the epic concludes creates, despite its rather savage Counter-Reformation piety, a truly heroic world in which both Christian and Pagan are ennobled by the courage with which they confront death on a dusty and tragic plain that recalls the setting of the *Iliad*. Solimano's death (20.73–76) has an epic grandeur which suggests the death of Rodomonte at the end of the *Orlando furioso*. It seems to me that one must, finally, regard Tasso's masterpiece, despite the many ways in which it anticipates Baroque stylistic traits, as one of the last great monuments of Renaissance style.[14]

After the *Gerusalemme* and *The Faerie Queene*, the *romanzesco* epic, like the secular epic in general, goes into marked decline in the western European literatures. Such is not altogether the case in the literatures of eastern Europe—possibly because of a cultural lag which, though not preventing the eastern poets from being exposed to the influence of the Baroque manners, exempted them from experiencing the characteristic attitudes which, in the west, weakened the impulse toward secular epic. Possibly, also, the Christian national cultures along the hostile frontier of the Ottoman empire retained in their common life folkways and assumptions which were hospitable to the creation of epic poetry. In Croatia, with its strong indigenous tradition of heroic poetry, the influence of Tasso and, to some extent, of Marino led to the production of a number of impressive epic

13. Wölfflin's formulation slights, I believe, the element of careful mimesis in Tasso's poem.
14. My placing of Tasso, like my entire conception of the Baroque, differs radically from that of H. Hatzfeld, who, seeing Tasso, Cervantes, and Racine as centrally Baroque, relegates to a kind of limbo of vanities a large number of the authors whom this study regards as definitive for the age. See esp. H. Hatzfeld, "A Clarification of the Baroque Problem in the Romance Literatures," *Comp. Lit.* 1, no. 2 (Spring 1949): 113–39, and *Estudios sobre el barroco* (Madrid, 1964).

poems, chief among them the Osman of Ivan Gundulić, in which the contemporary struggle of the Slavs against the Turks provides the material for an epic wherein the Christian seriousness of Tasso merges with patriotic motifs reminiscent of Trissino and Camoẽs. A similar combination characterizes the *Obsidio Szigetiana* of the Hungarian poet Miklós Zrínyi and the *Wojna Chocimska* of the Pole Wacław Potocki. Elsewhere on the periphery of Christian Europe the Baroque produced some vigorous epics based on secular materials—in Sweden, for example, where an epic tradition extends from Stiernhielm's *Hercules* (1648) to Gunno Dahlstierna's allegorical *Kungascald* (1697).[15]

As previously indicated, however, the chief strength of the Baroque epic lies in the subgenre of the Christian epic. Normally the Christian epic takes its subject from the Bible and exposes it to a treatment imitative of epic tradition from the ancients down through the Renaissance poets. Among the subjects most favored by the Baroque poets are the Creation (as in Du Bartas's influential *La Sepmaine* and the Dane Anders Arrebo's *Hexaëmeron*) and episodes from the life of Christ (as in Fray Diego de Hojeda's *La Christiada,* Giles Fletcher's *Christ's Victory and Triumph,* and Milton's *Paradise Regain'd*), but the total range of biblical subjects covered by the Baroque poets is wide indeed: the slaughter of the innocents (Marino's *La strage degl'innocenti*), the life of David (Cowley's *Davideis*), the finding of Moses (Saint-Amant's *Moïse sauvé*), the life of John the Baptist (Vondel's *Joannes de Boetgezant*).

15. My lack of the relevant languages prevents me from commenting on these works. For an impression of some of them I am indebted to Sonja Valčić of the University of Zagreb (Gundulić), Judith von Lichtenberg of Amsterdam (Zrínyi), and Walter Johnson and Andrew Hilen, both of the University of Washington (Stiernhielm). Information is also available in A. Preminger, F. J. Warnke, and O. B. Hardison, eds., *Encyclopedia of Poetry and Poetics* (Princeton, 1965).

These epics vary widely in merit; among the finest are those of Milton, Fletcher, Hojeda, and Vondel. One of the most impressive of Christian epics, however, diverges from the norm in that it derives its material not from Holy Scripture but from current history: Agrippa d'Aubigné's *Les Tragiques* (1616) describes and comments on the religious wars of late sixteenth-century France from a violently partisan Huguenot point of view and in a style which is, in its extremeness, grotesqueness, and extravagance, strikingly Baroque. *Les Tragiques* is not, despite its subject, an historical poem: it makes few gestures toward literal verisimilitude (fewer, perhaps, than the *Gerusalemme liberata*), and its settings range from the throne of God to ravaged France to Hell. The poet focuses relentlessly on the struggles and sufferings of God's elect, the Protestants, but more in the manner of a prophet than of a chronicler; consistently, and with gloomy relish, he looks forward to the day when the elect will receive their reward and their enemies their allotted punishment.[16]

D'Aubigné's poem does not strive overtly to imitate the devices or effects of the classical epic, but nevertheless it achieves, in its grandeur of vision and its cosmic sweep of setting, an effect which is unquestionably epic. In structure and in the implications of structure *Les Tragiques* does present a contrast with earlier epics, and this contrast may tell us something about the Baroque imagination as it expresses itself in epic form.

Earlier heroic poems—the epics of the ancients, the vernacular epics of the Middle Ages, the *romanzesco* epics of the Renaissance—assume the form of linear narrative: they chant the sequential story of great actions. Epos is of its nature story, but in

16. Among the helpful studies of d'Aubigné in English are I. Buffum, *Agrippa d'Aubigné's Les Tragiques: A Study of the Baroque Style in Poetry* (New Haven, 1951); de Mourgues, *Metaphysical;* and Greene, *Descent.*

its heroic form it places finite narrative in a context of eternal
recurrence and infinite renewal; the hero's mortality defines
itself against the unchanging aspects of the nonhuman cosmos,
as Achilles is defined by the existence of "the gods who live at
ease," and as Gilgamesh is defined by the melancholy knowledge
brought to him by his voyage to the underworld.[17] The tension
between the finite, mortal, and heroic, on the one hand, and the
imperishable, perpetually renewed, on the other, explains perhaps the constant device of the beginning in medias res, the re-
sultant suggestion of timelessness, or of circular time, providing
the setting for the delimited experiences of the humanly heroic.

Occasionally the hero's actions bring him into vital contact,
or even temporary identification, with the natural and permanent: Achilles chooses a short but heroic life over a long and
inglorious one, and the dying Beowulf can derive some consolation from the glory of his deeds. Even the mad Orlando of
Ariosto's poem, however grotesquely comic he is in his amorous
madness, assumes an unquestionable grandeur as he becomes
identified, in his quest for Angelica, with the seasonal pattern
of the unchanging year:

> Tra il fin d'ottobre e il capo di novembre,
> Ne la stagion che la frondosa vesta
> Vede levarsi, e discoprir le membre
> Trepida pianta fin che nuda resta,
> E van gli augelli a strette schiere insembre,
> Orlando entrò ne l'amorosa inchiesta:
> Né tutto il verno appresso lasciò quella,
> Né la lasciò ne la stagion novella.[18]

More than mere description is operative here, and more than

17. *The Epic of Gilgamesh,* trans. N. K. Sanders (Baltimore, 1960).
18. Ariosto, *Orlando furioso* (9.7), ed. N. Zingarelli (Milan, 1949),
p. 72.

mere narration: in a manner essentially mythic the epic hero enters on his amorous quest, regardless of winter or spring and yet, in the primitive force of the passion which dominates him, he is equated with the seasons themselves. It is a momentary apotheosis, for the action of the poem reduces Orlando and the other heroes to their human finiteness, restores to them their mortality in time.

Les Tragiques has neither the sense of movement in time nor the affirmation of active individual heroism that we find in the earlier epics. The static rather than dynamic nature of the poem, its continuous circling around the drearily repeated spectacle of the oppression of the just, constitute an effective denial of both history and the possibility of active heroism. Related to this conception of time is d'Aubigné's striking use of the device of scriptural prefiguration, a device which, in his hands, incorporates not merely the scheme of the fulfillment of the Old Testament in the New but rather the repetition of the Old Testament in the events of human history, including contemporary history. Greene takes note of the fact that, though there are antagonists in full supply, there is "virtually no protagonist" in d'Aubigné's poem, heroism consisting not in the capacity for achievement but in the capacity for passive endurance shared by the whole group of the elect. He persuasively relates both the "passive heroism" of d'Aubigné's characters and the static conception of history to the poet's Calvinism:

> D'Aubigné sacrificed the Virgilian frame for the Christian. He rejected the traditional panegyrical pattern of history, based on an ideal of dynastic power, for a Christian pattern of recurrences with fixed terminal limits—creation and judgment . . . The orthodox Christian pattern . . . implied that no individual action could essentially alter human destiny. The Virgilian pattern implied that a man might so alter it, as

Aeneas was supposed to have done. It implied that the divine might effectually intervene in human affairs, because human affairs were capable of progress. The Christian pattern limited direct divine intervention to the two termini of history and to the incarnation (which plays no role in *Les Tragiques*).[19]

Greene's observations apply very justly to *Les Tragiques* in the detail of its vision, but in a larger sense the concept of passive heroism and the sense of history as recurrence without progress are hallmarks of the Baroque epic in general. The theme of passive heroism is so important as to require treatment in a separate chapter; the handling of time in the Baroque epic consistently implies a major shift from the Renaissance sensibility, and that shift, if related to the intensified religious awareness of the age, is not necessarily related only to the Calvinist Christianity of d'Aubigné.

Giles Fletcher's heroic poem *Christ's Victorie and Triumph* (1610) has not generally been accorded the prominent place it deserves in English literary history, perhaps because Spenserianism has been uncongenial to twentieth-century critics, at least until recent years, but perhaps also because it is difficult to know what to make of *Christ's Victorie*. To a more marked degree than *Les Tragiques* it is a static poem, and the passive heroism of its divine protagonist supplies little in the way of dramatic tension or absorbing narrative. Lacking the violence, the scope, and the ideological commitment of *Les Tragiques,* Fletcher's poem does not succeed in being even the approximation of an epic. Its pervasive tone and its finest moments are lyric, as in the following stanza describing Christ's reception in heaven after the Ascension:

So Him they lead into the courts of day,
Where never war, nor wounds abide Him more;

19. Greene, *Descent*, pp. 276–89, 291–92.

But in that house eternal peace doth play,
Acquieting the souls, that new before
Their way to heaven through their own blood did score,
 But now, estranged from all misery,
 As far as heaven and earth discoasted lie,
Swelter in quiet waves of immortality.[20]

Fletcher is interested not in the unfolding of an action in time against a context of implied timelessness but rather in the rendition of timelessness itself as an aspect of the divine reality. All his poetic energies are bent to the fashioning of a language capable of capturing that reality.

Cowley's *Davideis* (1656), the chief English Christian epic between Giles Fletcher and Milton, lacks both the felicities of *Christ's Victorie* and the towering greatness of *Paradise Lost*. In its own way it is as much of a failure as *Gondibert,* and for rather similar reasons. (Cowley, like Davenant and Ronsard, left his epic unfinished out of boredom and despair, not, like Spenser, because time ran out on him.) The poem displays the static and descriptive features typical of most Baroque epics, but it does not compensate for a loss of narrative drive by providing the lyric beauty of a Fletcher or the apocalyptic force of a d'Aubigné. Furthermore, the *Davideis* is undercut from its very conception by Cowley's proto-Neoclassical distrust of poetic fiction: condemning the false fables of the ancients and exalting the truth of biblical history, he nevertheless attempts to write a regular epic in imitation of the ancients and in so doing induces a fatal dichotomy between narrative and ornament. He gives up, in the name of piety and rationality, the spirit of myth without which epic poetry cannot live.[21]

20. P. and G. Fletcher, *Poetical Works,* ed. F. S. Boas, 2 vols. (Cambridge, 1908–09), 1:80. See also above, pp. 35–36.

21. For Cowley's epic, see D. Bush, *English Literature in the Earlier Seventeenth Century* (Oxford, 1945), pp. 357–58, and Greene, *Descent,* pp. 366–73.

The principal Christian epics on the Continent after *Les Tra-giques* (published in 1616 but composed over a period of time beginning forty years earlier) are *La Christiada* (1611) and *Joannes de Boetgezant* (1662). Hojeda's epic has been praised as "the work of a splendidly inspired and visionary imagination,"[22] but it shows also the intensified emphasis on the descriptive and the stress on the theme of passive heroism characteristic of the narrative poetry of the age. Like Giles Fletcher, Hojeda concentrates finally on the expression of theological mysteries which transcend the world of time and action as completely as they do the possibility of human comprehension.

Joost van den Vondel's *Joannes de Boetgezant* is far from being the masterpiece of this poet whose genius is, in a definitively Baroque manner, essentially lyric and dramatic.[23] Nevertheless, despite its exploitation of descriptive, meditative, and nonactive elements, the poem is among the most valid Baroque achievements in the epic genre. Although the descriptive passages are often weighted, like Fletcher's, with symbolic evocations of transcendent reality, they usually have at the same time a dimension of solid realism which recalls Ariosto. Although the poem as a whole has a feeling for the personally mystical which seems at variance with the traditions of epic, it shows a sense of narrative pacing quite absent from the epics of Fletcher or Cowley. Most importantly, Vondel demonstrates throughout a sense of the validity of myth—not for decoration derived from Greco-Roman mythology but for Christian history felt as a series of divine interventions in human affairs, permeating every image of earthly experience and endowing them all with significance. The dominant image of the poem is water—appropriate, of

22. Greene, *Descent*, p. 231. This critic notes also the important role of theological mystery, specifically that of the Incarnation, in Hojeda's epic (p. 232).

23. On Vondel, see W. Kramer, *Vondel als Barokkunstenaar* (Antwerp and Utrecht, 1946).

course, to the sacramental function of John the Baptist, but working also as a symbol of the divine mercy which sends to the spiritually arid earth both John and the Messiah, whom he announces, and as a symbol of the inspiration of the poet himself, who, in the invocation, observes that his effort will remain a *woestijngedicht* ("desert poem") unless he is refreshed and bathed by the living waters that issue from the heavenly throne.[24] Vondel is one of the few authors to retain, as late as the 1660s, that sense of the radically metaphorical nature of poetry which was one of the casualties of European rationalism.

Another poet who retains this sense is the greatest poet of the seventeenth century, the author of the last great epic poem of Western civilization. John Milton's *Paradise Lost* is virtually inexhaustible, in the manner of the highest works of art. Among the most popular and profitable of recent approaches to the poem have been those which concentrate on its style, its structure, and its dimension as myth. It has also been considered from the point of view of its features as a specifically Baroque work.[25] In the context of this book, and of this particular chapter, it may be useful to augment earlier analogies drawn between *Paradise Lost* and works of Baroque painting and sculpture by a consideration of some of the ways in which Milton's poem confronts the problems of theme and style discernible in the lesser Baroque epics and resolves them through a grandly heroic conception

24. J. van den Vondel, *Joannes de Boetgezant*, in *Werken*, ed. A. Verwey (Amsterdam, 1937), p. 1007.

25. Various approaches are exemplified by: A. Stein, *Answerable Style* (Minneapolis, 1953); I. G. MacCaffrey, *Paradise Lost as "Myth,"* (Cambridge, Mass., 1959); J. I. Cope, *The Metaphoric Structure of Paradise Lost* (Baltimore, 1962); and J. Summers, *The Muse's Method* (Cambridge, Mass., 1962). The question of *Paradise Lost* as a Baroque work is confronted by R. Daniells in *Milton, Mannerism and Baroque* (Toronto, 1963) and, less effectively, by W. Sypher, *Four Stages of Renaissance Style* (Garden City, 1955).

faithful at once to the traditions of the genre and the vision of the age.

Paradise Lost shows several of the tendencies already noted in other Baroque epics: it makes use of an overtly Christian subject; it has a kinship with the dramatic mode, most evident in Satan's soliloquy on arriving in Eden (4.32–113),[26] but perceptible throughout the work; it shows a marked affinity for the descriptive, the elegiac, and the pathetic, particularly in the treatment of the character of Eve; it is built on what amounts to a complete abrogation of time as a prescriptive and inescapable reality; its vision of history (as overtly presented in Books 11–12) recalls that of d'Aubigné's epic in its emphasis on recurrence rather than progress; and it espouses specifically the concept of passive heroism (see 9.27–41).

Milton's handling of time requires some detailed comment. Beginning traditionally, in medias res, the poet narrates in Books 1–2 the crucial events in Hell after the fall of Satan and his cohorts. The sense of linear narrative is strong, but with the introduction of the conventional epic catalogue, the list of the principal demons (1.376–521), chronology and character alike begin to undergo some radical distortions: the demons—Moloch, Chemos, Belial, and the rest—are presented under the names and aspects which they are to assume after the beginning of history. There emerges thus a kind of double perspective on the infernal characters: on what they are in the narrative moment of Book 1—fallen angels with some traces of glory still clinging to them—and on what they will become and in a sense are already internally committed to becoming—grotesque monsters

26. John Milton, *Poetical Works,* ed. H. Darbishire (Oxford, 1958), pp. 74–76. Further references to *Paradise Lost* will be to this edition and will appear in the text. With reference to the dramatic features of Milton's epic, see also A. Barker, "Structural Pattern in *Paradise Lost,*" *PQ* 28 (1949): 17–30.

of ugliness and cruelty. The narrative thrust is irresistibly strong
in Book 2, with its account of the great infernal council and
Satan's departure for earth, but the reader's sense of chronology
is wrenched out of all repair by the opening of Book 3, in which,
after an invocation to light, the poem brings us into the presence
of God the Father, beholding Satan "from his prospect high, /
Wherein past, present, future he beholds" (3.77–78). From this
point on it will be impossible for the poem to exhibit that thoroughgoing submission to time which practically defines the traditional epic.[27]

Nevertheless, to a far greater degree than any other Baroque
epic, *Paradise Lost* achieves the narrative thrust, the texture, the
very feel of traditional heroic poetry. In part this is due to a kind
of doubleness in both narrative technique and structure: the
point of view of omniscient Godhead has been introduced, and
with it has come a kind of stasis characteristically Baroque, a
stasis which is reinforced by the poet's habit of darting about
chronologically from Creation to Apocalypse with a freedom
which is both stimulating and unnerving to the reader. At the
same time, however, the deeds, the *gesta,* of Satan and of Adam
and Eve are conveyed to us with such immediacy and with such
a finely achieved sense of these characters' awareness of things
happening in time that we cannot help but identify with their
points of view to the extent of feeling, along with the stasis in-
duced by the poet's chronological legerdemain, the dynamic and
irreversible force of time as the element in which narrative lives.

Just as Milton incorporates the static Baroque vision without
losing the dynamic traditional feeling for narrative, so too he
enunciates the familiar conception of passive heroism, but in a
poem which centers on figures of extraordinary energy and
enterprise. Satan is, of course, the poem's most striking embodiment of heroic energy, and it is not necessary to fall into the critical heresy of seeing him as the hero to do justice to what he con-

tributes to the enormous sense of action which fills the work.[28] Adam and, especially, Eve have also a good share of enterprise, if not of the infernal sort, and the paradox of the *felix culpa* which casts its equivocal glow over the whole last part of the poem forces the reader to wonder if the culpable forcefulness of our first parents does not indeed have its share of true heroism.

The epic motif of the confrontation with mortality plays a prominent role in *Paradise Lost* as well. Adam anticipates "A long days dying to augment our paine" (10.964), and the promise of redemption later given him can confirm a delivery from death but not a cancellation of its initial horror—a horror which, as Books 11–12 tell us, is the definition of history.

Like Vondel, Milton captures a sense of the validity of myth which many of his Baroque contemporaries were unable to achieve. In part, of course, Milton's sense of myth derives from his extensive allusions to the body of Greco-Roman mythology, but those allusions are not, like those of many of his contemporaries, merely decorative, fashionable, and illustrative: they are rooted in a feeling for the identity existing between the fables of the ancients and the recurrent realities of the seasonal earth. Two familiar passages will perhaps illustrate the depth of Milton's sensitivity. The first occurs in the initial description of Paradise, in lines which, before the entrance of Eve, prefigure her person and her destiny:

> . . . Not that faire field
> Of *Enna*, where *Proserpin* gathring flours

27. L. Nelson, *Baroque Lyric Poetry* (New Haven, 1961), pp. 41–52, 64–76, examines Milton's "Baroque" manipulation of time as manifested in two shorter poems.

28. C. S. Lewis, *A Preface to Paradise Lost* (London, 1942), has ably refuted the Blake-Shelley contention that Satan is the hero of the poem, but in so doing has failed to take the true stature of the antagonist into account. Greene, in *Descent*, p. 404, notes the "separation of energy from human heroism" which occurs in *Paradise Lost;* his phrase perhaps does less than justice to Eve's spiritual energy.

Her self a fairer Floure by gloomie *Dis*
Was gatherd, which cost *Ceres* all that pain
To seek her through the World; nor that sweet Grove
Of *Daphne* by *Orontes,* and th'inspir'd
Castalian Spring, might with this Paradise
of *Eden* strive . . .

[4.268–75]

In a very real sense Paradise and Eve are always identified;[29] the guiltless capacity for fecundity which is associated with Eve repeatedly throughout Book 4 reminds us that her identification with the mythical embodiment of spring is not fortuitous, and the somber destiny of Proserpina relates alike to the negative aspect of the cycle of the year, to the Greeks' transformation of that fact of experience into a human tale of the greatest pathos and appeal, and to the Christian's awareness of the death of the year as simultaneously a symbol and a consequence of the primal sin.

The extraordinary inclusiveness of Milton's epic manifests itself over a still greater range of association: it is, as Frank Kermode justly observes, a poem about loss.[30] Hapless Eve, "Defac't, deflourd, and now to Death devote" (9.901), combines with the vulnerable, ravished maiden of the Greek myth to stand, one might say, for all the losses our race can undergo, committed to our incommodious planet but haunted by the irretrievable vision of something, whether womb or dream, better than we know, where flourish, impossibly, "Flours of all hue, and without Thorn the Rose" (4.256). *Paradise Lost* is about loss, and the ideal settings and emotions of Books 4–5 are created specifically to be destroyed. The ideal settings and emotions

29. Arnold Stein's observation *(Style,* pp. 56–57) of the womb-imagery associated with Paradise in Book 4 is relevant in this connection.
30. F. Kermode, "Adam Unparadised," in *The Living Milton,* ed. F. Kermode (New York, 1961).

exist, however, by virtue of having been imagined, and even though doomed by the linear action of the poem, they are recapturable, and recaptured by every imaginative experience of the poem. *Paradise Lost* is a total myth, incorporating and expressing in a manner simultaneously Christian and supra-Christian the total positive and negative possibilities of human existence.[31]

The quality of inclusiveness distinguishes *Paradise Lost* whether we consider its overall structure or the detail of its imagery, and that quality explains finally how Milton is able to achieve the effect of traditional epic while still giving very complete expression to the spirit of his own nonepic age. The action of the poem shifts from Hell to Chaos to Heaven to Earth and back, and with every shift the reader is carried along by Milton's narrative sense. Nevertheless, the geographical parallels existing among the separate realms are consistently stressed, with the result that we are confronted not only by the illusion of an experience in time but also by the illusion, more difficult to bring about, of an observation in space. Milton's achievement of epic dynamism and Baroque stasis derives from the quasi-architectural quality of his poem's structure.

Parallel and echo often become parody in Paradise Lost: the ironically unconscious and yet commendable parodies of celestial actions performed by the still-innocent couple in Eden (e.g. 4.720–35, 5.137–208), and the corrupt, sterile, infernal parodies of Satan and his followers, parodies which remind us that Hell's vulgarity consists very largely in its imitativeness, its total lack of creativity. Mammon asks rhetorically of his fellow-devils, with reference to the darkness sometimes assumed by the Al-

31. MacCaffrey, *Paradise Lost as "Myth,"* uses myth in a rather more restricted sense, dealing particularly with the Christian myth as it recapitulates universal patterns. But she also stresses myth as a mode of seizing experience. See also W. Shumaker, *Unpremeditated Verse* (Princeton, 1967), pp. 3–25.

mighty, "As hee our Darkness, cannot wee his Light / Imitate when we please?" (2.269–70), and Satan's subsequent expedition becomes, from its very inception, a piece of third-rate copying. Nowhere is this aspect of infernal character more marked than in Satan's encounter with his progeny, Sin and Death, an encounter in which one becomes aware that the three protagonists constitute an infernal trinity to balance the Blessed Trinity of Father, Son, and Holy Ghost. The daughter-figure Sin proceeds from the father of all evil, and the unholy spirit of Death proceeds from their union: the blasphemous parallel emerges plainly in the passage in which Sin yields to Satan's suggestion that she disobey the divine command:

> Thou art my Father, thou my Author, thou
> My being gav'st me; whom should I obey
> But thee, whom follow? thou wilt bring me soon
> To that new World of light and bliss, among
> The Gods who live at ease, where I shall Reign
> At thy right hand voluptuous, as beseems
> Thy daughter and thy darling, without end.[32]
>
> [2.864–70]

Satan's voyage itself is a shoddy imitation, as Book 3 makes us aware. In Book 2 he undertakes the task of destruction in language charged with egotism (2.402–16); in Book 3 Christ undertakes the task of redemption in language expressing passive acceptance (3.236–65). Joseph Summers, in his admirable analysis of these passages, points to the contrast between the questions "whom shall we find / Sufficient?" (2.403–04) and "where shall we find such love?" (3.213), as well as to the difference between Satan's use of the first person nominative pronoun and the sacrificial Christ's use of the first person objective. He goes

32. See B. Rajan, *Paradise Lost and the Seventeenth-Century Reader* (London, 1947), pp. 47–48.

THE BAROQUE EPIC   183

on to point to a further analogy with these passages when, much
later in the poem, the repentant Eve reconciles herself to Adam
in words which unknowingly echo the redemptive offer of
Christ:

> While yet we live, scarse one short hour perhaps,
> Between us two let there be peace, both joining,
> As joind in injuries, one enmitie
> Against a Foe by doom express assign'd us,
> That cruel Serpent: On mee exercise not
> Thy hatred for this miserie befall'n,
> On mee already lost, mee then thy self
> More miserable; both have sinnd, but thou
> Against God onely, I against God and thee,
> And to the place of judgement will return,
> There with my cries importune Heaven, that all
> The sentence from thy head remov'd may light
> On mee, sole cause to thee of all this woe,
> Mee mee onely just object of his ire.[33]
>
> [10.923–36]

Such elements of structure as these, arching a kind of vault of
mutual reference over the whole vast extent of *Paradise Lost,*
help to bestow on the poem its character as an aesthetic construct
existing in space as well as moving in time; they give to it its
double structure as linear narrative and static composition. A
similar doubleness obtains in Milton's descriptions, which, mov-
ingly vivid and evocative in their own right, play on a whole
range of associations beyond the local—as the descriptions of
Paradise create the nonexistent world of our desires, and as the
descriptions of Hell, as Martz has pointed out, describe the world
we know.[34]

33. Summers, *Muse's Method,* pp. 176–85.
34. L. L. Martz, *The Paradise Within* (New Haven, 1964), pp. 110–16.

Even on the level of the single metaphor Milton's poetry possesses a remarkable density of meaning which relates each part of the poem to the work as a whole and to the entire cultural tradition of which it is a part. One example of the way in which his metaphors function may be found in the extended simile which appears near the end of the first book, as the poet pictures the assembly of demons:

> ... As Bees
> In spring time, when the Sun with Taurus rides,
> Poure forth their populous youth about the Hive
> In clusters; they among fresh dews and flowers
> Flie to and fro, or on the smoothed Plank,
> The suburb of thir Straw-built Cittadel,
> New rubd with Baume, expatiate and conferr
> Thir State affairs. So thick the aerie crowd
> Swarmd and were strait'nd ...
>
> [1.768–76]

Highly effective in its simplest function as description, the passage gains resonance by reminding the cultivated reader of Homer *(Iliad* 2.87 ff.) and of Virgil *(Aeneid* 1.430–35; 6.707–09), affirming again the position of the poem in the tradition of its genre. But it does many more things. Just as, in the *Iliad,* Homer's similes flash into the dusty, bloody plain before Troy to remind us, in their references to freshness, coolness, and the pursuits of peace, that there is another world besides that of war, so Milton here, after some 700 lines largely devoted to the sterile, anguished atmosphere of Hell, with its "darkness visible," reminds us that Hell is not the only place in the universe. Furthermore, the analogy between the demons and bees shifts abruptly the focus previously maintained: initially the fallen angels were presented in their stunned and harmless state, "Thick as Autumnal Leaves that strow the Brooks / in

Vallombrosa" (1.302–03), but immediately thereafter, as the angels recover some of their power, a great chain of similes extending from 1.304 to 1.355, likened them to figures of progressively intensified size, potency, and menace. But even the first simile has its hidden threat: "Vallombrosa" is "shady valley," an image of peace and contentment, but it is also "valley of shadow," and as such an image loaded with fatality. But the bee-simile reverses all these connotations, introducing what might be called the God's-eye-view in anticipation of God's entrance *in propria persona* in 3.56 ff. From this point of view the fallen angels are no longer figures of terror but rather figures of almost pathetic innocuousness, and the mighty edifice of Pandemonium becomes no more than a "Straw-built Cittadel." Even Satan comes indirectly into a new focus: his followers are like bees "New rubd with Baume" in that they have been dipped in the honey of their leader's rhetoric—that mighty, dishonest oratory which has misled so many readers into believing it as helplessly as the demons themselves.

The inclusiveness and density of *Paradise Lost,* characteristic of its structure, imagery, and metaphor, explain perhaps how the greatest of Baroque epics manages to be also the last utterance of the Renaissance, how a profoundly Christian work is at the same time a myth of wider than Christian reference, and how an artist firmly committed to the concerns of his particular time and place is able to speak to us in a language deriving from the entire history of our culture. A simpler explanation would be to say that, in an age in which the writing of a great epic poem should have been an impossibility, Milton wanted to write one and proceeded to do so.

The Christian-humanist fusion which enabled Milton to synthesize the most disparate elements of faith and culture proved impossible for later poets to maintain. Milton himself could not sustain it in his *Paradise Regain'd,* in which Classical culture is rejected in the name of Christian revelation.[35] The epic poem of Western culture had become extinct, and such mock-epics as Boileau's *Le Lutrin* (1672) and Dryden's *Mac-Flecknoe* (1682) symbolized its passing. The mode of epos was destined to assume a different shape as the novel, and as the Baroque age shaded off into the era of Neoclassicism, the new genre of prose epos prefigured itself in works as different in character and yet as similar in narrative force as Grimmelshausen's *Der Abentheuerliche Simplicissimus* (1669) in Germany and Bunyan's *Pilgrim's Progress* (1678) in England.

35. D. Bush is surely right in ascribing such an important role to the poet's Christian Humanism *(English Literature*, pp. 359–98). For views differing from mine on Milton's attitude toward Classical culture in *Paradise Regain'd*, see Martz, *Paradise Within*, pp. 195–99, and A. Stein, *Heroic Knowledge* (Minneapolis, 1957), pp. 96–111.

8

The Sacrificial Hero

Book 9 of *Paradise Lost* opens with some observations by the poet on his epic material. Though not invoking his celestial muse directly, he refers to her, and to the necessity of her aid to the success of his undertaking:

> Not sedulous by Nature to indite
> Warrs, hitherto the onely Argument
> Heroic deemd, chief maistrie to dissect
> With long and tedious havoc fabl'd Knights
> In Battels feignd; the better fortitude
> Of Patience and Heroic Martyrdom
> Unsung...[1]
>
> [9.27–33]

The lines which follow make it clear that Milton is rejecting as unworthy of epic treatment the subject matter of the *romanzesco* epic, including that of his beloved Spenser:

> ... Races and Games,
> Or tilting Furniture, emblazond Shields,
> Impreses quaint, Caparisons and Steeds;
> Bases and tinsel Trappings, gorgious Knights
> At Joust and Torneament...
>
> [9.33–37]

1. John Milton, *Poetical Works*, ed. H. Darbishire (Oxford, 1958), p. 183. Further references in the text will be to this edition.

The introduction as a whole affirms Milton's conviction that his sacred subject is innately superior not only to romance material but to all secular material, even that of Homer and Virgil. The attitude is typically Baroque in its insistence on a direct confrontation with religious themes; it is equally Baroque in its conception of heroism as passive rather than active, of the will as a faculty to be directed not toward achievement but toward endurance.

An apparent paradox presents itself to any reader familiar with Milton and with his forceful, crotchety, and determined personality. Nevertheless, the concept of heroism as the will to endure is a fully consistent one for Milton: both early and late his imagination and his intellect are captured most fully by situations in which the will is tested by temptation and in which triumph consists not in accomplishment or external conquest but in resistance. The Lady in "Comus" successfully holds out against a seducer who cannot touch the freedom of her mind, although he has power over her "corporal rinde"; the speaker in "Lycidas" finds the inner resources to reject the temptations of doubt, despair, and disgust with the world. The two major works with which Milton concluded his career— *Paradise Regain'd* and *Samson Agonistes*—deal definitively with the figure of the passive hero whose will manifests itself in resisting temptation and whose triumph ultimately resides in his making himself a sacrifice. Milton's emphases in these works relate him to a whole tendency of the Baroque imagination—a preoccupation with the sacrificial protagonist which is observable in narrative and dramatic works alike.

Despite his concern with the passive hero, Milton seems never to have found the crucifixion an attractive subject, from the time of the early poem on the Passion, which he left unfinished as being "above the years he had, when he wrote it" (p. 413), until the very end of his career. Thus in *Paradise*

Regain'd he eschews the event which, for the Christian, constitutes the atonement and hence the actual regaining of Paradise and chooses instead the temptation of Christ in the wilderness (Luke 4:1–13). One might speculate on the reasons for this choice: Milton's rationalistic temperament perhaps found the supralogical mystery of the blood-atonement disturbing, at least sufficiently so that his imagination was not inspired to dwell on its details in the manner of Crashaw, La Ceppède, or Vondel. Furthermore, the episode of the temptation furnished Milton with a subject emphasizing not the physical fact of suffering and sacrifice but the fixing of the heroic will on the decision to undergo suffering and sacrifice. His protagonist has learned, before the temptation begins, that his heroic course lies not in rescuing Israel by force of arms from the Roman yoke (1.215–20) but in undergoing "many a hard assay eev'n to the death" (1.264); with unconscious irony he later remarks to Satan that a crown "Gold'n in shew, is but a wreath of thorns" (2.459), and still later he expresses overtly the poem's doctrine concerning the positive function of passivity:

> ... who best
> Can suffer, best can do; best reign, who first
> Well hath obey'd; just tryal ere I merit
> My exaltation without change or end.[2]
>
> [3.194–97]

In such ways does Milton's brief epic point to the paradox of proper will central not only to the English poet's vision but to that of the entire Baroque.[3]

2. The viability of Christ as a protagonist in *Paradise Regain'd* is largely dependent on the fact that his knowledge of his own divinity is something that emerges only gradually. Indeed, there are even hints in the poem of a concept of that divinity as being metaphorical.

3. W. Sypher, *Four Stages of Renaissance Style* (Garden City, N.Y. 1955), pp. 289–95, gives some attention to the "Late Baroque" quality of Milton's style in this work.

A stricture on *Samson Agonistes,* heard frequently since Dr.
Johnson first formulated it, is that the tragedy, though it has a
beginning and an end, lacks a middle.[4] The criticism is irre-
futable as long as the critic requires that a drama have at its
center externalized conflicts between an active protagonist and
his opponents. If, however, one is willing to recognize the
existence of a dramatic art based instead on the protagonist's
internal struggle with spiritual weaknesses activated by external encounters, *Samson Agonistes* emerges as a tragedy of
force and grandeur. Samson is, like Christ, a hero of passivity,
setting his will toward endurance and the resistance of temptation and achieving his triumph as he achieves the sacrifice of
his life. Each of the successive episodes which make up the
center of the play is a temptation, each subtly tests a different
area of potential weakness in the hero's virtue, and each, as it
is successfully resisted, contributes to the regeneration of his
will and his spirit. The visit of Manoa, Samson's father, affords,
with the greatest good will, a temptation toward self-pity and
the transfer of guilt for his downfall from Samson himself to
God; the visit of Dalila offers a temptation toward granting a
forgiveness corrupted by weakness and uxoriousness; the visit
of Harapha directs a temptation toward impotent rage and idle
boasting. In each case Samson's resistance is successful: he
resists his father's plea, forgives Dalila "at distance" (line 954)
and without desire, and defies the threats of Harapha not as a
champion in his own right but as one who was once God's
champion and has come to hope that he may again be. A kind
of double movement makes itself felt throughout the middle
part of the play: each visit leads to a deeper reconviction of his
sin on the part of Samson and suggests thus a kind of progressively downward movement of his spirits, and yet, paradoxical-

4. Samuel Johnson, "Life of Milton," in *Lives of the English Poets*
(1779–81), ed. L. Archer-Hind, 2 vols. (London, 1925), 1:111–14.

ly, the acceptance of his burden of guilt progressively liberates him from the despair of his opening speech—as well as from his unconscious bondage to his own self-esteem in the days of his prosperity, when

> Fearless of danger, like a petty God
> I walkd about admir'd of all and dreaded
> On hostil ground, none daring my affront.
>
> [lines 529–31]

With the departure of Harapha, Samson's internal transformation is complete, and his words to the Chorus after he has been summoned by the Philistine lords show that he is aware of that transformation:

> Be of good courage, I begin to feel
> Some rouzing motions in me which dispose
> To something extraordinary my thoughts.
> I with this Messenger will go along,
> Nothing to do, be sure, that may dishonour
> Our Law, or stain my vow of Nazarite.
> If there be aught of presage in the mind,
> This day will be remarkable in my life
> By some great act, or of my days the last.
>
> [lines 1381–89]

Milton's tragic hero has undergone a spiritual purification which has made him worthy of becoming a sacrifice, manifesting thus that "better fortitude" exalted in *Paradise Lost*.

Martyrdom and sacrifice are glorified as acts of the highest heroism throughout the literature of the Baroque age, narrative as well as dramatic, in the works of both Catholic and Protestant authors. The forces of virtue and true faith in d'Aubigné's *Les Tragiques* have little to go on besides their fortitude and their capacity for endurance, and the poem makes it clear that oppression will cease to be the lot of the just only when the Judgment Day arrives. In Hojeda's *La Christiada,* as in Fletcher's *Christ's Victorie and Triumph,* emphasis falls similarly on "the lonely and passive heroism of the afflicted saint,"[5] and in such a work as Marino's *La strage degl'innocenti* (a portion of which was translated into English by Crashaw) even positive and purposeful saintliness is abandoned for a subject (the slaughter of the innocent infants by Herod) in which the simple vulnerability to suffering is sufficient.

The Baroque drama, even more strikingly than the epic, focuses on the sacrificial hero as the center of imaginative attention. The later Shakespeare, whose style and thought show so many Baroque traits, does not share significantly in the use of this theme: his tragic heroes remain active in their suffering, and the protagonists of his romances, if they are often the playthings of chance, do not hasten to embrace their uncontrollable destiny in the characteristic Baroque manner (although, to some extent, Hermione in *The Winter's Tale* does so). Two other giants of the drama of the age, Corneille and Calderón, show equivocal treatments of the theme. The Cornelian hero is proverbial for the force of his will and his active confrontation of experience, but, as Rousset has suggested, even the motif of will in Corneille implies a compensation for the dramatist's obsession with the phenomena of instability and metamorphosis. From the tension between the conviction of inescapable change and the hero who firmly defies change the drama of Corneille derives its distinctive character.[6]

Corneille's chief exemplar of the sacrificial hero is, of course, Polyeucte, and the tragedy (1643) which bears his name forces

5. T. M. Greene, *The Descent from Heaven* (New Haven, 1963), p. 238. His specific reference is to Hojeda. Greene also points out (p. 240) the curious weakness of will which permeates Marino's *Adone.*

6. J. Rousset, *La Littérature de l'âge baroque en France* (Paris, 1954), pp. 212–13.

on us even more powerfully than the works of Milton the Baroque paradox of the aggressive will dedicated to its own eradication. It is difficult to see or read the play without sympathizing to some degree with André Gide's aversion to its hero.[7] There is something inescapably repellent about the way in which Polyeucte asserts himself against the pagan society in which he lives: ostensibly his destruction of the pagan idols is an affirmation of religious truth, but one is tempted to see in it an aggressive manifestation of the hero's conviction of his own superiority to his fellows:

> Ne perdons plus de temps: le sacrifice est prêt;
> Allons-y du vrai Dieu soutenir l'interêt;
> Allons fouler aux pieds ce foudre ridicule
> Dont arme un bois pourri ce peuple trop crédule;
> Allons en éclairer l'aveuglement fatal;
> Allons briser ces Dieux de pierre et de métal:
> Abandonnons nos jours à cette ardeur céleste;
> Faisons triompher Dieu: qu'il dispose du reste![8]

But even here the last line, with its abdication of the individual attempt to determine a future, expresses the Baroque paradox of will and passivity in its extreme Cornelian form.

However unattractive the hero of *Polyeucte* may sometimes make himself, he is finally both a complex and a successful character. The great scenes (4.3, 5.3) in which he resists the appeals to his wife Pauline and takes his final leave of her express the conflict between natural and Christian attitudes toward life and death with a force which recalls the devotional lyrics of Andreas Gryphius, and the conclusion of the play, with its

---

7. Gide's remarks occur in his *Journal*, August 12, 1941. Quoted by G. May in his introduction to his edition of Corneille, *Polyeucte and Le Menteur* (New York, 1963), pp. 25–26.
8. Corneille, *Polyeucte and Le Menteur*, p. 56.

implausible but effective spate of conversions occasioned by the
martyrdom of Polyeucte, increases his stature as an agent of the
Baroque awareness that the mortal world is neither desirable
nor real.

Corneille's hero, rudely self-assertive and yet finally passive,
exemplifies one of the key tenets of Corneille's dramaturgy, a
principle which is related to the aesthetic assumptions of
Marino, a poet whose differences from Corneille are generally
far more striking than his similarities. For Marino, as for the
Italian Baroque in general, the principal aim, indeed the only
aim, of poetry is wonder, surprise:

> E del poeta il fin la meraviglia
> (Parlo de l'eccelente e non del goffo):
> Chi non sa far stupir, vada alla striglia![9]

For Corneille, quite consistently, the emotion of "admiration"
—to be translated as "wonder" rather than as the English
"admiration"—is indispensable to theatrical success.[10] The
hero of Baroque drama, like the texture of Baroque poetry and
prose in general, exists in large measure to excite our wonder
rather than to elicit our pleasure at seeing reality well imitated.
In this way he exemplifies both the extravagance and the transcendence of the mundane toward which the age was so obsessively compelled.

Fernando, the hero of Calderón's *El príncipe constante*
(1629), is another martyr-figure who inspires admiration, not
only in the sense that he is an exceptional human being whose
fortitude strikes us with wonder, but also in the sense that he is
an epitome of virtue, both Christian and courtly. The constancy

---

9. G. B. Marino, *Poesie Varie*, ed. B. Croce (Bari, 1913), p. 395.
10. See May, in Corneille, *Polyeucte and Le Menteur*, pp. 20–23. Helpful treatments of Corneille may also be found in O. Nadal, *Le Sentiment
de l'amour dans l'œuvre de Pierre Corneille* (Paris, 1948), and R. J.
Nelson, *Corneille, His Heroes and Their Worlds* (Philadelphia, 1963).

of Calderón's hero is untainted by the egotism, the determined
pursuit of *la gloire,* which marks Polyeucte's. Indeed, once he
is captured by the Moors, Fernando displays notable humility,
treating the king of Fez with respect, and offering complete
obedience to his captor in every matter which does not involve
inconstancy to his religion. The king, for his part, treats Fernando with courtesy until angered by his captive's refusal to
allow the Christian city of Ceuta to be exchanged for his freedom. The king has him subjected to extreme cruelty, reduced to
the status of the basest slave, and, in effect, starved to death.
Fernando's situation in the final act of the play denies him the
rhetorical posturings available to Polyeucte and a number of
other martyr-heroes: like Milton's Samson, he is ragged, sick,
and pale, and he smells bad. By dwelling on the details of
Fernando's physical degradation, Calderón demonstrates again
the complete degree to which he incorporates in his work the
central attitudes and emphases of the Baroque age: the contrast between the hero's beautiful and constant soul and a body
which has been rendered ugly and repellent asserts, like La
Ceppède's picture of the suffering Christ in his sonnet "Voicy-
l'homme," the metaphysical irrelevance of everything physical.

This theme receives added emphasis in one of the most powerful scenes of *El príncipe constante*—the garden conversation
between Fernando and the Moorish princess Fénix. As Spitzer
has demonstrated, it is, despite its subdued and indirect quality,
a love scene: the prince is a martyr to his Christian faith, but
he is by no means an ascetic saint totally free of susceptibility
to earthly beauty, and the flowers which he offers to Fénix are
the gift not of a slave to his mistress but of a courtly "servant"
to his beloved.[11] The egotistical princess is moved to a pity
scarcely typical of her nature, but, as later scenes demonstrate,

11. L. Spitzer, "The Figure of Fénix in Calderón's *El príncipe constante,*" in B. Wardropper, ed., *Critical Essays on the Theatre of Calderón* (New York, 1965), pp. 137–60.

she will be unable to sustain even her pity in the face of Fernando's physical repulsiveness.

The inconstancy of Fénix serves as an articulation of Calderón's obsessive theme of *desengaño,* or disillusionment, a version of the central Baroque attitude of rejection of the physical: haunted by a prophecy that she is destined to be "the ransom of a dead man," Fénix is troubled by what she feels to be an offense to both her beauty and her worth. At the play's denouement the prophecy is fulfilled as the Princess and her two suitors, captured by the Portuguese, are exchanged for the corpse of the constant prince, which is then given Christian interment in a church, as Fernando in life had desired. His words to Fénix at their last meeting are thus confirmed:

> ... es bien que sepáis,
> aunque tan bella os juzgáis,
> que más que yo no valéis,
> y yo quizá valgo más.[12]

In Calderón's poetic calculus, just as Fernando is not worth as much as the many Christian souls of Ceuta, Fénix, with her physical beauty flawed by egotism and motiveless passivity, is not worth as much as the dead Fernando.[13]

The texture of the great garden scene is as representative of the Baroque sensibility as is its thematic content. The flowers presented by Fernando work as conventional emblems of transience, but they are also specifically equated with the individual lot of the prince:

> flores, de la suerte mía
> geroglíficos, señora,

12. P. Calderón de la Barca, *El mayor monstruo del mundo y El príncipe constante* (Buenos Aires, 1952), p. 170. Further references in the text will be to this edition.
13. Spitzer, "The Figure of Fénix."

> pues nacieron con la aurora,
> y murieron con el día.

[p. 149]

With the effect of unceasing metamorphosis already noted as characteristic in the lyrics of such poets as Góngora and Marvell, the flowers identified with the prince become equated with the stars identified with the princess. In the context of a reality which is not subject to measurement, the numbered days of Fernando and the doomed beauty of Fénix are equatable with the duration of the flowers or of the stars—a duration equally brief in the light of eternity. As Fénix says of the stars in the exquisite sonnet in which she replies to Fernando:

> Flores nocturnas son, aunque tan bellas,
> efímeras padecen sus ardores;
> pues si un día es el siglo de las flores,
> una noche es la edad de las estrellas.

[p. 151]

In a manner typical of the style of the age, her *précieux* observation that the life of the stars is limited to the night merges with a speculative suggestion about the brevity of all material things.

In Calderón, as in so much Baroque lyric poetry, the fusion of images with one another implies a vision of the material world in which all physical entities have ultimately the same worth or the same worthlessness. Only the spiritual constancy of the sacrificial hero makes possible a transcendence of the earthly. The "summation schema,"[14] or set of parallel examples followed by a brief recapitulation, one of Calderón's favorite devices, gives expression to this attitude as well, and its operation in Calderón's plays recalls not only the imagery of Góngora but also the char-

14. E. R. Curtius, *European Literature and the Latin Middle Ages*, trans. W. R. Trask (New York, 1953), pp. 289–91, coins the phrase and discusses its occurrence in Calderón and others.

acteristic rhetoric of Andreas Gryphius, with its strong reliance on asyndeton.[15] The constancy of Fernando, like Polyeucte's avowal of faith, exemplifies a will fixed not on earthly achievement but on transcendence. To a greater degree than Corneille's, however, Calderón's tragedy is permeated with a symbolic language expressive of a whole philosophical view which gives justification to the theme of martyrdom.

Polyeucte and *El príncipe constante* are among the greatest of Baroque martyr-dramas, but neither is fully typical of that genre. The representative martyr-drama of the seventeenth century has approximately the following shape: a male or female protagonist, either Christian at the beginning of the play or converted during its course, is threatened with persecution and death by some secular authority opposed to Christianity; resisting both the threats of the tyrant and the emotional appeals of a beloved, the protagonist embraces death, often with joy. Minor motifs frequently encountered include the hero's conversion of his beloved, the conversion of a large number of other characters as a direct result of his martyrdom, and the appearance of the martyr after death to encourage a Christian army in combat with the pagans. This last motif is prominent in *El príncipe constante,* but in most respects *Polyeucte* traces more completely the typical pattern. It is chiefly the aggressiveness of its hero which sets Corneille's play apart from the standard martyr-drama of the age.

Examples of typical Baroque martyr-dramas may be cited from all over western Europe: among others, Massinger and Dekker's *The Virgin Martyr,* Calderón's *Los dos amantes del cielo,* Corneille's *Théodore,* Vondel's *Maeghden,* Gryphius's *Catharina von Georgien,* and Dryden's *Tyrannic Love.* It is in-

15. See F. Strich, "Der lyrische Stil des 17, Jahrhunderts," in R. Alewyn, ed., *Deutsche Barockforschung* (Cologne and Berlin, 1966), pp. 229–59. See also Curtius, pp. 285–86.

teresting to note that five of the characteristic martyr-dramas mentioned above have female protagonists; the sixth *(Los dos amantes del cielo)* has a hero and a heroine of equal importance. Possibly the extreme of passivity which constitutes heroism in plays of this genre tends to find its most eloquent embodiment in a female figure, a St. Ursula *(Maeghden),* a St. Dorothea *(The Virgin Martyr),* or a St. Catharine *(Tyrannic Love);* possibly, also, the mythic stratum underlying the figure of the sacrificial hero has something to do with the mysteries of fertility, a primal awareness of the interrelatedness of life, death, and rebirth and of the role of willing sacrifice in effecting participation in these mysteries. Such an interpretation is suggested by the Latin anagram which Vondel affixed to another of his martyr-tragedies, *Maria Stuart, of Gemartelde Majesteit: "Maria Stuart erat Matura Arista."*[16] The Scottish queen, regarded by Vondel as a martyr to his own Catholic faith, is seen as a ripe ear of corn, destined to be cut down but, like the grain in 1 Corinthians 15:36, to be quickened through dying. At its best, the Baroque martyr-tragedy incorporates into its religious concerns and its preoccupation with the vanity of earthly things a profound feeling for the archetypal motif of the life-death-rebirth cycle.

Two particular variations of the martyr-figure deserve notice —the martyr as actor and the martyr as monarch. Vondel's *Maria Stuart* and Gryphius's *Carolus Stuardus,* exemplify the latter type; Rotrou's *Saint-Genest,* Desfontaines's *L'Illustre Comédien,* Lope de Vega's *Lo fingido verdadero,* and Jacob Bidermann's Latin *Philemon Martyr* supply treatments of the former.[17] Each of these variations in its own way gives special

16. J. van den Vondel, *Werken,* ed. A. Verwey (Amsterdam, 1937), p. 303.

17. E. M. Szarota, in *Künstler, Grübler und Rebellen* (Bern and Munich, 1967), supplies an exhaustive study of the martyr-drama in England, France, Spain, Germany, and Holland. She perceives three major types of martyr-hero—the artist, the meditative intellectual, and

expression to the Baroque rejection of the world: in the destiny
of the martyr-monarch a tension is established doubly, between
earthly glory and earthly misfortune, and between temporal
misery and eternal bliss; in the experience of the martyr-actor
equations are set up in which "real" life is role-playing and role-
playing is spiritual reality. Such a play as Gryphius's *Catharina
von Georgien* shows an overt concern with the contrast between
time, the dimension of the tyrant Chach Abas, and eternity, the
dimension toward which the martyr Catharina strives. One is
reminded of the garden scene in *El príncipe constante.*

The Baroque figure of the sacrificial hero, discernible in epic
and drama alike, appears also in situations which are not, strictly
speaking, those of martyrdom. Calantha, the heroine of John
Ford's *The Broken Heart,* is a figure to inspire Cornelian *admiration* or Marinistic *meraviglia,* but her proud stoicism and
her determined will make it impossible to regard her as a martyr, a sacrifice, or, indeed, a passive figure. The Duchess of Malfy,
in John Webster's tragedy of that name, is, in contrast, a definitive embodiment of the sacrificial heroine in her secularized
form. Neither saint nor ascetic, the Duchess is a warm-blooded
and tender woman, but in the powerful fourth act, in which she
is subjected to mental tortures by the equivocal Bosola on the
orders of her wicked brothers, she accepts death in a manner
suggestive of the martyr-protagonists considered earlier:

> What would it pleasure me to have my throat cut
> With diamonds? or to be shot to death with pearls?
> I know death hath ten thousand several doors
> For men to take their exits; any way, for Heaven sake,
> So I were out of your whispering.[18]

the rebel or resistance-hero. She also recognizes the martyr-monarch as a
subtype. See also G. Gillespie, "The Rebel in Seventeenth-Century Tragedy,"
Comp. Lit. 18, no. 4 (Fall 1966): 324–36.

18. John Webster, *Complete Works,* ed. F. L. Lucas, 4 vols. (London,
1927), 2:99.

In the midst of her sufferings Webster's heroine achieves the *contemptus mundi* which the Baroque temperament shares with the medieval, but she retains, like Polyeucte and the Fernando of *El príncipe constante,* an unshakable sense of her spiritual identity: "I am Duchess of Malfy still."

The Duchess of Malfy is a conspicuous triumph of the Baroque imagination, not only in its concentration on the theme of sacrificial heroism, but also in its extravagance of imagery, its atmosphere of lurid chiaroscuro, and its expressively wrenched and distorted poetic rhythms. Such a line as Ferdinand's cry of remorse on seeing the corpse of the sister murdered on his orders —"Cover her face; mine eyes dazzle: she died young"—reminds us forcefully that Webster was a contemporary (and an acquaintance) of John Donne.

Szarota sees in the history of the seventeenth-century martyr-drama a pattern of progressive secularization.[19] Such Continental phenomena as the tragedies of Daniel Casper von Lohenstein, composed between 1653 and 1675, suggest such a pattern, but *The Duchess of Malfy,* performed as early as 1614, implies a rather different possibility: the Baroque sensibility, rather than taking the martyr-figure as its point of departure and then, with the passage of time, stripping it of its religious implications, started with the obsessive figure of the sacrificial protagonist and found, naturally enough, that such a protagonist readily fitted into plots having to do with Christian martyrdom. Psychologically, the Baroque, preoccupied by its convictions of the unreality of the phenomenal and the necessity of transcendence, found the sacrificial hero, whether Christian martyr or not, a central embodiment of its vision.

As the Baroque shades off into the Neoclassical age, the sacri-

---

19. Szarota, *Künstler,* pp. 267–73 and passim. She does, however, take note of mingled secular and religious elements in *The Duchess of Malfy* and *El príncipe constante.*

ficial hero either loses his vigor or is transformed into a hero distinguished by his capacity for action. The St. Catharine of Dryden's *Tyrannic Love* (1669) stands in marked contrast to the St.
Ursula of Vondel's *Maeghden* (1639) by virtue of her rationalism and her lack of any positive or mystical orientation toward
a martyr's death. The distance of Dryden's play from the Baroque tradition of the martyr drama is indicated further by the
fact that the play belongs not so much to Catharine as it does to
the villain Maximin, whose energetic atrocities make him a
monster to rival Shakespeare's Richard III in theatrical charm.

It would be inaccurate to see the sacrificial hero as omni-
present in the Baroque drama. I have been giving some account
of a significant tendency of the age, not of a ubiquitous quality.
As Szarota observes, the figure of the political hero, prominent
in several works of Corneille and Gryphius, shares with the
martyr-hero the interest of the Baroque playwright. Although
the martyr-hero continues to appear in dramatic literature until
the very end of the seventeenth century,[20] new dramatic centers
of attention come to dominate in the decades after 1660. Racine's characters possess a metaphysical dimension, and both
their passionate predicaments and their responses to them imply
an entire religious vision of experience, but the total dramatic
being of such heroines as Andromaque or Phèdre is shaped by
the fact that, despite longings toward transcendence and purity,
their emotions remain bound to earthly objects. The extraordinary tension of Racine's work—which has led some commentators to classify him as a Baroque artist[21]—derives from his sense
of the terrible gulf between human aspiration and human limitation. From his awareness of limitation comes his governing feel-

20. Szarota, *Künstler*, pp. 267–69.
21. H. Hatzfeld, "Die französische Klassik in neuer Sicht. Klassik als
Barock," *Tijdschrift voor Taal en Letteren* 23 (1935): 213–81; L. Spitzer,
"Die klassische Dämpfung in Racines Stil," *Romanische Stil- und Literaturstudien* 1 (1931): 135–270.

ing for strict form, and both feeling and form characterize him
finally as a Neoclassical rather than a Baroque figure.

The Neoclassical theatre of France is the chief achievement
of later seventeenth-century European literature. In England,
despite the comic triumphs of Wycherley and Congreve, the
drama does not achieve the heights reached by the Baroque.
Dryden's plays, despite an extravagance of language which constitutes a kind of Baroque reminiscence, demonstrate a breakdown of the Baroque conception of character without the formulation of a new conception to take its place. Conditioned by their
own impressive rhetoric, formed by the very poses they strike,
such heroes as Antony in *All for Love* and Don Sebastian in the
play which bears his name do not so much possess attitudes as
they are possessed by them. Character has become not the vehicle but the instrument of abstract ideas and conventions.

The finest tragedies of Thomas Otway are more persuasive
than Dryden's as representations of the human condition, but
their mode of operation is radically different from that of the
plays of Webster or Middleton. In *Venice Preserv'd*, for example, emotional attitudes, though projected with great power, do
not manifest themselves as forces working on individual figures
who are consistent mimeses of human beings. Jaffeir's love-
honor conflict, for example, may be conceived of in two opposed
ways: love for Belvidera versus honor toward Pierre, or love for
Pierre versus honor toward Belvidera. The erotic focus of the
play shifts between the ideally pure Belvidera and the courtesan
Aquilina, the function of hero shifts between Jaffeir and Pierre,
and the plot itself is presented in a thoroughly ambiguous way,
as a murderous conspiracy and as a noble blow for freedom.
Venice Preserv'd is not so much a drama, in the Renaissance or
Baroque sense, as it is a dramatic fantasy on a series of subjec-
tively obsessive themes. Otway's lack of objectivity or a sense of
controlled form makes it difficult to regard him as in any sense a

Neoclassical artist, and the breakdown in his work of both the Baroque conception of character and the traditional conception of dramatic form indicates the distance between him and the definitive creators of the Baroque drama. He may perhaps be most accurately viewed as a decadent Baroque writer, although a writer of genius.

In late seventeenth-century France the drama was reformulated by the genius of Molière and Racine; in England the drama, restored in 1660 after eighteen years of absence, failed to achieve the eminence it had formerly possessed. In both countries the Baroque preoccupations and obsessive characters, including the sacrificial hero, either disappeared or were altered beyond recognition.

9

The End of the World

The vision of the end of the world is one of the most frequent of Baroque topoi. The lugubrious prognostications of Donne in the "Anniversaries" and Browne in "Urne-Burial" come readily to mind as examples, and the apocalyptic obsession of d'Aubigné in *Les Tragiques* serves equally well to typify this aspect of the imagination of the age. These works participate in the mood of melancholy which is a recurrent feature of the literature of the period, but the apocalyptic preoccupation, as we encounter it in such lyric poets as Théophile de Viau, Saint-Amant, Gryphius, and Kuhlmann, often communicates not a sentiment of regret but rather a feeling of enormous zest and satisfaction, as if the accuracy of the poet's imaginative picture of the world were somehow confirmed by the inclusion of that world's abolition.[1]

A fascination with the Four Last Things, and a certainty that the race of man will very soon confront them, are both perhaps implicit in the assumptions which I have suggested as definitive for the Baroque—the illusory nature of the phenomenal world, the insuperable mutability of an experience always in a state of

---

1. On the apocalyptic element in the poetry of the Baroque, see esp. O. de Mourgues, *Metaphysical, Baroque and Précieux Poetry* (Oxford, 1953), pp. 85–88, and I. Buffum, *Studies in the Baroque from Montaigne to Rotrou* (New Haven, 1957).

flux, and the consequent vanity of all human desires.[2] A conviction that the soul's uneasy balance with an unreal world cannot last for long underlies the dark rhetoric of "Urne-Burial" and the somber lyrics of Gryphius, and it finds eloquent utterance in two dramas central to the spirit of the age: *The Tempest* and *La vida es sueño*. That conviction permeates the metaphor of the world as theatre and it is perhaps the source of the conception of art as play. It intensifies the meditative and devotional impulses of the Baroque poet, and it does much to explain his tendency to locate the utmost heroism in acts of passive sacrifice.

Jean de Sponde's *Stances de la mort* and *Sonnets de la mort*, composed well before the end of the sixteenth century, predict in a number of ways the direction to be taken by the seventeenth-century religious lyric.[3] Like his younger compatriot Jean-Baptiste Chassignet, Sponde dwells with rather suspicious fervor on the desirability of death from a Christian point of view:

> O la plaisante Mort qui nous pousse à la vie,
> Vie qui ne craint plus d'estre encore ravie!
> O le vivre cruel qui craint encor la mort!
> Ce vivre est une mer où le bruyant orage
> Nous menace à tous coups d'un asseuré naufrage:
> Faison, faisons naufrage, et jettons-nous au Port.[4]
>
> [p. 64]

Like Gryphius, he expands his meditation on personal death to embrace the eventual annihilation of everything material, and

---

2. See also, passim, J. Rousset, *La Littérature de l'âge baroque en France: Circé et le paon* (Paris, 1954).

3. For Sponde, see A. M. Boase, "Jean de Sponde, un poète inconnu," *Mesures*, (Oct. 15, 1939), pp. 129–51; T. C. Cave, *Devotional Poetry in France* (Cambridge, 1969), pp. 171–82, 208–12; and de Mourgues, *Metaphysical*, pp. 56–64.

4. Jean de Sponde, *Poems of Love and Death*, ed. G. F. Cunningham (London, 1964). Further citations are to this edition.

his expression of that theme often has an extraordinary poignancy:

> Ce beau flambeau qui lance une flamme fumeuse,
> Sur le vert de la cire esteindra ses ardeurs,
> L'huyle de ce Tableau ternira ses couleurs,
> Et ces flots se rompront à la rive escumeuse.
>
> [p. 72]

As Odette de Mourgues remarks of these lines, "the irony [is]
reinforced by using these verbs in the active form; it is the torch
which puts itself out, the picture which tarnishes itself, and life
destroys itself, so to speak, from within."[5] Theologically, the
poet rejoices in the prospect of death and the annihilation of the
physical, but his psychological honesty establishes a stark tension between what the Christian must believe about death and
what the human being cannot help but feel about death. His
poems strike often the note of terror.

That note resounds in the work of a good many poets of the
Baroque—Donne in such *Holy Sonnets* as "Oh my blacke
Soule! now thou art summoned" or "This is my playes last
scene"; Quevedo in such poems as "¡ Como de entre mis manos
te resbalas!" and "Todo tras si lo lleva el año breve."[6] Andreas
Gryphius treats the theme rather differently: he regards the extinction of life with an equanimity that almost amounts to pla-
cidity, and the element of terror is seldom present. Nevertheless,
his great somber sonnets and odes, with their tolling insistence
on the certain fact of mortality, have a cumulatively oppressive
effect which gives his work a central position among seventeenth-century treatments of the themes of the death of the self
and the death of the world.

5. De Mourgues, *Metaphysical,* p. 58.
6. John Donne, *Poetical Works,* ed. H. J. C. Grierson, 2 vols. (Oxford, 1912), 1:323, 324; Francisco de Quevedo, *Obras completas,* ed. F.
Buendía, 2 vols. (Madrid, 1966–67), 2:38, 37.

Gryphius resembles Sponde and differs from many earlier writers on similar subjects in his insistence on the completeness of bodily annihilation. The soul is immortal, Gryphius is in no doubt about that, but his imagination is repeatedly seized by a harried sense of the completeness with which everything *physical* is destroyed:

Der hohen Taten Ruhm muss wie ein Traum vergehn.
Soll denn das Spiel der Zeit, der leichte Mensch, bestehn?
Ach, was ist alles dies, was wir vor köstlich achten,

Als schlechte Nichtigkeit, als Schatten, Staub und Wind,
Als eine Wiesenblum, die man nicht wieder findt!
Noch will, was ewig ist, kein einig Mensch betrachten.[7]

Some fifteenth-century poets, notably Villon, had been comparably obsessed by intimations of mortality, but whereas they had placed their emphasis on the facts of decay and putrefaction, on the worms that devour the corpse and on the ugliness to which human beauty is turned,[8] Gryphius and the other poets of the Baroque stress the utter nothingness into which the body is transformed:

Was itzund Atem holt, muss mit der Luft entfliehn,
Was nach uns kommen wird, wird uns ins Grab nachziehn.
Was sag ich? Wir vergehn, wie Rauch von starken Winden.

[p. 31]

or:

... Lass ferner keinen Dunst
Verhüllen mein Gemüt, und alle Phantasie

7. Andreas Gryphius, *Gedichte,* ed. H. M. Enzensberger (Frankfurt-am-Main, 1962), p. 28. Further citations are to this edition.
8. For a consideration of the motif in fifteenth-century literature, see J. Huizinga, *The Waning of the Middle Ages,* trans. F. Hopman (Garden City, N.Y., 1954), pp. 138–51. For a confrontation of Villon and Sponde, see de Mourgues, *Metaphysical,* pp. 59–60.

Der eitel-leeren Welt sei für mir als ein Traum.
Von dem ich nun erwacht! Und lass nach diesem Tod,
Wenn hin Dunst, Phantasie, Traum, Tod, mich ewig stehn.

[p. 45]

The shift in treatment suggests once again the dominant Baroque conviction of the unreality of the physical. The pathos of the late-medieval treatment rests in the picture of a world of physical beauty continuing to flourish while one's own body decays; seventeenth-century treatments visualize individual dissolution as a foreshadowing of the imminent dissolution of the entire physical world.

If Gryphius's emphases recall Sponde, they suggest also the Donne of the *Sermons,* the eloquence of which is typified by the following passage:

Aske where that iron is that is ground off of a knife, or axe; Aske that marble that is worn off of the threshold in the Church-porch by continuall treading, and with that iron, and with that marble, thou mayst find thy Fathers skinne, and body; *Contrita sunt,* The knife, the marble, the skinne, the body are ground away, trod away, they are destroyed, who knows the revolutions of dust?[9]

They suggest also the works of Sir Thomas Browne, most clearly his *Hydriotaphia, Urn-Burial,* in which the theme of death modulates into a vision of the approaching death of the world. Like the *Religio Medici,* the *Hydriotaphia* operates through a submerged thematic structure which, in the later work, runs under the surface for the first four chapters and comes out into the open only in the great final chapter. Overtly an archaeological treatise on "the Sepulchrall Urnes lately found in Norfolk," the

9. John Donne, *Poetry and Prose,* ed. F. J. Warnke (New York, 1967), p. 376.

Hydriotaphia begins with an erudite preliminary survey of the various forms of burial and cremation practiced by the human race. Chapter 2 centers on the particular urns discovered in Norfolk and raises the complex question of their provenience; chapter 3 continues the physical description of the Norfolk urns and the comparison of the implied burial customs with those of other nations and times; and chapter 4 returns to more general observations, stressing two themes: the vanity of all attempts to preserve the memories of the dead, and the absoluteness of human ignorance in the face of the mysteries of the past. But the vanity of all human undertakings has been Browne's true subject from the very beginning. Even the initial description of the Norfolk urns conveys, together with its scientific information, a version of the "metaphysical shudder":[10]

> In a Field of old *Walsingham,* not many moneths past, were digged up between fourty and fifty Urnes, deposited in a dry and sandy soil, not a yard deep, nor farre from one another: Not all strictly of one figure, but most answering these described: some containing two pounds of bones, distinguishable in skulls, ribs, jawes, thigh-bones, and teeth, with fresh impressions of their combustion. Besides the extraneous substances, like peeces of small boxes, or combes handsomely wrought, handles of small brasse instruments, brazen nippers, and in one some kinde of Opale.[11]

In style the paragraph is a good example of seventeenth-century anti-Ciceronianism, with distinct affinities to Bacon. At the same time, however, the passage has something of the rhetorical effect of zeugma: subtly an equation is effected between the

10. I take the term from G. Williamson, *The Donne Tradition,* paperbound ed. (New York, 1958), pp. 90–98.
11. Sir Thomas Browne, *Religio Medici and Other Writings,* ed. F. L. Huntley (New York, 1951), p. 144. Further citations are to this edition.

pathetic scattered bones and the never-animate objects possessed by the once-animate dead. Chapter 3 exhibits passages in
which the meditative dominates the descriptive even more significantly:

> How the bulk of a man should sink into so few pounds of
> bones and ashes, may seem strange unto any who considers
> not its constitution, and how slender a masse will remain
> upon an open and urging fire of the carnall composition. Even
> bones themselves reduced into ashes, do abate a notable pro-
> portion. And consisting much of a volatile salt, when that is
> fired out, make a light kind of cinders.
>
> [p. 162]
>
> Teeth, bones, and hair, give the most lasting defiance to cor-
> ruption. In an Hydropicall body, ten years buried in the
> Churchyard, we met with a fat concretion, where the nitre of
> the Earth, and the salt and lixivious liquor of the body, had
> coagulated large lumps of fat, into the consistence of the
> hardest castle-soap; whereof part remaineth with us. [p. 165]

Such passages cannot help but remind the reader of Hamlet's
sententiae over the skull of Yorick, and they may remind him
also of the anguished question of Lear: "Is man no more than
this?"

Browne reserves his answer for the mighty peroration of chapter 5, one of the greatest of Baroque meditations on death and
immortality. His meditation is unequivocal in its statement of
the completeness of physical annihilation: not only will each
man unfailingly die, but his name will also die, as will, rather
sooner than later, the earth on which he has lived:

> And therefore restless inquietude for the diuturnity of our
> memories unto present considerations, seems a vanity almost
> out of date, and superannuated peece of folly. We cannot

hope to live so long in our names, as some have done in their
persons, one face of *Janus* holds no proportion unto the other.
'Tis too late to be ambitious. The great mutations of the world
are acted, or time may be too short for our designes . . . But the
iniquity of oblivion blindely scattereth her poppy, and deals
with the memory of men without distinction to merit of perpetuity . . . Time hath spared the Epitaph of Adrians horse,
confounded that of himselfe . . . The night of time far sur-
passeth the day, and who knows when was the Aequinox?
[pp. 178–80]

The awareness of the total impermanence of the physical in
any sphere heightens Browne's sense of the spiritual as the only
dimension in which permanence or even reality is located—
"There is nothing strictly immortal, but immortality; whatever
hath no beginning, may be confident of no end" (p. 182)—and
leads directly to his resolution:

Pyramids, Arches, Obelisks, were but the irregularities of
vainglory, and wilde enormities of ancient magnanimity. But
the most magnanimous resolution rests in the Christian Religion, which trampleth upon pride, and sits on the neck of
ambition, humbly pursuing that infallible perpetuity, unto
which all others must diminish their diameters, and be poorly
seen in Angles of contingency. [p. 184]

For Browne, as for Donne, Sponde, Gryphius, Quevedo, and
d'Aubigné, the vision of universal destruction is a concomitant
of deeply held religious views, an aspect of the heightened religious sensibility which manifests itself so often in the literature
of the first two-thirds of the seventeenth century. It would be
fallacious, however, to attribute the apocalyptic imagination of
the Baroque age quite simply to religious fervor. Several works
of the period demonstrate that the theme of universal destruction exerted its fascination also on authors who were tepid

Christians or not Christians at all, as the great ode "A Monsieur de L., sur la mort de son père," by the free-thinker Théophile de Viau, may perhaps suggest.

Théophile's ode is in the familiar genre of the "consolation," but in contrast to most poems of its species, it ignores altogether the motif of personal immortality and the promises of the Christian religion. It begins with an evocation of landscape, and to this manifestation of external nature the poet ascribes his inspiration:

> O beaux prés, beaux rivages verds,
> O grand flambeau de l'univers,
> Que je trouve ma veine aisée!
> Belle aurore, douce rosée,
> Que vous m'allez donner de vers![12]

Nature, the setting and the condition for all human joys, is in the next stanzas placed in opposition to death, the remorseless termination of all things:

> Mon Dieu, que le soleil est beau!
> Que les froides nuicts du tombeau
> Font d'outrages à la nature!
>
> [p. 93]

In the context of this opposition the bereaved Monsieur de L. is offered as consolation not an assertion of his father's immortality and not an affirmation of divine plan but simply a reminder that the father, being dead, is wholly obliterated and thus in no position to make a claim on the concern of his son:

> Vostre père est ensevely,
> Et, dans les noirs flots de l'oubly
> Où la Parque l'a fait descendre,

12. Théophile de Viau, *Oeuvres choisies,* ed. M. Bisiaux (Paris, 1949), p. 92. Further citations are to this edition.

Il ne sait rien de vostre ennuy,
Et, ne fût-il mort qu'aujourd'huy,
Puisqu'il n'est plus qu'os et que cendre
Il est aussi mort qu'Alexandre,
Et vous touche aussi peu que luy.

[p. 94]

As in the *Hydriotaphia,* so in Théophile's ode the contemplation of individual extinction leads directly to a consideration of the extinction of the entire universe:

Les planettes s'arresteront,
Les éléments se mesleront
En ceste admirable structure
Dont le Ciel nous laisse jouyr.
Ce qu'on voit, ce qu'on peut ouyr,
Passera comme une peinture:
L'impuissance de la Nature
Laissera tout évanouir.

Celuy qui, formant le soleil,
Arracha d'un profond sommeil
L'air et le feu, la terre et l'onde,
Renversera d'un coup de main
La demeure du genre humain
Et la base où le ciel se fonde;
Et ce grand désordre du monde
Peut-estre arrivera demain.

[p. 95]

The crucial difference is that Théophile makes no reference whatsoever to the spiritual immortality so strongly affirmed by Browne. Without underestimating the vast importance of orthodox Christianity for the majority of Baroque writers, one should note that the popularity of the topos of the end of the world is based on a feature of sensibility more widespread than either devotional fervor or concern over the new science. It is based, it seems to me, on the expansive nature of the Baroque imagination as a whole, that feature, noted so often in this study, which stresses the unreality of the phenomenal and, discontent with the classicistic contemplation of an ordered and enclosed world, is incapable of imagining a world without imagining also its dissolution.

The heavens did not open, as the seventeenth century moved toward its close, nor did the great globe dissolve, but nevertheless there is a sense in which the writers of the age, with their awareness of an impending end, were entirely justified. As Nicolson has observed,[13] the world of tradition did in fact die before the end of the seventeenth century, and the modern world was born to replace it. The Baroque, in its varied manifestations, was the last age to sustain a mode of vision—poetic, symbolic, theologically centered—which had lasted for more than a thousand years. Noting—in the heavens, in the human intellect, in the institutions of church and state—the evidence of huge and unpredictable change, the European literary sensibility could only assume that such change portended the lifting of the veil which had always hidden reality from the eyes of living men. For the lyric poet or dramatist, as for the thinker like Browne or Pascal, the sense of something ending, and ending forever, is inescapable. And the styles of the age—experimental, extravagant, capable of a wider range of response than the style of the Renaissance—expressed that sense of conclusion with an eloquence mournful, exhilarated, or both.

The last third of the seventeenth century witnessed an alternative response, however, different from that which found expression in lament over or celebration of the death of the world. It was, of course, the response of writers who, observing that the world of experience had become different from that of their

13. M. H. Nicolson, *The Breaking of the Circle* (Evanston, Ill., 1950), pp. 188–89.

fathers (or that of their own youth), forged a new style capable of expressing the new world which had come into being. In the work of some of the writers traditionally labelled "Neoclassical" and more recently designated as "Late Baroque," we encounter new terms of vision and a new style in which to express those terms.

"Late Baroque" may mean (and in recent scholarship has meant) at least three different things: (1) a style in which the characteristic Baroque tensions and extravagances assume forms of highly exacerbated excitement and irregularity; (2) a style in which such tensions, though recognized and justly estimated, do not determine literary form, being rather subjected to ironic expression through forms which are chastened, ascetic, and clearly ordered; and (3) a style which, in its orderly schematization of the phenomena of experience, implies a world-view from which the Baroque tensions have been exorcised. "Late Baroque" applies in the first sense to the dramas of Otway and Lohenstein and, in a rather different way, to the lyrics of Traherne, Kuhlmann, and Luyken.[14] The term applies in the second sense to the tragedies of Racine and the late works (*Paradise Regain'd* and *Samson Agonistes*) of Milton.[15] It applies in the third sense to the poems and plays of John Dryden.[16]

There are, of course, numerous overlaps and interrelation-

14. H. Hatzfeld, *Estudios sobre el barroco* (Madrid, 1964), conceives of a "barroquismo" which is a late, "mannered" form of Baroque. Since Hatzfeld locates his quintessential Baroque among rather earlier figures (e.g. Tasso, Cervantes) than do most authorities, his "barroquista" poets include many writers (e.g. Marino, Calderón) who are traditionally seen as High Baroque.

15. The term is used in this sense by such divergent authorities as L. Spitzer, "Klassische Dämpfung in Racines Stil," *Romanische Stil- und Literaturstudien* 1 (Marburg, 1931): 135–270, and W. Sypher, *Four Stages of Renaissance Style* (Garden City, N.Y., 1955). See also L. Spitzer, *Linguistics and Literary History* (Princeton, 1948), pp. 87–125.

16. The underlying assumption of this study—that European literature from the late sixteenth century to the late seventeenth century constitutes a literary period, distinct from Renaissance and Neoclassicism—implies that I would accept the first two uses of the term "Late Baroque" and

ships among the three stylistic phenomena: the plays of Otway pretend to a schematized reduction of passionate experience, and those of Dryden noisily assert the reality of uncontrollable emotion. But on closer examination the alternative directions remain clearly separate. Love and honor in *Venice Preserv'd* are pretexts for what I have called a psychological fantasy, a work in which human figures, driven by uncomprehended agonies of existence, establish arbitrary and self-contradictory ideals which they strive, unsuccessfully, to turn into principles of order. In *All for Love* the emotions of the protagonists fit neatly into the abstract categories of love and honor: in that play there are, effectively, no other emotions, surely none of those equivocal and death-oriented passions which make the reading or seeing of *Venice Preserv'd* such a disturbing experience.

Dryden reduces the chaos of passion to a rhetoric of order; Otway attempts to do so, but ends by celebrating the all-destructive power of a passion which does not even know its own object. In the work of the greatest dramatist of the later seventeenth century, a more complex relationship obtains between passion and order. The motivation of Racine's characters is relentlessly passionate, and the clarity with which they understand their predicaments only intensifies the cruel sense of human helplessness which defines Racine's tragic vision. Phèdre's longing for purity lends a metaphysical dimension to a consuming and guilty lust which, in the absence of such a longing, would be merely psy-

---

reject the third. Given my conception of Baroque, Milton would appear as a Baroque artist whose late works begin to shade into Neoclassical austerity; Racine, as a Neoclassical artist with strong reminiscences of the Baroque; and the mature Dryden, as a Neoclassical artist with relatively few Baroque reminiscences. My terminology, like that of many Continental scholars, thus differs radically from that of Arnold Hauser, whose sweeping conception of Mannerism obliges him to define the Baroque exclusively in terms of a small selection of writers who would be more conventionally classified as either late Baroque or early Neoclassical. See his *Mannerism: The Crisis of the Renaissance and the Origin of Modern Art,* 2 vols. (London, 1965).

chological. The characters of *Andromaque,* fully aware of their own inability to conquer their various passions, can contemplate horrible courses of action with a desperate equanimity which is the measure of both their grandeur and their bondage. Racine's style—balanced, reserved, controlled, and yet infinitely expressive of psychological distress—answers to the demands of a vision which includes at once the passionate disorder which is man's inheritance and the ideal of order which man can imagine but never achieve—except perhaps in art.[17]

The controlled, ascetic, essentially nonsensuous style of Milton's last works bears a certain relationship to that of Racine, but in place of victims of destructive passion we find heroes— Christ and Samson—who are liberated, by a more than human will to endure, from a world of disorder and temptation. As already noted, the theme of temptation is central to all of Milton's work, but the terms in which the theme is handled in the late works reveal a personal development closely parallel to one of the major developments in the later Baroque period in general—the purgation of sensuous elements and the assertion of a strict rational control over the emotions. Samson's illumination, it may be noted, comes with a transcendence of the world of images, not, like that of the speaker in "Lycidas," with a proper comprehension of a world of images.

In Racine and Milton, both artists of the highest rank, Baroque conceptions persist but find embodiment in forms which, however ironically, are more settled and harmonious than those typical of the earlier writers of the period. In Dryden, an artist of almost the highest rank, the Baroque conceptions yield to conceptions of a very different sort. After the "metaphysical" extravagances of his youthful poetry (examples of Baroque-Mannerist style in decadence), Dryden created a style appropriate to

17. A recent authoritative study of Racine's style is to be found in O. de Mourgues, *Racine, or The Triumph of Relevance* (Cambridge, 1967).

a new and different vision of life. In his hands both heroic play
and tragedy assume a schematization of emotion which implies,
as noted above, a new order of things. And the other genres cultivated by Dryden—satire, mock epic, verse essay—reveal, like
the work of Boileau in France, a rationalistic, critical, and order-
conscious sensibility oriented toward values which the earlier
epoch had underplayed. Basically Dryden is not a late Baroque
writer but an early Neoclassical one.

Like the Baroque writers, Dryden has a sense of change and
passage, an awareness of the ending of something, but for him
it is not an apocalyptic vision of the end of the world but rather
an observation that one historical age has yielded to another.
The implicit historicism of the attitudes underlying Dryden's
discursive poems and critical essays contrasts strongly with the
sense of history as recurrence without progress, earlier noted as
characteristic for such Baroque epic poets as d'Aubigné. In lines
written near the end of his life Dryden cast a sublimely ironic
eye on the century that was ending, on the whole Baroque age
of conflict, aspiration, and turmoil:

> All, all of a piece throughout:
> Thy chase had a beast in view;
> Thy wars brought nothing about;
> Thy lovers were all untrue.
> 'Tis well an old age is out,
> And time to begin a new.[18]

Jonathan Swift was born in 1667, Alexander Pope in 1688,
Voltaire in 1694: the new age had arrived.

The achievement of the literature of the Baroque can scarcely be assessed without superlatives. The age of Shakespeare,
Webster, Corneille, Rotrou, Lope de Vega, and Calderón is
one of the supreme ages of the drama, comparable only to the

18. From "The Secular Masque," in John Dryden, *Poems,* ed. J. Sar-
geaunt (Oxford, 1913), p. 203.

fifth century B.C. in Athens. The lyric poetry of the period, Mannerist and High Baroque alike, is no less remarkable, and that poetry is unique in its capacity for incorporating the expression of personal emotion with subtle intellectual perception and philosophical speculation. The age witnessed further, in the works of Montaigne, Cervantes, Burton, Browne, and Pascal, the perfection of individual, idiosyncratic, eloquent prose styles which were to disappear from Western literature with the passing of the Baroque age.

The contribution of the period may be summarized in more general ways as well. Its capacity for rendering simultaneously the specific and concrete and the universal and transcendent has been both the inspiration and the envy of many modern artists. Its theme of disenchantment, *desengaño,* the refusal to entertain either a facile sense of order or a facile faith in progress, gives the writers in question an obvious modern relevance, as does their feeling for the absurd, issuing as a preoccupation with paradox and complex irony.

The foregoing observations seem to praise the literature of the late sixteenth and seventeenth centuries as being modern. They are not intended to. Whatever similarities may exist between those centuries and our own, between the Baroque sensibility and the modern, it would be just to remark that, in general, the Baroque writers knew how to make art out of their agonies, lusts, frustrations, and doubts. In our century only the occasional giant—Yeats, Rilke, Mann, Pasternak, and a few others—has discovered how to do so. Not misled by either a naïve faith in art as the mimesis of observed reality or a naïve faith in art as expression of the self, the Baroque artist was free to create his art as art—something of himself and yet separate from himself, something which renders truly the world that we inhabit and which yet renders with equal truth the unseen world that we also inhabit.

Index